Into the Deep

Into the Deep

An Unlikely Catholic Conversion

Abigail Rine Favale

CASCADE *Books* · Eugene, Oregon

INTO THE DEEP
An Unlikely Catholic Conversion

Cascade Books
An Imprint of Wipf and Stock Publishers
199 W. 8th Ave., Suite 3
Eugene, OR 97401

www.wipfandstock.com

PAPERBACK ISBN: 978-1-5326-0501-7
HARDCOVER ISBN: 978-1-5326-0503-1
EBOOK ISBN: 978-1-5326-0502-4

Cataloguing-in-Publication data:

Names: Favale, Abigail Rine.

Title: Into the deep : an unlikely Catholic conversion / Abigail Rine Favale.

Description: Eugene, OR : Cascade Books, 2018.

Identifiers: ISBN 978-1-5326-0501-7 (paperback) | ISBN 978-1-5326-0503-1 (hardcover) | ISBN 978-1-5326-0502-4 (ebook)

Subjects: LCSH: Favale, Abigail Rine. | Catholic converts—United States—Biography. | Catholic Church—Relations—Evangelicalism. | Evangelicalism—Relations—Catholic Church. | Biography.

Classification: BX4668.F38 A3 2018 (paperback) | BX4668.F38 A3 (ebook)

Manufactured in the U.S.A.   10/23/18

For my children, who have changed me

Contents

Acknowledgments

There were many people praying for me as I wrote this book, and those prayers, more than anything, are what made it come to be: Joshua and Brittney Hren; Stephen Kenyon; Kathy Kier. My beloved friends, Thaddeus and Lindsay Tsohantaridis, both prayed and read an early draft, providing invaluable feedback (and a quick heresy check).

My parents, Ric and Becky Rine, opened their snowy Idaho abode for a writing retreat, letting me disappear upstairs for hours at a stretch while they watched my children.

I am grateful to the Faculty Development Committee at George Fox University, which generously supported me with a summer writing grant. Many colleagues at George Fox gave me frequent encouragement, especially Brian Doak, Nicole Enzinger, Javier Garcia, Jane Sweet, Leah Payne, and Joseph Clair.

Thanks to my editor at Cascade Books, Charlie Collier, for first reaching out to me about the prospect of writing this book, and for waiting patiently until I felt ready.

The real man behind the curtain is my husband, Michael Favale, who provided continual support, love, childcare, and helpful comments on the manuscript. Nothing I accomplish happens without his steady hand.

December 2017
Feast of the Holy Family

PART I

The Shallows

"Let me, then, confess what I know about myself, and confess too what I do not know, because what I know of myself I know only because you shed light on me, and what I do not know I shall remain ignorant about until my darkness becomes like bright noon before your face."

—St. Augustine, *The Confessions*

Saved

My earliest religious memory is not really my own. It is an inherited memory, a story handed to me that has, after the fact, been given the flesh and fabric of true memory. Even now, as I call it to mind, specific images appear; I can see the moment unfold, but from a third-person distance, as if I am watching what happens, rather than experiencing it firsthand.

This is the night I was saved, the night that I first accepted Jesus into my heart. I am three years old, driving with my father and brother in a Toyota Land Cruiser. We are coming back from a basketball game. It is mid-March, March 17 to be exact, the Feast of St. Patrick—although of course the ideas of feasts and saints are not yet part of my world. We live in central Idaho, so there are, no doubt, still piles of snow along the road, glowing momentarily in the passing headlights. Probably trees too, evergreen and snow-laden, but nothing more than tall, flickering shapes in the dark. I'm probably staring out the window, listening to my dad talk to us about Jesus; my brother, two years older, is asking questions, wanting to know more. Then Dad asks us The Question, the one that, in this world, is the most important to answer. It is a question with eternal consequences, and a simple "yes" has the power to permanently mark one's soul. *Are you ready to accept Jesus into your heart?* Yes, we say, and my dad pulls over and prays with us.

I actually don't know if it was dark. Maybe the surrounding night in this post-hoc reconstruction is imported from the darkness of my own recollection. Or perhaps it heightens the drama of the moment, expressing its spiritual meaning. *For those who were in darkness have seen a great light.*

There is another facet of this story—one told to me much later, but now fully integrated into my rendering: at the same time my dad was praying with us, my mother was at home in bed (a detail that lends credence to the darkness) and a feeling of sudden suppression came over her, a great, crushing weight, an invisible force bearing down. For the record, my no-nonsense, levelheaded mother is not one to see demons regularly lurking in the shadows. Once told, this experience, with its uniqueness and intensity, was fully ingrained into the story of that night.

My brother, being a little older, remembers the moment in the car directly. I do not. This lack of recollection was a continual source of anxiety throughout my childhood. Not being able to know my own thoughts or feelings in that moment—had I really understood? Did I really *mean* it?—made me wonder if the salvation actually took. I felt as if, somehow, I had been saved by accident, mere proximity, riding on my brother's coattails and sneaking into glory on a technicality. What if I hadn't been in the car that night? Would I have had my own salvation experience later, giving me a real memory to which I could cling in subsequent years?

In those moments, late at night, happening not infrequently, I thought about hell and wondered whether I was really saved. It all seemed so easy. Too easy. To be safe, I made sure to repeat the salvation prayer at regular intervals, just in case. I don't know what the original prayer was like, that long-ago March night, but soon enough I learned the A-B-C formulation, thanks to formative experiences like Vacation Bible School. *Accept* that you are a sinner, *Believe* Jesus Christ is the savior, *Confess* your sins and ask Jesus into your heart. A-B-C, 1–2-3. Without meaning to, I began to see this prayer as an incantation, a spell that must be meticulously cast to take hold, a spell I worried might wear off after awhile.

There was a time I almost got re-saved by accident. I was probably seven, sitting in the sanctuary of our small Bible church in southern Utah with dozens of other restless children. It was high summer, the week of Vacation Bible School, the sun pummeling through the windows, reminding me that it was almost noon, time for lunch. We'd just finished singing a round of rousing, clap-infused songs, the lyrics written on bright poster board and held aloft by enthusiastic teenagers for us to see. *I am a C. I am a C-H. I am a C-H-R-I-S-T-I-A-N. And I have C-H-R-I-S-T in my H-E-A-R-T and I will L-I-V-E E-T-E-R-N-A-L-L-Y.*

Then we were quieted and coaxed into our seats, and the pastor came up front to prime us for an altar call—though I can't resist pointing out the misnomer now, as there was no altar at the front of the sanctuary, only a pulpit.

"Everybody close your eyes and bow your heads," the pastor was saying, and we complied; the movement was second nature. "Good. Now. . ."

He went on, and my attention wandered. I opened my eyelids ever so slightly, blurrily looking down at my fingers, then to the right, to the left. I couldn't see much with my head down.

". . . Jesus Christ as your personal savior, raise your hand."

I raised my hand, taking the chance to peek a little more, but I didn't see any other hands, which surprised me.

"Good. Lots of hands. You can put them down now, thank you."

He prayed, we sang one last song, and then we were excused, two minutes past noon, bolting out the doors and outside, hoping for a few last minutes of outside play before parents began to collect us.

I was stopped just outside the sanctuary by one of the teachers, a gentle, smiling woman who invited me into a small room off to the side. Reluctantly, I followed.

"Thank you for being brave and raising your hand, Abby."

"You're welcome." I stood there awkwardly, fidgeting, looking longingly outside as she began to explain the A-B-C formula. I was confused. I already knew this. I had already accepted Jesus as my savior. That's why I'd raised my hand.

"Can I pray with you?" She asked, and before I knew it, we were launching in, getting ready to save my soul.

"It's okay," I finally interrupted, my desire to be outside overpowering my fear of saying the wrong thing. "I don't need to say the prayer. I've already said it."

She looked at me, dubious. "Oh? When did you say it?"

"A long time ago."

"Then why did you raise your hand?"

"I thought, I thought you were supposed to raise your hand if you knew Jesus Christ as your personal savior."

She seemed unsure, like she didn't believe me. "Wait here a minute." She left, and came back with the pastor. They both sat down and the pastor began to ask a few questions, trying to gauge whether I needed saving. I must have answered to his satisfaction, because after a moment he thanked me and said I could go, but I could sense a tinge of disappointment in both of their smiles. I felt embarrassed, wondering if I should have just played along and said the prayer again, rather than making a fuss. At times, I couldn't fully trust the simple prayer, but I was also wary of abusing it and faking my own conversion, spawning a new salvific story that gave my pastor and teacher the satisfaction of believing they'd led me to Christ. This story, I sensed, would eventually clash with the founding narrative of my salvation, and even though I had a hard time believing "once saved, always saved," I knew that was what I was *supposed* to believe, so I decided to trust that I'd done the right thing.

Looking back, through a now-Catholic revisionist history of my own life, I see in my child-self a nascent Catholic sensibility, an instinctive desire for continual reconciliation with God, a persistent suspicion that the need for sanctifying grace was ongoing, and doubt that one prayer, no matter how carefully worded, could encase one's soul in celestial amber, forever preserved from a damning fall.

Mormonland

My family moved to Utah when I was five. This was my third move, though I barely remember the other two. My memories of McCall, Idaho, the town of my birth, were mostly limited to our small cul-de-sac, and our brief year in Corvallis, Oregon, is only a mosaic of scattered images: the gray, melancholy ocean; pots of simmering blackberry jam on the bright green stove in our compact apartment; getting in trouble for chewing a wad of gum I found on the sidewalk; learning how to pump my legs on the swings and count off my age on my fingers 1–2–3–4–5; the sticky glazed donut holes we got to eat after church; waves of shock ripping through my chest and out my fingertips, when I sat on an electric fence in a nearby field; my brother standing in the doorway of our apartment, backlit by lightning, after a brief panic when he went AWOL during a thunderstorm. For our move to Utah, my dad drove a bright yellow moving truck, impossibly huge, and sitting next to him on the black leather seats, I was on top of the world, indestructible, and could feel the thrill of the unknown ahead.

Southern Utah seemed like a different planet. The bright sun, dry wind, and bare, orange hills contrasted starkly with the lush gray-greenness of Oregon. The cultural landscape was just as foreign, though I was less aware of that at the time. For our first few weeks in Cedar City, we stayed at The Crest Motel, a brick 60s-era motel, with a sign decorated by large colorful balls on spikes. The motel was run by a polygamist family, something my mom whispered to me after we checked in. I'd noticed the woman at the front desk, with her elaborately coiffed hair and clean, simple dress; she looked like Ma from Little House on the Prairie. There were several women like her around the motel, doing the laundry, cleaning the rooms, and lots of children, the girls with long braids and dresses, the boys in suspenders and trousers. We didn't interact much; they seemed wary of us, perhaps similarly perplexed at our strange, modern clothing and small family.

One afternoon, my dad was playing with my brother in the grassy courtyard of the motel, batting softballs for my brother to field. There were a few of the other children around, watching curiously, but standing at a distance, behind some bushes. My dad noticed them and waved them over, batting a grounder toward one of the boys who, after a moment of hesitation, ran out to grab it and throw it back. After that, the invisible barrier breached, the other children ventured forward, our separate worlds, for a moment, forgotten. There were probably a dozen of them, enough to start a makeshift softball game with two teams. My dad was the perennial pitcher, easing slow lobs toward each batter, some of whom were as young as me.

There's one girl in particular I remember, the clearest image I have of this game; she was probably seven, with two blonde braids stretching down her back, wearing a long purple dress dotted with tiny flowers. She came up to the Frisbee serving as home plate, holding the bat high but firmly, a hard determination in her eye. And then the crack of the bat, the softball curving through the air and landing over the hedge beyond the grass, the hedge behind which she'd been hiding and watching before. She ran and ran, past first base, second, on and on, and that's where I still see her, suspended in flight between second and third, her braids streaming behind her, legs churning beneath that purple dress.

Before long we moved into our house, a big bungalow with a wide front porch stretching across like a smile, two windows above like eyes. A happy house. The house was on the east side of town, facing the mountains—Cedar Mountain a little to the south, and due east a bright limestone hill that, to this day, I simply think of as My Mountain. At sunset, this mountain caught the light, glowing bright orange, as if lit up by some divine presence. Even now, my soul has been marked by that luminous, sunburned landscape that will always somehow feel like home.

There is another aspect of the Utah landscape that revealed itself more slowly, growing more and more pronounced as I got older. This was the social terrain, which, in contrast with the topography, I never quite learned how to navigate, feeling always somehow like an outsider looking in, like that girl at the Crest Motel, peeking over the hedge at the strangers. And it's certainly true that, like that girl, I was a religious minority in the land of Zion, an evangelical Gentile in the Mormon Promised Land.

This created a sense of cognitive dissonance. My best friend was LDS; we lived across the street from each other, played every day, her family was like my extended family. The Mormons I knew well, I loved. But the sense of social alienation was bigger than any one person or family; it was in the atmosphere. When I entered public school, I was the only non-Mormon in my class, and we were one of only two non-Mormon families on our block. The LDS culture was endemic, and although it wasn't usually hostile, it was never one to which I could belong. I could never see it from the inside.

Once, when I was in fourth grade, our class was going on a field trip to Brigham Young's historic home in St. George. On the way back, we were going to drive by the LDS Temple; I was sitting by myself, as usual, looking out the bus window, when my teacher turned toward me. "In just a minute," she said, "We'll be driving past St. George Catholic Church. It's a beautiful old building. You can see it just up here." Then she smiled at me, almost apologetically. Of course, at that time, Catholicism was almost as alien to me as Mormonism, but I appreciated the gesture nonetheless, simply for its kind, momentary awareness that it must be weird and hard to be a non-Mormon girl growing up in southern Utah.

In the midst of Mormonland, my family took refuge in a conservative evangelical bubble. We went to a non-denominational Bible church about twenty minutes from where we lived. The geographical isolation of the church befitted our sense that we were, spiritually, in exile—a small but vibrant troupe of God's chosen holding our own in Canaan. The church was tiny and in the proverbial middle-of-nowhere, suspended between towns, tucked behind two immense water tanks. There were a few scattered juniper trees here and there, but the landscape was mostly rocks and dirt, prime for lizard chasing, which was our regular post-church pastime.

Our first pastor was warm and light-hearted, with two daughters and a petite, mouse-voiced wife with a professed "lead foot" when driving. I befriended the younger of the daughters and, later, when we got a new pastor, I similarly befriended his daughter until she hit adolescence and traded me in for some more stylish friends. This later pastor had a different vibe, more serious, more intense; he took *sola scriptura* to a new level, making sure there was no more guitar music, however mild, in the sanctuary. His wife played the piano; we sang along from a blue hymnal, and the forty-minute sermon was the centerpiece and climax of the service. The clearest image in my mind from that sanctuary is the small analog clock that hung over the entrance doors. During the service, one had to turn around surreptitiously to see it, and it seemed forever suspended at 11:55 a.m., as if, no matter how long I'd been there, there were always five more minutes, five eternal minutes, of sermon left to go.

My dad taught my Sunday school class for a while when I was a little older, maybe nine or ten. I don't remember a word from any of the Sunday sermons, but I do remember my dad teaching us about "absolutes," drawing compelling diagrams and lists on a white board for us to take in. This material seemed complex and sophisticated, like theological mathematics, although I doubt I would have known the word "theological" at that time. In our circle, the term of use was "biblical." We were concerned with biblical truth, biblical absolutes, biblical guidelines for living. We sang songs about the Bible, held Bible studies, dutifully carried our Bibles to each church service, so we could follow along with the words being preached.

I was grateful for this last practice, because I could always, when stranded in the timelessness of a never-ending sermon, have something to read. My go-to books tended to be the weird ones, like Genesis, or Revelation. The latter was always an exciting, dizzying read. Once Christian post-apocalyptic fiction became a fad in my preteen years, I would try to read between the lines and decode the prophecies; even now, in my childhood Bible, I can read comments like "Meteor???" and "Russia??" in the margins.

Perhaps my most immersive biblical experience in childhood was auditory rather than visual. When we were very young, my parents bought some audiotapes with dramatized stories from the Old Testament. They were produced by an LDS company, but my parents vetted them carefully, deciding they were orthodox enough for our consumption. On these tapes, the biblical stories were not simply read aloud, but acted out, complete with very convincing sound effects like sheep bleating, swords clashing, people milling about, men shouting. Every night, I fell asleep listening to one of these tapes, the stories of that strange, violent, God-filled world funneling through my ears and settling into my imagination. There were only two tapes I avoided: Job, and the Witch of Endor, because the distorted, sinister voices of Satan and Samuel's ghost terrified me.

Soon enough, I had my favorites, tapes I listened to over and over, featuring the most epic biblical heroes: Jacob, Samuel, David and Saul, Elijah. But what entranced me most about these stories were not the men in the foreground, but the women who loved and hated them. Rachel and Leah, sister rivals, one blessed with beauty, the other with abundant fertility, one cursed with an early death, the other with being second in her husband's affection. Hannah, barren yet beloved, with a bitchy sister wife, whose prayers for a son are heard. Esther, the humble underdog turned queen who won a beauty contest and saved her people from a deadly conspiracy. Two of David's many wives: Michal, a pawn between husband and father, a loyal wife turned contemptuous; Abigail, my namesake, rewarded for her wisdom, generosity, and diplomacy by the timely death of her asshole first husband and subsequent remarriage to the super hunky King David—it was clear, even from his voice, that David was young and easy on the eyes.

But ruling supreme over this cast of formidable biblical women, the reigning, raging Queen of my youthful attention, was none other than. . . Jezebel. Even now, it is hard for me to think of a more compelling villain than the Queen Jezebel of my childhood Bible tapes. She was strident; she was ruthless; she was filled with passion and rage, a female Achilles, commanding and terrifying, completely outstaging her wimpy husband, Ahab. She could have gobbled him up. She could have slain him with a glance, had she the inclination. Instead she went for the prophets of Yahweh, slaughtering scores of them. When her gods were bested in the fire-from-heaven test—the fire from Yahweh incinerating hundreds of Jezebel's priests as a cheeky bonus—her thirst for vengeance forced Elijah into hiding. She was a worthy foe for Elijah and his God. Jezebel's pathos, bloodlust, and ready armies versus an aged prophet, a widow with a jar of plenty, and a still, small voice in the desert. Power-and-might versus strength-in-weakness. Damn, that's a good story, and one told and retold, in various incarnations, throughout Scripture. Our God is a God of the underdog.

Speaking of dogs—even Jezebel's death is glorious in its horror, worthy, like the queen herself, of being forever seared into my imagination. She outlasted her husband, whose life eked out from an arrow wound; she outlasted her nemesis Elijah, who was whisked up to heaven in a blazing chariot. But Yahweh was playing the long game. Jezebel, adorned like a goddess, pushed out a window by eunuchs. Jezebel, hitting the ground, trampled to death by horses. Jezebel, eaten by dogs, nothing left to bury. A bloody, harrowing death, befitting a blood-spattered life.

The stories of these Old Testament women entranced me. When I was nine, my parents gave me my first study Bible for Christmas. It was beautiful and leatherbound, with gilded pages that whispered when you turned them. My full name was inscribed in gold lettering on the cover. This was an NIV Student Bible, and in the front matter were a series of thematic study tracks on various topics with tiny boxes to check once you read them. Competitive by nature, and very into checking things off lists, I was sure I would read through all the tracks—nay, *the entire Bible*—and I regularly combed over the lists, anticipating the moment I could place an X in each box with permanent ink. I never did make it through all the tracks. There was one in particular that consumed my attention: Women of the Bible. I read and re-read the stories on that list, never tiring of them, already having fallen for these heroines and villainesses on those audiotapes.

The same year that I received that study Bible, on a wet August day, I was baptized. Summers in southern Utah are prone to thunderstorms and flash flooding, unexpected torrents of water that come pouring down the limestone hills. The baptism was supposed to be held in a creek on Cedar Mountain, but there was a deluge that morning, and I spent several hours waiting to hear if all would continue as planned. That's my clearest memory of the day, aside from the plunge itself: looking out my kitchen window as the rain began to clear, wondering anxiously if my baptism was going to be canceled.

But it wasn't. The clouds burst and departed, the sun rolled in, and we made our way up the mountain in a caravan of cars. Because of the rain, the creek was running high and fast, and the water was the color of chocolate milk, thick with sediment. I was not clothed in a white robe, but multi-colored florescent shorts and a t-shirt, my hair in two braids. I waded out into the creek, guided by my pastor. With his hand bracing the base of my neck, he ducked me backwards into the water, holding me under for a few seconds, long enough to invoke the Trinity: *I baptize you in the name of the Father, the Son, and the Holy Spirit.* I came out of the creek looking much filthier than when I went in, as if I'd been marinating in the mud. But within me, there was a warmth that glowed white and flowed down into my frigid limbs, a joy I couldn't yet name.

* * *

When I was eleven, already in the throes of puberty, my family relocated from Southern Utah to Eastern Idaho, to an isolated town of only one thousand people. This geographical move was timed in such a way that it demarcated a clear break from my childhood. I was literally and figuratively exiled from those enchanted red hills, from a land that, despite its aridness and high winds, even now seems charged with the supernatural.

The place we moved to was no less endowed with natural beauty, tucked within sight of the Grand Tetons and only miles from a remote edge of Yellowstone Park. We lived on five acres near a river, surrounded by a sublime landscape of sprawling farmland and majestic mountains on the horizon. The winters were long and brutal, with regular blizzards, but that was my favorite time of year, the season when the earth was transfigured, clothed in miles of luminescent snow. Despite this beauty, in the emotional terrain of my memory, this place is not enchanted, but haunted: desolate. This is not the fault of the place, really, but more the season of my life while I lived there, a time when the geographical isolation reflected a great spiritual and social isolation within me.

Although we hoped that leaving Utah would take us out of the Mormon belt, it turned out that this Idaho town was just as Mormon, and because of its small size, the non-Mormon population was minimal and fragmented. There were five Christian churches in the town, all Protestant, each with its own tiny congregation that mingled little with the others. During our tenure there, we attended two of these churches: a charismatic fellowship church and a Missouri-Synod Lutheran church, from which the former had split off, years ago. The fragmentation of the Christian community, in contrast with the monolithic LDS unity, seems to me now a clear sign of tragic disunity. If this could be seen as a microcosm of American Christendom, we had fallen far from the New Testament vision of one cohesive, harmonious body.

The fellowship church in town was helmed by a wonderful pastor, dynamic and warmhearted. The charismatic flair was new and diverting at first. In our Utah church, we sang traditional hymns and guitars were banned from the sanctuary, but here, the worship time opened with praise songs before dissolving into an improvisational musical theater, with folks singing and prophesying and speaking in tongues alongside dizzying riffs on the piano.

As strange as this commotion might seem to the outsider, the worshippers were heartfelt and sincere. Few seemed to take advantage of this open period of worship in a self-serving way, although there was one woman who attended sporadically and always seemed to have a prophetic word to share. She'd wait for the diminuendo, when the music had faded almost into silence, and then she'd blare forth with a fake trumpet sound to preface her forthcoming prophecy, or begin stomping her feet on the floor and clapping loudly. My dad and I would look at each other with raised eyebrows and barely contained smiles; I loved this part of the show. I also loved communion, mostly because the bread they used was a whole unleavened loaf, handmade by an elderly congregant, and we'd each get to tear off our own piece as we filed by in a line.

Most of the folks involved in youth ministry at the church took an extremely countercultural stance toward "the world"; they homeschooled their children, eschewed pop cultural influences of any kind, dressed in prairie chic. I was a public-school kid, and there was great scrutiny on my appearance. I can remember being chided for getting my hair layered, for sporting wide-leg jeans (a poor fashion choice, to be sure), and wearing a friendship ring with a peace sign on it. "Don't you know that's an upside-down, broken cross?" On the flipside, when I started wearing the trendy WWJD? bracelet at school, I was teased by a classmate, who tauntingly asked, "What would Jack Daniels do?" These kinds of comments now strike me as so minor, so benign. Yet, at the time, I was a hypersensitive, emotional teenager, hungry for the approval of my peers and religious authorities, and deeply unsure of my place in either sphere.

I responded to this insecurity and anxiety with an increasingly recalcitrant attitude as my high school years unfolded. I abandoned contemporary Christian music and Christian fiction and went totally secular, hiding this from my parents when necessary. I became skilled at lying and pretending, being whomever I needed to be, depending on whom I was trying to please. I was the inverse of St. Paul: I became all things to all men to protect my anxious ego. This pretense, at least initially, wasn't premeditated or particularly methodical, but rather reactive, instinctive. A knee-jerk reflex to guard myself from social censure.

Throughout this period of my life, from ages thirteen to seventeen, a very consistent pattern to my spirituality emerged. For most of the year, while I was in school and surrounded by my close friends and peers, none of whom were evangelical, I immersed myself in that world; I defined myself by those standards. I minimized, as well as I could, any startling differences that would distinguish me from my secular friends.

Then, in the summer, when the epicenter of my world shifted away from school and back to home, I'd be overcome with guilt about being such a shitty Christian and scramble to make things right. During those months, I would typically have some immersive religious experience, like a mission trip or camp, that would sweep me back into the arms of Christ and have me vowing never to fall away again. These would be "mountaintop" spiritual experiences, where I was temporarily relieved of spiritual isolation and surrounded by likeminded believers; emotions ran high; bonds formed quickly and deeply; the secular world seemed weak and remote. In these settings, I'd pick up long dormant practices, like reading the Bible daily, praying, singing praise songs with my hands raised, eyes closed, tears streaming. I was having a teenaged love affair with my faith, intense and short-lived. All too quickly, summer would end, the emotions ebbed, and things would reset for another cycle.

One of these summers, amidst one such rotation, I was in Montana with a mission group, having a celebration of some kind at a beautiful house on a lake. The youth pastor from the charismatic church was there, as we both had connections with this group. My family had since begun attending the Lutheran church, and it had been awhile since I'd spent much time with him. After an afternoon of praise, prayer, and volleyball, a group of teens was going to the lake to be baptized, and I decided to go with them.

I knew I had already been baptized, but I wanted some outward sign of the determination I felt in that moment to recommit my life to Christ. Somehow, nothing seemed to anchor me, to keep me grounded. Maybe my first baptism was too premature, I though, and it didn't quite take. I had no sense of sacramental theology at that time. To me, baptism was an outward sign, a public proclamation of a private faith commitment; it didn't actually *do* anything. It was a symbolic pronouncement, albeit a powerful one. Yet, underneath this belief was a desire for it to mean more. I wanted to plunge into the cold waters of that alpine lake and emerge a new creature; I wanted to be overpowered by something stronger than my faltering will.

My turn came. I went under the water, felt the jolt of cold on my skin, my breath arrest then begin again. I came up. I was soaked, shaking, exhilarated, but also the same person I was a moment ago. The youth pastor looked at me with tears in his eyes—he was not an emotional guy, and I was surprised in that moment to realize that he cared so much. "We lost you for awhile," he said, "But you've finally come back." I remember feeling embarrassed, ashamed as I saw myself reflected in their faces. I was a cliché. The black sheep, the prodigal son, and for the beaming people around me, this familiar story had just had its climactic, redemptive ending. A soul had been reclaimed for Christ. Yes, I'd come back. But only for a time. Another fall was yet to come. I knew, deep down, this was a charade, a fake baptism, a flailing attempt to secure my fickle love.

* * *

During my last year of high school, we started driving an hour to attend a community church in the nearest city. This church had a large, growing congregation, an active youth group, a worship band—all the trappings of a bustling evangelical community. My parents changed to this church primarily for my benefit, but by then I had checked out entirely, seeing church as little more than an opportunity to troll for boys. The years of double-mindedness had worn me down, and I was now just burnt out. I was sick of church; I was sick of failing; I was sick of yo-yoing between faith and apostasy. I was not, however, sick of getting attention from guys. That was a bottomless desire. That year, I went careening from boyfriend to boyfriend, from love to crush to meaningless hook-up, without much care or awareness of how anything I did affected anyone else. When my first intense love, a nice Mormon boy, confessed he'd cheated on me, I cried in the mall food court for about half an hour, before driving to church and throwing myself at a cute Californian I met at youth group. I became adept at lying, sneaking around, so much that I would lie sometimes just for fun, just to pretend to be someone else, to escape the web of webs I was weaving, ensnaring mainly myself.

I could give you a litany of sins from this time, but it's hard to construct a coherent narrative—there was no order to my life in that year. The school year began with a growing chasm between my parents and me, because of my clandestine first love and failure to keep the purity vow I'd made when I was twelve. Then two suicides in quick succession in my small high school, one of whom was the fourteen year-old little sister of my best friend. Everything seemed to be shattering, spinning out into entropy. My best friend and I withdrew from each other, coping with grief and confusion in different ways. My drug of choice was male attention. I was driven by impulse, by emotional and sexual whims, by shame and pain and desire. I slept around, at first for love and young passion, but then, after the fall, because I began to think of myself as good for little else. I misused people and allowed them to misuse me.

Toward the end of that year, I smoked and drank a bit, as if to round out the archetype of the rebellious teenager. I even dabbled in the occult by playing with a Ouija board, which worked surprisingly, eerily well. Even though I was living in an array of colorful sins, marooning myself from the grace of God, I was not particularly concerned for my soul and fancied myself impervious to demonic forces—because, after all, I was "saved." I could act with impunity, and if all the Jesus stuff turned out to be true—an open and remote question for me at the time—I'd sneak into heaven by the back door.

This time of moral chaos hit an apex the summer before college, a three-month countdown to leaving that haunted corner of Idaho for a Christian university in another state. This was the summer after my junior year. I was seventeen, but I'd decided to graduate from high school early, because, well, everything had gone to shit. I wanted out; I was miserable; I knew my behavior was not sustainable, but I didn't know how to make it stop. For some months that hellish year, I'd harbored a secret desire to fall accidentally pregnant by my Mormon love, even though I knew that likely meant a teenage marriage, forgoing college, and remaining trapped in eastern Idaho. The prospect of that fate was terrifying, but also alluring, because it would force an external limit upon my reckless freedom.

Somehow, though, a pregnancy didn't happen—something I now find miraculous, to be honest. An exodus to college it would be, and a Christian college to boot. Part of me knew a reformation loomed, so I made sure to enjoy myself in the meantime. If I'd been praying at the time, maybe I would have riffed on St. Augustine: Lord, I'll be chaste, but not quite yet.

At the end of August, my parents accompanied me on the two-day trek to Western Oregon, the car laden with the trappings of dorm life, along with a handful of beloved artifacts from childhood, like my stuffed bear, George. That's who I was at the time, a contradictory picture: a teenaged girl toting her teddy bear off to college, and also a fallen woman, like those who haunt the pages of tragic Victorian novels, for whom things usually didn't end well. Somehow, I was both of these things.

There was something healing about that trip, a long road to a new chapter, all of us eager to bring the current one to a close. Despite the fraying of our relationship over the past year, my parents and I comfortably shared that crowded space as it moved westward. To pass the time, I read aloud *Far from the Madding Crowd*, a book I didn't particularly understand, but reciting the words on the page had a soothing effect, drawing the three of us together into a shared narrative, where the drama and betrayal and agony belonged to a fictional world, and not to us.

Our Mother Who Art in Heaven

Picture a green, sprawling quad around a clocktower, academic buildings skirting the edges. Youths scattered across the grass in various states of leisure and repose: frisbees flying, unread books open on the grass, guitars strumming in a major key. Boys with blond-tipped hair and puka shell necklaces, girls with high-waisted denim shorts and flip-flops. This was like summer Bible camp, but better; this lasted all year, and there were no campers, only cute counselors.

Such was my utopic first impression of college. Everyone, except the skittish freshman like myself, seemed so mature, so confident, so wholesome. This was an alluring new world, and I was determined to conquer it, to make it my own, to become a native. I'll be a good Christian girl, and I'll meet a good Christian guy, I'll behave myself this time, I swear.

I didn't waste any time adapting to the new environment. No longer trapped in a house with my parents and our recurrent skirmishes, I began to feel bad for how I'd treated them and resolved to reform my ways. I cut off all contact with boys from back home, even the Mormon love, who I'd dreamed of someday marrying. I threw away pictures, letters, keepsakes—I even took out my belly button ring, which, being underage, I'd lied to get in the first place and successfully concealed from my parents. It always seemed to be perennially infected and crusted over anyway, a wound that wouldn't quite heal. Fate conspired with me to make this a clean break: shortly after I went to college, my parents moved to Wyoming, so there would be no mid-semester return to Idaho, no reconnection with old friends and loves and habits. Everything could be made new.

I wish I could say that all this self-renovation stemmed from a radical inner conversion, a resolve to devote myself, once again, to God. There was some of that, sure. My longing for God never quite died away, even when I was distracted by other desires, and in this Christian setting, a spiritual hunger began to reawaken. But I was also following the same old patterns;

18

I was adapting myself to the world around me, wanting to fit in, to succeed in this new social milieu.

Plus, it was much easier to move on from the boys back home when I was suddenly surrounded by an ample supply of hymn-crooning hotties. I immediately began trolling for The One, the man destined by divine providence or fate or whatever to be my husband. At first, I kept a particular eye on boys with P-names, because I'd been told in one Ouija session that my mate would have the unfortunate initials P-U-G. Those pickings proved slim, so I soon expanded the search.

As it turns out, I did meet my future husband that first weekend of college; we were thrown together in the same group on a frenzied, campus-wide scavenger hunt, one of those many high-octane events designed to terrorize introverts. He was quiet, bearded, and hiding under a baseball cap, silently enduring the festivities around him. We didn't speak to each other, and for some reason I thought his name was Jeremiah (it is actually Michael). Our love was not instant, nothing memorable at first sight; it would not end up following the usual script. And, after that first semester of trying to fit in, neither would I.

I started out as a freshman with fairly run-of-the-mill evangelical views about women. I remember surprising a male peer during a Bible study with my assertion that women should not be pastors—at least not *head* pastors. In the back of my journal, I kept a running list of traits to look for in a future husband, an exercise encouraged in my church circles. At the top of that list? "A leader in the home, and in the world." I'm not entirely sure what I envisioned in terms of "world leader," as I didn't harbor any ambitions to marry a head of state, but the first part of that criterion is pretty straightforward. I believed that, in the home, the man should be the leader, even if I had only vague notions of how that might play out in practice.

Midway through my first semester, I acquired a nice Christian boyfriend who I'll call Dave. We were poorly matched, but it would take over a year for me to acknowledge this; he was very fun-loving and extroverted, with an buoyant youth pastor vibe. He once confessed to me that he'd rather have dozens of superficial friendships than only one or two close ones. During the pre-dating phase of our relationship, we spent a lot of time in his dorm lobby, where he shared his various hobbies with me, which I would adulate enthusiastically. He'd croon self-penned worship songs on his guitar, perform feats of daring on his scooter, and read me his poems, including one entitled "Void"—which was just a blank page.

When we finally worked up to the requisite Define the Relationship (DTR) talk, this consisted of me following him on a meandering walk all over campus for several hours, while he waited for a word from God regarding whether or not we should date. God didn't seem to be chiming in with his opinion, so Dave picked up a rock and pointed to a stop sign twenty feet away. "If I hit the stop sign, that means we should date," he said. It took several tries, but eventually God gave his approval.

As is typical, we quickly fell into the pseudo-marriage model that is emblematic of Christian dating. We spent all our time together. We made future plans around each other. We became inseparable, except when dorm rules forced us apart. I even brought him to an advising session with me, to see if we could sign up for all the same classes. In my freshman composition class, I wrote pious, maudlin essays about how much I loved Dave, how it was God's will that brought us together, how no man would put us asunder, etc. On paper and in practice, I was on the road to marrying a future youth pastor by the age of twenty. I hardly seemed a likely candidate for a sudden feminist awakening. Yet that is precisely what happened.

In spring of my freshman year, I was taking a required New Testament course. My boyfriend was unable to take the same section, due to his groundskeeping work schedule, so I'd sit by the window in the back row, and he'd arrange to prune the bushes just below, so I could wave at him and gaze at the top of his head now and then. Another back row occupant in this class turned out to be that quiet Jeremiah guy I'd met during orientation. By now, however, I knew his real name; it was often humming through my mind, a clandestine incantation. Ah yes, my faithless, fickle heart.

Of course, Michael Favale was totally out of my league, so this was an innocuous crush, like a crush on a celebrity, something that had no hope of fruition and could therefore be secretly indulged. Only a freshman, he was already taking the campus theater scene by storm. My schoolgirl desire for him was first awakened during auditions for *A Midsummer Night's Dream* several months prior. Dave and I prepped and attended auditions together (neither of us were cast), and toward the end of the night, a tall, dark-haired guy with a serious, unassuming air took the stage to read for the role of Puck. He was captivating; a hush fell over the room. In his deep, honeyed voice, the language of Shakespeare suddenly seemed to throb with life. I was sitting next to Dave, but in that moment, he ceased to exist, as did every other man in the world, until the dark-haired one stopped speaking, breaking the spell. *And this weak and idle theme, no more yielding but a dream . . .*

Yet here we were, months later, in the same class, the same row, and I found myself idly doodling his name in my notebook during lectures, making sure to spell it backwards in case he ever glanced over (he didn't): *Elavaf Leahcim*, like the name of an exotic Jewish elf from Rivendell. Evalaf Licheam.

With the ongoing distractions of an actual boyfriend and the boy-friend of my fantasies, it is remarkable that I nonetheless managed to pay attention in that class. Despite my Bible-infused upbringing, I found myself regularly startled by passages that seemed totally unfamiliar, thinking to myself, "Wait, that's actually in there?"

One such verse was 1 Corinthians 11:3, which in the NIV reads: "But I want you to realize that the head of every man is Christ, and the head of the woman is man, and the head of Christ is God." At the time, I practiced the reading strategy, ingrained through years of memory verses, of dismember-ing the text into isolated, digestible parts. So I read this verse as if it were plastered by itself on a lit-up marquee, rather than enclosed within the arc of the text as a whole. And I was unnerved, suspicious. I had a naïve trust in the Bible; I was used to it comforting me, consoling me, urging me close to God. But this verse implied a stark separation between God and myself, simply because of my sex.

When the instructor glossed over this verse in his lecture, I raised my hand and asked him directly: "What does this mean? Are women not as close to God as men?" I don't remember his response, but whatever it was, I found it less than satisfactory, and resolved to find the answer myself. I took for granted that there *was* an answer to be found, a way to disarm this verse, to make it palatable, to make the Bible safe again.

This was the early days of the internet; there was no such thing as "googling," so I found myself wandering the halls of the library instead. It was there that I made a life-altering discovery: Christian feminism. On these shelves, I found ample resources to interpret the Bible in a way that confirmed my belief in the equality of the sexes before God. By the end of the semester, just weeks away, I had embraced an evangelical feminist hermeneutic and wrote a term paper for that class with the provocative title "God is a Feminist."

This sudden embrace was somewhat surprising, as I was not raised to view feminism as a positive word, or indeed to consider it much at all. I grew up in an evangelical cocoon inside a Mormon bubble in thoroughly red states; "feminist" was not in the common lexicon. In fact, I was more familiar with the term "Femi-Nazi," coined and popularized by Rush Lim-baugh, whom my dad used to listen to on the radio. Those were the Clinton years, so Hillary, the Queen Femi-Nazi, was often pilloried, and I gleaned a vague notion of feminists as angry women in suits who wanted to be men.

When I look back and consider what inspired me to adopt a feminist identity so quickly and wholeheartedly, a few things come to mind. First, the ability to reconcile several enduring interests: my Christian faith, my fasci-nation with women's experiences, and my awareness of gender dynamics.

Before, these had seemed like separate spheres; church was a pretty masculine space overall, with male pastors, hymns to Jesus, Lord, and Father God, sermons preoccupied with Paul, or other male figures from the Bible. I might hear a story about Ruth or Esther in Sunday School, but never from the pulpit. Women's stories were edifying for women and children, but not for the congregation at large.

Christian feminism, as I first encountered it, turned a spotlight on these overlooked stories, paying careful attention to Jesus's interactions with women, how he healed them, spoke with them, exhorted them, listened to them, invited them to sit at his feet, and chose them to be the first witness and proclaimers of the Resurrection. Paul's letters reveal women's active involvement in the early Church, with forty percent of those he names as his co-workers in Christ being women—this became a favored talking point of mine, when engaged in feminist apologetics. In Christian feminism, I had discovered a form of my religion that seemed to take the Bible seriously, the gospel seriously, and women seriously.

This discovery also opened a new horizon of biblical reading. No longer was the Bible to be taken at face value as a clear-cut instruction guide for life, free from tensions and ambiguities. No, this Bible was richer, scarier, multivalent, and in need of careful interpretation. Christian feminism introduced me to the idea of hermeneutics, the idea that we read through lenses of meaning, through presuppositions we bring to a text that shape how it speaks to us. For the evangelical feminist, the foundational belief in the equal dignity of the sexes tends to translate into a praxis of egalitarianism, a rejection of strict gender roles. Verses that affirm this egalitarian sensibility are used as hermeneutical keys to reinterpret passages that seem to reject it. A closer look at the original linguistic meaning of certain words can disarm passages that seem to demand the silencing of women. This technical, academic study of the Bible opened up the text in new ways, renewing my fascination with and faith in sacred Scripture. At least at first.

There's another reason I fell so quickly for Christian feminism: it enabled me to reclaim a positive feminine identity. While there is much I now appreciate about my evangelical upbringing, there is one aspect I can say was spiritually damaging—the undue emphasis on female sexual purity. Once I was no longer a virgin, it was made very clear to me that I now occupied a permanent, second-class status among my peers. I was damaged goods. Even though I'd repented and, for the time being, reformed my ways, there was nothing I could do to regain my purity in the eyes of God, or in the eyes of fellow Christians. My past transgressions were something I would always have to carry with me. I was marked, if not with a visible scarlet letter, with the inner corrosion of shame.

"Imagine it's your wedding day," said a girl from my dorm floor, first semester. We were in the back of a van, driving to the beach for a girl-bonding
retreat. "Picture your beautiful white dress, the one you've always dreamed
of wearing. You're walking down the aisle to meet your future husband, and
everyone is watching you, your family, your friends." She paused dramati-
cally. "Now, imagine a bright red handprint on your body, everywhere a guy
has touched you."

I laughed, a default defense mechanism for me. "Well, looks like I'd
have a lovely red dress!" I joked, brazenly outing myself as a non-virgin to
my shocked dorm mates. I laughed at this and other equally bizarre prophy-
lactic thought experiments: Imagine you're a lollipop that's been unwrapped
and sucked on! Imagine you're a piece of gum that's already been chewed!
I laughed, yes, but I got the message, well familiar by that point. I knew
I was trapped in the wrong side of a dichotomy—not the virgin, but the
whore. And I knew I'd have to break the news to any boy I dated, let him
examine my past sins, decide if I'm still marriage material. I received the
message, and worse, I believed it. I believed that I had transgressed beyond
the bounds of restoration, that I was permanently damaged, and this belief
abetted continued poor choices, because there was no longer any purity to
protect. This does not absolve me of personal responsibility. I made those
choices. But I made them under the assumption of my irredeemability.

In this new paradigm of Christian feminism, however, a woman's value
was not contingent on her sexual history. I could begin to rethink myself beyond that dichotomy, as a whole person again. Instead of virginity, a passive
virtue that can be permanently lost, this paradigm prized active virtues like
fortitude, mercy, justice. Discovering feminism did not magically heal my
shame—that would come later, from a different source. But it allowed me
to regain a sense of self-respect, a renewed belief in my worth as a human
being, one made in the image of God.

For the first two years of college, my feminism more or less stayed
in the evangelical sphere. I was not yet trying to dismantle the underlying
premises of my tradition, namely the view of Scripture as divinely inspired
and authoritative. I operated within this presumption, trying instead to re-
cover what I believed to be more faithful, accurate readings of Scripture, to
discern what Paul et al. were *really* trying to say.

Admittedly, I was also importing some premises to guide this interpretive project; I was working backwards, beginning with the assumption
that Christianity, rightly understood, would uphold an egalitarian ethic
between the sexes. The verses that affirmed this I was happy to read at face
value; it was those passages that seemed more hierarchical that needed careful examination. I spent most of my energy researching and compiling a

compelling biblical argument for women in ministry, reading Jesus against Paul, Paul against himself.

Turning to the Old Testament, I revived my childhood interest in the stories of women, attempting to reclaim obscured female figures. At first, I focused on those whose example confirmed the idea of women's leadership—like Deborah, who leads Israel in the book of Judges, or Miriam, the prophetess. Eventually, however, my attention turned to the so-called "texts of terror," stories about women that were horrifying, rather than inspiring. These narratives were not highlighted in the study guides of my NIV Student Bible, but left buried, like landmines, for the hapless reader to stumble upon. The gang rape and dismemberment of the unnamed concubine in Judges 19 is an iconic example, or Jephthah, who sacrifices his beloved daughter to fulfill a rash vow.

The story that most haunted me was that of Tamar, David's daughter. David is the celebrated hero of the Old Testament, a prefiguring of Christ the King, the poet of the Psalms, slayer of Goliath, the man after God's own heart. Even his primary failing, committing adultery with Bathsheba and arranging the death of her husband, is incorporated into his favorable edit, because he repents; he humbles himself before God and accepts the consequences of his sin. Absalom, his proud, longhaired son, is a villain who rebels out of envy and personal ambition. This was the story of King David, as I knew it, as it had been told to me.

Then I read 2 Samuel 13. I read about Amnon, David's firstborn heir, and his burning lust for his sister Tamar. I read about his methodical conspiracy to trap her in his room so he could rape her. I read her protestations. I read about the rape. I read about how Amnon's lust turned to hate as soon as the deed was done. I read about Tamar's disgrace, her life-altering shame, her exile into the household of her brother Absalom, and her disappearance from the text altogether. That is where she leaves us: stripped of virginity, she is no longer relevant, no longer able to play a role, through childbirth and marriage, in the world of men. According to the text, King David is furious, but this is an impotent rage. He does nothing to Amnon, who remains his heir. Tamar bears all the punishment of a crime done to her. Absalom, as it turns out, does not usurp his brother from mere ambition, but out of vengeance, out of love for his sister, Tamar.

What haunted me was the rape, yes, and how Tamar was treated afterward—permanently disgraced. That, and her eventual silence; she is swallowed by the text, her ultimate fate unwritten. Recovering this story completely altered my opinion of David—how could this be a "man after God's own heart?" Unlike the episode with Bathsheba, there is no repenting here; David does not realize his mistake and come to the defense of his daughter. Yet this is never part of the story of David, as told in church circles. I never heard a sermon on Tamar. I'd never even heard her name mentioned, until I read the story for myself.

This marked a turning point in my feminist outlook—a growing resentment, even anger, toward the Bible, and toward a Christianity unquestioningly mired in it. For the evangelical, the Bible is the sole divine authority, the pristine source of right doctrine and sound living—the primary means of understanding God and our relationship to him. I began to wonder: how can stories like the rape of Tamar be incorporated into this view of the Bible? How can I understand myself, as a woman before God, through this story? I was still, more or less, assuming a didactic and piecemeal reading of Scripture. God's failure to weigh in with narrative authority and condemn David's passivity seemed like tacit approval. I did not yet have a holistic, overarching view of scriptural narrative; I expected each isolated story to have a clear, unambiguous spiritual message. The Bible was supposed to be safe and good, but it no longer felt safe. It no longer felt good.

If I were to speak of my personal feminist revolution as having "waves," the first wave would be the evangelical wave, characterized by an effort to reinterpret Scripture in a way that confirmed feminist assumptions about equal dignity and mutuality between the sexes. The second wave, breaking in my latter years of college, began to push against the notion of biblical authority, against the boundaries of evangelical orthodoxy. This wave was marked by a hermeneutics of suspicion and resentment. Paul no longer needed to be reinterpreted as an egalitarian ally; I could simply disregard what seemed sexist as being shaped by the patriarchal culture of his time. Instead of trying to save the Bible from seeming misogynist, I wanted to dig up those very passages and execrate them. I wanted to put the Bible on trial—no longer as defense attorney, but as lead prosecutor.

My faith in the Bible as inspired and authoritative was severely eroded by my senior year. An iconic feminist pastime in my first wave would have been working through a reinterpretation of 1 Timothy, trying to reclaim the truest meaning of the text in favor of women's ordination. An emblematic activity of my second wave? Rewriting the Lord's Prayer in my own words, excising the Father-language and replacing it with Mother.

During this subsequent wave, I began making an effort to pray to God as Mother, convinced that masculine language for God was a hangover from patriarchy. But this felt forced and inauthentic, like it was something I felt I *should* do, like something that *should* work, but didn't. At the time, my explanation for this was simple: I was too indoctrinated by the patriarchy. My concept of "woman" was too sexualized, "mother" too mired in regressive gender norms. As a product of a misogynist culture, I couldn't make myself *believe* that God could be feminine. It never occurred to me to question the legitimacy of the practice itself, to consider what important meaning the Father metaphor might bring to prayer. I'd become something of an ideologue; anything could be interpreted in a way that confirmed my assumptions about reality. Patriarchy was always at fault, somehow.

Over these college years, my faith was in gradual exodus, shifting from my heart to my head. Being Christian had become an intellectual endeavor, a work of deconstruction and critique, an ongoing effort to reinterpret my religious tradition through the ideals of feminism. It was no longer my soul that needed saving, nor Christianity that could save. Rather, Christianity was in need of redemption, and I was the feminist prophet come to rescue my religion from itself.

Common Prayer

M y first impression notwithstanding, college, as it turns out, is not at all like Bible camp. I discovered this in my first philosophy class, which I took the spring of my freshman year. While I grew up in an inquisitive familial environment, the evangelicalism of my youth was suspicious of hard-hitting questions that confronted foundational Christian truths. We were trained to defend our beliefs, rather than investigate them. I developed a somewhat protective posture toward my faith, as if I was standing in front of it, facing away, guarding it from attacks from the outside world.

But in that first philosophy class, I was asked—required—to do something I'd never done: to face my faith and examine its premises, to prod them with the rudimentary philosophical tools I was acquiring. Over the semester, we had to write four papers arguing the following: 1) there is no God; 2) no human has a soul 3); abortion is always right; 4) trees have moral rights. It may seem scandalous that such paper topics were assigned at a Christian college. In a different, secular context, these assignments would likely be a transparent effort to dismantle the naïve evangelical faith of the students. And they were, I think, meant to dismantle something—not the faith, but the naiveté. These papers were an effort to force us to thoroughly consider an alternative perspective that we'd never been allowed to entertain, in order to help us understand why Christianity affirms the opposite.

Being forced to argue the opposite of what I'd been raised to believe was exhilarating. Here was a discipline that took nothing for granted, except perhaps Aristotle's principle of non-contradiction, and demanded that the truth-seeker strip reality down to its barest bones, down to the scaffolding that bolsters a worldview. I felt a new intellectual horizon opening. Truth was no longer a small terrain, easily and already mapped out for me, an enclosed kingdom to be guarded against invaders. Truth was a land wild and unknown; I had maps, but the clear edges blurred into a wilderness, full of mountains yet unnamed.

The professor of this class was a philosopher-priest. He was a burly, middle-aged Canadian, who had the air of a benevolent but formidable Scottish warlord. He was gruff, intimidating, no-nonsense, and he wore the exotic black garb and white collar of a priest—he was probably the first person that I ever saw wearing clerics. He was not Catholic, but Anglican, though the distinction meant little to me at the time. Over the next four years, this professor became a guide, like Frodo's Gandalf or Dante's Virgil, through a dimension of Christendom I'd yet to encounter. This was the advent of the other awakening I experienced in college, one that unfolded in tandem with my turn toward feminism—indeed these two threads were initially intertwined, until one began to unravel. This awakening is harder to label; there is no trite –ism to affix. It was a spiritual quickening, an initiation to tradition, to liturgy, to sacrament, to a Christianity more ancient, more enigmatic, more enthralling than I'd previously known.

* * *

The philosopher-priest lived in an old farmhouse on the edge of town, once probably surrounded by farmland, but now flanked by lookalike houses with tiny yards and massive garages. In the midst of these new settlements, he held on to at least an acre of land, where a few sheep wandered listlessly, as if trying to make sense of their suburban surroundings. On Sunday evenings, in his small living room, while a teacup dog in varying stages of alopecia yapped and wriggled around our legs, the philosopher celebrated the Eucharist according to the Anglican rites. There were typically five or six in attendance, myself and a few fellow students, occasionally a neighbor or two, but my professor's towering bulk, clad in white priestly vestments, filled the space, which never seemed empty.

I'd had a taste of a more liturgical, eucharistic worship in high school, while briefly attending a Lutheran church in my small town. I did not make an effort to try to understand what was going on in the service—I was too caught up in the whirlwind of teenage passions—but I remember liking it. I liked the short-and-sweet homily rather than the sprawling sermon. I liked kneeling down at the altar rail, on a beige cushion that looked like a maple bar, to receive communion. But I had no awareness, whether intellectual or visceral, of the Real Presence, no inkling that the bread and wine were supposed to be anything other than what they appeared to be.

There, at the farmhouse altar, I began to develop a deeper sense of the sacred. I'd had "spirit-filled" experiences before, moments of emotional euphoria during group worship, but this was something different, something more profound. This did not make me want to raise my hands in jubilation. This made me want—need—to kneel and fall silent.

The Eucharist was the centerpiece of this new-yet-ancient form of worship. Not a sermon, not thirty minutes of guitar songs, but a holy meal shrouded in holy language. What exactly occurred during the priestly prayer was still vague to me, inchoate and mystical, mostly just a strong sense that *something was happening*. Some mystery was being broached, some veil being pulled back, but just for an instant, just for a glimpse. Christ's presence felt palpable, not so much in the bread and wine specifically, but in the midst of our unison voices, our shared gestures. A transmutation of the profane to the sacred; God breaking into the mundane fabric of our existence—that's what I was beginning to experience. In a cramped and dusty living room that smelled like dog.

Before long, after months of these Sundays, the Eucharistic liturgy became second nature, the words surfacing in my mind in tandem with the priest and the people. The liturgy was not rote; memorization did not make it dead and automatic, as I'd often heard liturgical worship characterized in evangelical circles. Rather, the words were a gift that had become my own, a gift from outside of myself, one I could bring inward and offer back with my own breath. Gone was the stress of having to produce an eloquent and profound prayer extemporaneously, prayers that ironically tended to all sound alike, despite their alleged authenticity. I did not have to search and grasp for the right language from the muddle of my own experience. I was given the words, and those words gave shape to my experience.

During the weekday evenings, a handful of us, mostly philosophy majors and ragtag disciples of the philosopher-priest, began to gather and pray the evening prayer rite from the Anglican Book of Common Prayer. Even now, I look back at this time in my life as the most spiritually rich of my pre-Catholic years. I was able to experience a robust integration of the intellectual and spiritual. Each week began with the Eucharist, shared with fellow students and a professor who taught many of my classes. Our conversations flowed from the classroom, to the farmhouse, to the dinner table after evening prayer. My life, for that time, maintained a liturgical rhythm. I'd never prayed so consistently, never been so rooted in my faith, never felt charged with such devotion. Of course, I was still boy crazy, still struggling with surging hormones and sexual boundaries. But I was moving in the right direction; I was struggling *toward* God, rather than away.

Eventually, I decided, along with several of my compatriots—including boyfriend Dave—to be confirmed in the philosopher-priest's small Anglican denomination. I was nervous about breaking the news to my parents. I'd already had some evangelical peers voice their disapproval. Anglicanism, they warned, was almost like *Catholicism*. It was a potential gateway drug to outright popery. (In all fairness, this did end up being somewhat true in my case.) My retort was always to point to the patron saint of evangelicalism: "But C. S. Lewis was Anglican!"

I waited for an opportune time, when my parents and I were visiting my brother at Wheaton College. I had been scouring the phone book for an Episcopalian church to attend on Sunday, so I figured I needed to break the news. We were in an Indian restaurant, nibbling on crispy appetizers, when I took a deep breath: "Mom, Dad, I need to tell you something." This was probably an overly dramatic intro; my mother's eyes widened and they both froze. What new and awful surprise could I be springing on them now? I'm sure my mom's mind lurched instantly to Worst Case Scenario, which was probably me getting knocked up and dropping out of college. "I'm becoming Anglican," I said. They stared at me. "It's basically, you know, Episcopalian." They looked at each other and started laughing. "Okay!" My mother sighed and laughed again. "Great!"

I was confirmed the fall of my sophomore year. Soon afterward Dave and I broke up; he transferred to a Bible college and, as far as I know, left Anglicanism behind. I continued to attend Sunday Eucharist and evening prayer, a habit I kept up while studying abroad in Oxford. There, I went to sung vespers in a beautiful college chapel. I learned to chant the Agnus Dei in Latin and began to pick up Anglo-Catholic habits, like bowing toward the crucifix as it passed by in procession. The higher the liturgy soared, the more I longed to follow. The more I could pray with my body, the better.

During these middle college years, my feminist and spiritual awakenings unfolded in tandem, feeding into one another seamlessly. My entry into a more ancient form of Christianity introduced me to the communion of saints, and my spiritual imagination was newly peopled with figures like Catherine of Siena and Julian of Norwich. Even Mary, Christ's mother, was emerging from the shadows; I carried her words with my voice every time I prayed the Magnificat in evening prayer. In Oxford, I spent most of my time and energy researching and writing about medieval women mystics. I discovered St. Hildegard of Bingen, a twelfth-century Benedictine polymath and theologian who would be my confirmation saint a decade hence. My feminism was leading me to encounter the female faces of Christianity, which ushered me more deeply into tradition, into a life of faith.

Until it didn't. At some point, my forage into feminism began to supplant my faith in Christianity. My time at Oxford and the summer following was the pinnacle of unification between my feminist fervor and my hunger for God—after that, the union began to disintegrate.

* * *

Even then, all those years ago, Catholicism beckoned from afar. Despite my initiation into liturgy and sacrament, there was still something set apart about Catholicism, something yet more strange and otherworldly. Anglicanism seemed to have one foot deeply planted in the world of today, even while it stretched back through time toward ancient Christendom. Catholicism, though, seemed almost an opposite movement, a long-ago world breaking in on the present.

After coming home from Oxford, I spent the summer in Laramie, Wyoming, where my parents had moved. There was a beautiful Episcopalian cathedral in town, built around the fin de siècle, cruciform in shape, with a jutting spire and bright-red arching door. In my time at Oxford, my palate had been formed by the high Anglo-Catholic liturgies, and the Episcopal cathedral, though much newer, was old by American standards, and seemed to evoke the same ornate, reverential spirit. I biked over for noon prayer when I could, joining a handful of gray-haired parishioners, and sometimes attended on Sundays, when I didn't go to church with my parents. The priest at the cathedral was a woman—my first experience with a female priest— and I liked her tremendously. I even began to ponder whether I was called to the priesthood myself.

A block away from the cathedral was the local Catholic parish, a more minimalist but equally beautiful Norman-style building dating from the 1920s. Sometimes, en route to noon prayer, I would find myself inside the Catholic church instead. This was not a pre-meditated decision, but something that seemed to happen on accident. The interior of the Catholic parish was smaller and painted in a warm, soft white—different from the cathedral, which was far more cavernous, with pews and ceiling of dark wood. The walls of the parish church were lined with religious art, carving after carving of Jesus carrying the cross—I'd not yet heard of the Stations of the Cross—interspersed with stained-glass scenes of unfamiliar saints. On either side of the main altar were two small side-altars with rows of votive candles, a few scattered flames flickering. And, of course, a large wooden crucifix looming above the center altar.

There was no one else in the sanctuary, but I did not feel alone. And this was more eerie than comforting. I felt so conscious of the presence of another person that I was sure a priest was nearby, about to walk in at any moment, or perhaps already there and obscured inside a confessional, listening to me breathe. I felt like an interloper, and I didn't want to be found out.

Once, I wandered into the church just before Mass, and I stayed on, trying and failing to fumble through the missal, before giving up and just listening, watching. So much of the Mass seemed familiar, an echo of the Anglican liturgy I knew well. Some of the responses were almost identical. Intellectually, I thought of Anglicanism and Catholicism as twin sisters, one born first with stodgier views about women, the other just as lovely and winsome, but without the prickly, legalistic personality. By being an Anglican, I was convinced I'd found the ideal combination—the ancient beauty and the modern, enlightened wisdom.

Yet something kept derailing me on my way to noon prayer. Even though I had it all sorted out in my mind—I belonged at the almost-Catholic church with the female priest, not the actual Catholic church that forbids female priests—my heart remained restless.

Two churches. In actuality, they are a block apart. Facing the Catholic parish, you can see the Episcopal cathedral behind it and to the right. But I only know this from looking at pictures. In my memory, you see, the churches are directly side-by-side. So clear is this memory, that I am shocked to discover it's not correct. They are quite close together, true, but on separate streets.

In a way, though, the version in my memory is more accurate. At that interval in my life, I stood before those two churches, which faced me in turn, one on my right, one on my left. My memory puts in spatial terms what was happening within me. I was at a crossroads. Two doors opening to me, two echoing halls, and within them, disparate paths unfolded.

So I chose. I followed my feminist convictions, which were fast and firm, rather than that unnamable, mysterious current that pulled elsewhere.

The Way of Sorrows

There's this phrase in latin, *fomes peccati*, that translates to "the tinder of sin." Tinder: dry, combustible material that only needs a stray spark to flare up into a consuming fire. This is a metaphor for understanding human fallenness; we carry within us, always, the capacity for sin. Grace can extinguish the fires when they break out, but the fuel, the tinder of our appetites, waits in our hearts—dormant, one hopes, but waiting nonetheless.

When my senior year of college began, I was on the rebound from a brutal heartbreak. Dave was long gone, having been replaced by a long-haired Wyoming cowboy who played the electric guitar. At just nineteen, I became engaged against my parents' wishes and went off to study abroad in England with a ring on my finger, in a state of cognitive dissonance. I was crazy about my fiancé, exhilarated at the thought of marrying him, but my inner feminist was scandalized that I was engaged so young, especially to a man whose most prized possession was a coffee mug emblazoned with the words ALPHA MALE—a mug I'd given him myself.

This dissonance didn't last long. At the beginning of the summer, just home from Oxford, my fiancé abruptly broke off our relationship. It was an ill-fated match, to be sure, although I couldn't face that at the time. I did love him, and his rejection of that love was devastating. At first, I was able to take that grief to God—at least I tried to. I tried to live in a state of ruthless trust, even though the future now seemed so vacant. At the same time, my pain made me weak. I let the ex-fiancé string me along over the summer months. He was sure we were done, but it's hard to quit the emotional and physical comfort of an intense relationship, and whenever he turned back to me—always temporarily, always without promises—I gave myself to him, heart and body, too freely.

One mid-summer night, I was back in his apartment. He'd visited my work earlier and wanted to see me, and I came over, not having the will-power to refuse, even though our momentary reconciliations always left the

33

open wound more festering than before. While we were dating and engaged, we'd never been sexually intimate—thanks more to his self-control, rather than mine—but after the breakup, he changed his mind. He asked, and I assented.

There's a language that the body speaks during sexual union. A wordless promise of total self-gift. The body says: I am wholly yours; I belong to you; I give you myself, even my capacity to create new life, a gift that can't be taken back. When there are no spoken promises alongside this corporeal speech, the language of the body becomes a lie. With his body, he said: I give myself to you. With his words, he said: I don't want you.

Afterward, when he'd left the room, I was by myself, feeling broken and empty. In that moment, tangled up in my own weakness and misery, I had a profound experience of Christ's presence—not an amorphous presence, but there, right there, in the corner of the room. I looked right at him, and he looked at me. Not with judgment, or anger, or even disappointment, but pure pity. What are you doing here? He asked me. You were made for love, he said, not this.

I'd like to say that encounter changed everything. That I was able to cling to those words and believe them. But the enduring sense of my own worthlessness was hard to give up. I believed in that more than I believed in him. And this became the spark in my tinder of sin.

By the time school began again, and the ex and I said our final goodbye, I was wrung out, hoping that my return to college would be a return to spiritual vitality. I'd been away eight months from the beloved farmhouse church, with study abroad and summer break, and in the interim, things had changed. The farmhouse was gone, and there were new marriages in our little tribe. My best friend and fellow student married his girlfriend, and the philosopher-priest had recently remarried as well, moving to another house across town. While a widower, he'd been able to dedicate himself to his student-parishioners unreservedly. Now, of course, he had to devote himself elsewhere. My friend, similarly, had moved off campus and became cocooned in married life. We no longer prayed evening prayer consistently during the week. I felt abandoned twice over, needing more than ever the consolations of a tight-knit Eucharistic community, but I came back to find that community scattered.

The seamless union between my Christianity and my feminism was likewise beginning to disintegrate. The anger simmering in my heart began to eat away at my faith. I was increasingly resentful of evangelicalism, which seemed hopelessly misogynist and simplistic. I sought solace in reading postmodern and liberal mainline theology. I found it freeing to move beyond the straitjacket of orthodoxy, where I could let go of unpalatable doctrines, like eternal damnation and the inherent sinfulness of fornication. The very idea of sin began to seem archaic. Better to speak and think in terms of "health," I concluded. Taking sin seriously, especially sexual sin, meant thinking of myself as irrevocably defiled, while moving beyond sin seemed to offer an escape from shame. Or so I thought. If I'd had a concept of chastity then—an active, lifelong virtue, rather than the one-and-done virginity—maybe that would've helped. But I didn't. And maybe it wouldn't have mattered anyway.

Gradually, I was coming to see Christianity as essentially a beautiful story, a profound metaphor for the human experience that, if purged of its regressive baggage, could illuminate one's existence. The virgin birth, the resurrection—even if not literally, actually true, those myths were charged with beauty and meaning. I had more or less a postmodern outlook: ultimate truth cannot be known by finite human beings, so we collectively create metanarratives of meaning to connect with what remains beyond us. Christianity is one such narrative, perhaps the best and truest one, but not necessarily *actually* or *absolutely* true in its entirety.

This vision of Christianity was intellectually freeing and invigorating, but spiritually deadening. Toward the end of my senior year, I spoke with my philosopher-priest about a growing sense of malaise. While I felt plenty of cerebral energy toward religion, and was deep-diving into postmodern theology, this energy didn't seem to reach my heart. I never felt like praying; I never sensed God's presence. If anything, I was beginning to find the idea of God quite alien. What in previous years had felt like a collaborative effort, like I was searching for God and he was beckoning to me, now seemed a solitary pursuit, a conversation I was having with only myself. "It's like God has moved behind a wall," I said, "And I can no longer see and reach him."

At the time, both of us concluded that that wall must be patriarchy. Because the word "God" is so charged with masculine language and imagery in Christianity, that would naturally create a barrier between us. This was a plausible hypothesis, to be sure. But, looking back, I can't help but notice it doesn't fit the evidence at all. I was more immersed in feminist theology than I'd ever been. I had been experimenting—fruitlessly—with using feminine language for God. I'd even re-written the Lord's Prayer as a prayer to God as Mother, and we used that prayer during our Sunday Eucharist gatherings. Feminist concerns and rhetoric were, now more than ever, an integral part of our little religious community. Yet it was precisely at this moment of feminist ascendancy that I felt God disappearing behind that impenetrable wall. It was when I tried to pray to God as Mother that I lost the desire to pray at all.

* * *

In the midst of all this, still on the mend from heartbreak, I fell into an unexpected love. One warm autumn night in late September, I shared a clumsy, beer-fueled kiss with one Michael Favale, the boy I'd admired from afar since my freshman year. We'd struck up an ongoing friendship over the past four years, but never dated. After that first kiss, we entered that ambiguous relationship zone of hanging out a lot, kissing a fair bit, but leaving things open-ended and undefined. Despite my fervent vows to swear off men, or at least any serious relationships, I fell hard for Michael, perhaps because I'd been slowly falling for years. Recklessly tumbling into love was always my fatal feminist flaw. I was an independent woman who needed a man by her side. And here I was, experiencing the consummation of a long-suffering crush.

But the stars were not aligning seamlessly for us. If I was in something like a slow spiritual decline, Michael was in a downward spiral. He was losing his faith—a faith he'd lived more devoutly than I had—and in the mire of a deep depression, the extent of which I didn't fully grasp at the time. He was living in an off-campus apartment with several roommates, all in the throes of existential crises, booze and pot in abundance. Though I was more outwardly functional, staying on top of my academic work and commitments, we were both walking wounded, seeking solace in each other.

After a couple of breakups, by the time I graduated we had settled into a bond that seemed like it would hold, even though I harbored a secret anxiety that eventually he, too, would reject me for good. Being with Michael was healing, restful in a way that I'd never experienced in all my previous couplings. He had absolutely no interest in examining my sexual history, unlike some boyfriends, who'd had to process and forgive my non-virginity. I'd heard throughout my life the truism that marriage takes work, relationships take work—but being with Michael never felt like work.

I remember one particular moment, walking up the hilly drive to my on-campus apartment, when I was struck with an epiphany: Michael is someone I could love for the rest of my life. Not just *try* to love, or *work at* loving, but someone I simply would love easily, unalterably. At the time, our relationship still new and rocky, this epiphany filled me with sadness, because I assumed we wouldn't last, that I would spend my life looking back and wondering, *what if. . .?* But the final, cataclysmic break up never came, and slowly but surely, our lives grafted together.

The year after graduation, Michael's nucleus of friends had relocated to Portland and we occasionally drove up to see them. As was my pattern when in love, the lover's world began to encompass my own, a process made easier with the dispersing of my college friends and the loss of community. Initially, the recklessness of this group had been a welcome novelty, seeming more like youthful revelry than anything destructive and enduring. On the midnight of my twenty-first birthday, for example, the guys ambushed me at my apartment and we spent the night playing Bible Pictionary and drinking too much wine.

Over the next few months, however, the existential crisis in this tribe of Lost Boys had lost its sense of urgency, quieting into a banal nihilism. Alcohol and drugs were omnipresent, but what went on there can't really be characterized as "partying"; there was no party, nothing being celebrated, just a sense of ever-present despair and a fleeting attempt to escape it. I orbited the group, but never fully entered it. Aside from a couple of ex-perimental efforts here and there, I remained wary of drugs—not due to moral resoluteness on my part, but because spending a lot of time around smart people made stupid by intoxicants makes it seem much less enticing. Despite my own spiritual upheaval, I could not fully relate to this abandon-ment to finitude, to the heat of the present moment.

One afternoon, Michael and I came over to the apartment to find the guys sprawled out in the bedroom, rolling on ecstasy. I wasn't in the mood to watch a scrum of sweaty, inebriated men profess their platonic love for one other, so I left and went for a walk. The apartment was on the eastern edge of Portland, in a non-descript suburban fringe, so I was surprised to find myself, barely five minutes into the walk, at the entry of an otherworld-ly sanctuary. Catholic spaces seem to have a magnetic effect on me, even without my conscious awareness. That particular afternoon, I stumbled into The Grotto, a sprawling, 62-acre outdoor shrine dedicated to Mary, Our Sorrowful Mother.

The Grotto is built around and atop a sheer, rocky cliff, over 100 feet high. On the ground level, there is a cave hollowed out into the side of the cliff, with a statue of Mary holding the body of her crucified son in her arms. On the upper level are the botanical gardens, filled with an array of images, shrines, and life-sized statues depicting the *Via Matris*, the seven sorrows of the Virgin Mary.

I knew nothing about the *Via Matris*, or the Stations of the Cross, or the Mysteries of the Holy Rosary, so the full meaning behind much of the iconography in the Grotto was foreign to me. Yet again and again, whenever we visited the Lost Boys, I'd quietly sneak away to wander the sanctuary—not to pray, a habit I'd given up, and not even to actively contemplate God or truth or what-have-you, but simply to wander, to probe the longings of my heart, to wait for a sense of Something, Someone. I wandered not with in-tention, but by instinct. Even as I longed to belong to this luminous world, I felt myself outside of it. The flame of my faith was flickering, alight one moment, dark the next. The statues were so lifelike, yet also mute and looking past me, through me, into another realm that I once, too, had perceived, but which now seemed full of wraiths and shades. I didn't know if these images were windows into that world, or if the world itself had been imagined, a fantasy of my youth. The beauty surrounding me was entrancing—but what was its origin? The collective imaginings of human beings, coalescing over millennia? Or the revelations of a Creator who loved us into being?

That March, in the dark heart of Lent, Michael and I wandered the Grotto together. I'd been accepted into graduate school in Scotland, and we were making plans to marry. We were both ready for a new start, ready to escape the downward spiral that had claimed our friends, on the edge of which we wavered. It was late March, the brink of spring, a warm day shot with sunlight breaking through the gloom. We roamed together, talking of God and sadness and hope, our conversation a eulogy for the faith we'd all but lost. By his side, I felt like I'd found the Someone I'd been waiting for; his presence was the only one I felt. The light touch of his hand was a tourniquet for my longing. We walked the *Via Matris*, with its statued depictions of Mary's sorrows, stopping at a bench to sit together, face each other. "I love you," he said. "I want you to know that. I will always love you. I will take care of you, and I need you to take care of me." He kissed me and gave me a malachite ring. The green of the stone was deep and bright, more real somehow than the flash of a diamond. We stayed there together for a few moments longer, in sweet silence. The bench on which we sat faced the last of the seven sorrows: the burial of Jesus in the tomb.

PART II

The Storm

"To such weakness is a soul reduced when it is not yet anchored in the solid ground of truth. It is tossed and turned, whirled and spun, by every breath of opinion from the mouths of those who think they know, its light obscured by clouds and it cannot see the truth. But look! Truth is straight ahead of us."

- St. Augustine, *The Confessions*

Adrift

I am feeling the need to be brutally honest. Here are some things I am afraid to admit, even to myself. I'll carve them onto this page in dark ink:

I don't like the Bible. It is teeming with things that completely contradict my most deeply held beliefs and ethics. I do not believe it is God-inspired, at least any more than any other text. It is a creation of men. Every. Single. Word.

I don't believe Jesus was divine. I don't believe his death to be anything more than a tragedy. He was a man, and we have little idea what the historical Jesus was really like. All four gospels paint a different picture. There are four Christs.

I don't know if there is divinity in the universe. I don't believe in "God" as a personal guy-in-the-sky.

I rarely pray. When I do, my words hit the ceiling and bounce back to me. A part of me longs for the existence of a loving, all-encompassing deity, but I am doubtful.

I don't believe in the afterlife, in any form, either intellectually or intuitively. I believe that we all die, and that's it.

I do not believe in any of the creeds.

I find the history of the Christian church to be tainted with misogyny, mass murder, theft, oppression, greed, deception—a litany of grave sins.

I do not like church. I never have. Except for those four lone fruitful years as an Anglican in college.

In sum: modern American Christianity asserts, in many ways, the complete opposite of what I actually do believe.

Why, then, is it so fucking hard to let go? Why do I still, at some level, want to be part of a religion that I pretty much loathe? I know what I miss. I miss the experience of having faith, of being able to look to someone greater than myself. I miss nothing about evangelicalism. I miss some parts of Anglicanism. But, honestly, I am not a Christian anymore. I cannot seem to muster an active faith in any god. And I cannot reconcile what I hate about Christianity with what I love about it. I don't even know what I love about it, if anything. I feel betrayed by it. Let down.

Yes, I believe in "Jesus" (if "Jesus" means peace and love between people).

Yes, I believe in "God" (if by "God," I mean "meaning" and "mystery").

Enough word games. I am not a Christian. I am nostalgic, somewhat mournful; I miss those years in college when I had such spiritual meaning in my life as an Anglican. But I am not there anymore. I am not plagued by doubt; I am plagued by non-belief. No matter how hard I wish otherwise, no matter how hard this is to write, it is true: I am not a Christian anymore.

I wrote this in my mid-twenties, midway through graduate school, in mid-March, in the middle of a years-long Lent. The following journal entry comes just a few weeks later, on Easter.

I found myself praying again. On Sunday, I felt like going to church, to an Anglican service, a setting that used to be so alive for me. After driving around for ages, cursing, looking for a parking spot, I was surprised how calming, how comforting, even exhilarating the service was for me. Yeah, I was rusty, and a little bumbly. Like I was stretching out a stiff, unused muscle. But it was really wonderful.

This was the era of the in-between. I was adrift in waters that moved in eddies, stranded between the island of what I once loved and believed and a distant, far-off shore—was it even real? Or was it a trick of the light?

Some days, I could see it. I trusted the land was there, trusted that I was moving toward something, was moved by Someone. Then that trust would disappear, and I would see only the ocean—a vast, impersonal expanse of existence that had nothing to disclose. I wavered, day to day, between faith and disbelief, never sure, never steady. I didn't know if I was a Christian, because I wasn't sure what the word even meant.

Yet the longing never left. When I think about this time, this is the image I see: a girl adrift in the ocean, no land in sight, clutching onto a tiny, wooden raft, just a row of logs tied together. Her feet churn in the water, touching nothing but dark fathoms beneath. She is clutching the raft, which holds her afloat, but the raft itself is anchorless, rudderless. They bob in the water together, waiting to wash up on some shore, any shore, so the world can seem steady again.

Untethering myself from tradition, Scripture, creed—at first this all seemed so liberating. Everything was boundless potential; I could salvage what was meaningful and purge myself from the rest of it. There were no limits. I lopped those branches from the great ancient tree, just enough to keep afloat, and I paddled away from the shore alone, without a clear heading, whispering to no one in particular, "I am free, I am free, I am free."

* * *

During one of these in-between years, I made a journey, a pilgrimage of sorts, to Iona, a tiny island off the western coast of Scotland. For centuries, in the early Middle Ages, Iona was a thriving hub of Celtic Christianity. Saint Columba and twelve companions were exiled there in the sixth century and founded a monastery, which was renowned in its day, until persistent Viking raids drove the monks from the island centuries later.

Today, Iona retains a connection to that medieval spiritual identity. The Abbey church offers ecumenical Christians services with an emphasis on eco-theology. Communion is open, a cup of wine passed from hand to hand for anyone to take. The liturgy echoes the Eucharistic liturgy of Anglicanism, with a soothing revisionist spin. The communal confession does not mention sin, instead urging those gathered to "rid ourselves of what we need to carry no longer." The creed—renamed "affirmation of faith"—proclaims belief in "God above us," "God beside us," and "God within us." The Father, the Virgin Mary, and Pontius Pilate have been excised to make room for references to sun and moon, water and earth. Words like *love, life, healing, hope* permeate the prayers. There is nothing to fear or dread, nothing to offend. At the time, I thought I'd never heard a liturgy so beautiful.

The only way to reach Iona is by ferry from the nearby island of Mull. The residents of Iona number fewer than two hundred, living in a village scattered along the eastern shore. The western shore, facing the open Atlantic, still feels wild and untamed, possessed only by the wind and herds of wandering sheep.

The wind on Iona is otherworldly, sweeping across the rolling, treeless landscape, blowing wherever it wills. That was the image from Scripture that filled my mind as I wandered off on foot to explore the back of the island: *The wind blows where it wishes, and you hear the sound of it, but you do not know where it comes from, or where it is going.* Despite my ambivalence about the Bible, I loved this fragment. It seemed to express and sanction the ultimate mysteriousness of God, the only religious tenet I was consistently able to affirm. The wind, for me, was at once a symbol of God and ultimate mystery. Those words enabled me to be reverent in the midst of doubt. *You do not know where it comes from, or where it is going. . .*

The wind on Iona left me awestruck, stealing my breath and whipping my hair back like a banner. I had heard talk that Iona was a "thin place," a place where the veil between the natural and supernatural is thin and easily pulled back, a place imbued with divine presence. The wind seemed to rip away that veil entirely; I saw it as sacred, as a reminder to always move, always become. That was part of my creed at the time: *becoming.* Never to remain static, but ever to evolve, to actively create and recreate my theology, never to blindly inherit what the men had created before me.

On my aimless hike over Iona, I wandered into The Hermit's Circle, the ruins of a hermitage from the monastic era, now just a small square of stones. Saint Columba, or one of his brothers, probably sat there, looking out toward the ocean and filling the hours with prayer.

Those dead men held no interest for me. Instead, I imagined someone else, a saint of my making—St. Iona, the isle personified. A shepherdess, her hair is the color of dark wool, long and wind-tangled. Her eyes mirror the land and surrounding sea, shifting from blue to green to grey. Skin the color of sand. She wears robes that whip and flurry, making visible mischief. The grass parts for her. The nettles lose their sting and bow. In her wake, between the blades of bending grass, winds a line of snails with colored shells. She throws her arms wide to the beauty of the island, of herself, as she enters the Circle. She is untamed. She offers no other miracles than the miracle of what surrounds her. The miracle of who she is. And the land responds with welcome. Time, for her, has no meaning, rising, falling, twisting back on itself like the wind. This morning, the world began, and tomorrow, the world will begin again. She does not pray; she listens. She listens to the rush of air and ocean, the call and response of her sheep, the lichen crackling over rock. She listens, and nods her assent, and the earth nods back, the stars spinning their strings of planets, each nods in turn and they whisper together *yes, yes, yes.*

When I asked for her wisdom, she replied: "You have within you all that you need."

This is the lie—the beautiful lie—that defined my life for the better part of a decade. I have within me all that I need.

St. Iona was a projection, a specter of who I longed to be—beautiful, wild, powerful, free. She was easier to imagine and believe in than the actual saints who had lived and died on that Island. Monks stooped by prayer with calloused knees and withered hands, ordinary men who shat and stank and sinned and offered their mundane hours to God. I preferred the fantasy, the goddess of my imaginings, a Christianity of my making. Yes, rewrite the creeds, keeping only what is necessary. Yes, purify tradition by pillaging it. This is how I could be a Christian again. This is how I could return. But who decides what is worth keeping? Who decides what is to be carried away, the rest left to ruin? Me, of course. I have within me all that I need.

It is clear to me now that the Christianity I fashioned for myself was not recognizably Christian. In my attempts to explain away and discard all the uncomfortable bits (sin, hell, self-sacrifice), all the offensive bits (masculine language, hierarchy), all the improbable bits (virgin birth, resurrection), I gutted Christianity of its salvific meaning to make it safe, palatable, easy. At least, that's how I see it now. At the time, I saw these revisionist efforts as heroic, breathing life into old bones. To choose to stay Christian, despite its faults, was to me a kind of martyrdom. In my journal from those years, I write about *taking on a burden, one that at times seems overwhelming, a commitment to cultivate change, to continue to wrestle and question and prod, to carry, for lack of a better term, a progressive cross, a woman-centered cross. A cross that doesn't really look like a cross at all.*

* * *

After finishing graduate school, I took a job at a Christian university. In order to take the job, I had to sign a statement of faith, which was essentially a rendition of the Apostle's Creed. I signed it with only a little hesitation. I'd spent the last several years swimming in the secular waters of graduate school, imbibing critical theory and postmodern feminist philosophy. In that setting, a specific worldview is assumed but never fully articulated. To describe it simply, the worldview is this: there is no inherent meaning in the cosmos, or if there is, it cannot be known directly by humans. Human beings are *homo narrans*, the story-telling beings, and all meaning is created by us. We tell stories to explain ourselves, our place in the universe, our purpose. The most compelling and all-encompassing of these stories are metanarratives, stories that offer an explanation for all that is and are accepted by whole communities, cultures, civilizations. Christianity is one such metanarrative, the reigning one of the West, until it was dismantled by the rationalizing tide of the Enlightenment. In the postmodern era, the metanarratives have been dismantled, revealed to be human efforts at meaning-making, rather than revelations from God. For the postmodern person, it is impossible to go backward into naiveté, to live within a metanarrative without recognizing it as such. Instead, one can choose to enter into a metanarrative, choose to believe it, choose to accept that vision of the world, even while acknowledging it is something created by humans, rather than revealed to humans by a self-disclosing Being.

I had unconsciously adopted this worldview over the years. I believed in an ultimate, divine reality beyond the mere human, but I nonetheless viewed all metanarratives as human attempts to understand and access this reality. I lived in a state of cognitive dissonance as a postmodern Christian. Although it needed revision, Christianity, to me, was the most compelling metanarrative on offer, one that could give life meaning if entered into. So I signed that statement of faith as an assent to take the Christian story as my own, even though, most days, I saw the creedal statements as powerful metaphors, rather than actual events. I couldn't truly *know* if the Resurrection actually happened, so there was no point handwringing about it, I thought. The Resurrection as a metaphor was enough.

In this Christian academic setting, I saw myself as an iconoclast in the trenches, battling for the soul of Christianity against the fundamentalists. I wanted to be a chaplain to the doubters, to show them how to remain. It's hard for me to not look back and see this as arrogant and self-deceived. Yet this was also heartfelt. Many of my comrades from my college years had left Christianity altogether, including my husband. I was trying to hang on, still grasping that tiny raft, and I wanted others to hang on, too.

But there was something I didn't understand at the time, a fatal flaw in my religion of reverent doubt. This truth was crippling me spiritually, yet I remained blind to it. That truth is this: *No one can love a probable God.* A metaphor can be inspiring, enlightening, but it cannot elicit devotion. It cannot save. In fashioning God according to my desires, I had made him impossible to worship.

Motherlove

In the twilight of my twenties, that decade of doubt, I became a mother.
I went into labor on the first Sunday of Advent. I didn't realize this at the time; I was flagrantly skipping church to linger in bed, trying to catch up on the sleep that was being robbed each night by back pain and frequent trips to the bathroom. I was still working full time during the week, toddling through each day behind an impossibly huge belly, only vaguely aware that I was about to give birth in the season of The Birth.

Not that I had to attend church to be reminded of Jesus, Mary, and Joseph and all that. I saw them constantly, most often and most depressingly in the forms of bobbing, inflatable lawn ornaments with cartoonish faces— Mary wearing a shapeless blue tarp like a rain poncho, Joseph looming limply over her, and somewhere in there a blow-up Christ child. These were only their nightly forms; in the day the little air pumps would get turned off, and the Holy Family would wilt completely into a pile of plastic on the front lawn.

That wasn't the only version of the nativity scene around, of course. But one commonality among them was that Mary tended to look remarkably clean and, well, *refreshed* for someone who just labored in a barn all night. I did not look so serene after giving birth. I looked traumatized, like a shade from the underworld, leaning back against a pillow literally soaked in sweat, my eyelids swollen from being clenched shut for hours, the eyes behind them marbled with burst capillaries.

What were we thinking on that long-ago St. Patrick's Day, my husband and I? What made us imagine we could do something as reckless as create another human being? There was no divine command; no angel appeared to me in a blaze of terror and light to say *this is what will come to pass*. It was just us, Michael and me, feeling frisky and perhaps a little bored and so full of love that we needed to make another body to contain it, to catch what was spilling over.

We had no idea what we were getting into, this business of incarnation. How can anyone? It must be entered blindly.

And blinded I was. I kept my eyes closed almost entirely during labor. I labored in darkness, descending deep within myself, trying to burrow under the pain that was radiating to my spine in hot jolts. All my research and preparation, all those breathing exercises, the mantras, the various laboring positions—all that was whisked away once I was thrown fully into the excruciating pain of back labor, pain so intense that I vomited with every contraction, between which the pain only ebbed and never quit. Pain that crescendoed for eleven hours.

At that last moment—at once an epiphany and an annunciation—my mother pulled away the cool cloth covering my eyes and in a rush of water and dazzling light my son spilled into life and onto my stomach, covered in blood and goo, and we touched for the first time, skin against skin, along the length of our newly split bodies.

So much is said about the ripped and tortured and dying body of God, but what about the body he came in? The one like my son's, tiny and hungry with skin soft as ash, and hands that spring open like little stars, grasping in the air for something, someone.

I am grasping, too, struggling to funnel this moment into language, to find words that can touch its vastness—such flimsy tools, these clusters of letters, but they are all that I have.

Even now, years and babies later, I can still remember that other me, the newly born mother, who felt traumatized by the excruciating, relentless pain she'd endured, the me who is like a ghost in those first pictures, as pale as her newborn son. She's looking around in a daze after returning from a place behind words, after having her eyes clenched shut for hours, and, as language slowly returns to her, she's wondering: *what just happened to me?*

I had a beautiful labor, yes, but beautiful in the way that perilous cliffs are beautiful, or God is beautiful—a terrible, overpowering, dangerous kind of beauty. A beauty that rattles your bones. I was like a warrior plucked from Greek mythology who descends deep into the horror of the underworld and returns, after hours of torment, with the most precious boon.

One of my favorite short stories is "Giving Birth" by Margaret Atwood. Long before I became a mother myself, this story fascinated me, and I've returned to it repeatedly, writing essays about it in college, in graduate school, even including an analysis of it in my master's thesis. What most captivates me is its portrayal of the sea change that happens to a woman once she gives birth, the inner transformation that occurs, one simultaneously subtle and earthmoving.

This is how Atwood's story ends, hinting at the transfiguration that has occurred in the life of Jeanie, the woman who just gave birth:

> After that the baby is carried in, solid, substantial, packed to-
> gether like an apple, Jeanie examines her, she is complete, and
> in the days that follow, Jeanie herself becomes drifted over with
> new words, her hair slowly darkens, she ceases to be what she
> was and is replaced, gradually, by someone else.[1]

Most of the time life moves at such a crawl that we remain blind to its constant change, but there are some experiences, like becoming a parent, that strike like lightning and, in just a flash, we are utterly altered.

This is what happened to me. When I first became pregnant, I was comfortably settled into my own unique brand of postmodern, feminist Christianity. I remember lounging on the couch amidst waves of nausea, watching news coverage of the controversial contraception mandate, rolling my eyes in anger and disgust at those regressive Catholic priests in their prim white collars, telling women what to do with their bodies.

Yet almost exactly two years later, I would be standing before such a priest at the Easter Vigil Mass, publicly confessing my desire to be received into the largest, oldest male-helmed institution in the world, the Roman Catholic Church.

Motherhood broke me open.

* * *

His coming was a cataclysm: Julian, my firstborn. Something I both knew would happen and could never have anticipated.

Even before he came, when his toothpick bones were welding together in my womb, he began to change me. Like with that second ultrasound, a peak inside his world within me—something he'll never be able to remem-ber, so I'll carry the memory for him. The first ultrasound had found a cyst on our umbilical cord, which could indicate a congenital abnormality, so we went in for another ultrasound to see how he was doing.

We were only twelve weeks in, just ten weeks after conception. The last time I'd seen him on that murky gray screen, he'd been only a lima bean huddled inside a life-giving bubble, his heartbeat a tiny window that opened and opened and opened. He was a baby then, a miniscule human, but I'd had to stretch my imagination to see it. Here we were, just a few weeks later; I assumed he'd be a bean still, only bigger.

But no! He was small enough that we could see his whole body at once on the screen. He was huddled no longer, but kicking and bucking around, the bubble of my womb his playpen. His head was round and perfect, his brain bloomed like cauliflower as he sucked his thumb and paddled his legs. I was shocked at how quickly he'd become recognizably, indisputably human. Still within the first trimester.

His brain in full bloom. His limbs on parade, waving and churning in his amniotic ocean. His heart with its syncopated chambers, an undeniable herald: *I'm alive, I'm alive, I'm alive.*

In that moment, catching a glimpse of the carnival inside my womb, I began to feel unsure about what I thought I knew. Though I'd never been comfortable with the idea of abortion, the first trimester had always seemed like an ambiguous safe zone to me. Later on, yes, it's pretty hard to argue comfortably that the unborn fetus is not a human being—but that first third of the pregnancy, that was before the baby was really a baby, right?

Seeing this declaration of humanity on the ultrasound screen only ten weeks after we lit the spark of his existence—this undeniable reality began to erode what I thought I knew.

And this was only the beginning.

After his arrival, I remember taking my first walk around the ward, leaving my son's side for the first time since meeting him. I shuffled along in an ill-fitting robe, trying to gauge the slope of the ground beneath my feet again, because everything had shifted. Strangely, only I seemed to notice. The nurses buzzed around me, going about their business. The December sun lit the earth behind the clouds as usual. The color of the walls remained the same warm beige. Everything continued to move and hum and flurry past, while I was yet suspended in a sense of timelessness. My body was broken, but in a way it was meant to break. This was purposeful suffering.

As I walked slowly along, I was aware of my breathing, each intake of air an effort. At first, this worried me—was something wrong with my heart? Then I realized it was just the weight of my breasts, which sat like rocks on my chest, filling with milk for my son. My body no longer carried him, but it was still working busily to keep him alive.

Yet something *was* happening with my heart. It no longer belonged to me, no longer sat easy under my ribs. My heart now lived outside of me, hovering in the space between, tethered now to another, impossibly fragile new life. And there was a wound leftover, a hole that will never heal. *And a sword shall pierce your heart also,* says Simeon to Mary, when she presents her infant son in the temple. This is true for her, and for every mother.

I shuffled down that hospital hallway, away from his side for a moment, but I left my heart behind, with him, to keep vigil, always.

* * *

Before becoming a mother, in an effort to make sense of myself, to find my place in the world, I'd adopted the mantle of feminism and its cardinal virtues: autonomy, self-sufficiency, equality, empowerment. These named and shaped my experience, my sense of identity. Motherhood and pregnancy had long dazzled and entranced me—but only as romanticized metaphors for a kind of selfhood that is compassionate, creative, welcoming of the other. I loved reading and theorizing and writing about these metaphors. The *reality* was more terrifying.

I'd watch friends and acquaintances become mothers and get swallowed into a child-centered world, where conversations about spit up and breastfeeding and birth plans reign, where once-clean houses are overrun with laundry and plastic toys, where time is both frenzied and monotonous, where no one has sex anymore, where wives and husbands become Moms and Dads and get a bit fat. I thought of this world as Mommyland, and the inhabitants as women who'd lost themselves in their children and their home lives, compromising their independence and ambition and freedom, ceding control of both body and mind. I wanted to be a mother—one day, I said—but I didn't want to disappear.

So I wouldn't, I resolved. It would be different with me. I prided myself that my marriage wasn't like that, no fusion of identities, no joint Facebook profile. I kept my own last name, our marriage an alliance of love between two autonomous beings. Like most, my twenties were a time of intense self-discovery, and aptly so. That is when we venture beyond the parental canopy and become adults. My sense of self so newly discovered, I was afraid to lose it.

While this is hard to admit, my feminism was, in good part, self-centric. It was very much concerned with my identity, my power and potential. Of course, this expanded to include an interest in womankind more generally, but my passion for feminism nonetheless sprang from an exaltation of my own experience. I lauded the ideals of autonomy and independence—until those ideals were utterly undone by the realities of pregnancy and motherhood, the reality of Julian.

His coming brought another revelation: the intractable reality of maleness and femaleness. These are not mere social constructs. My femaleness is not something I chose, not something I control. Motherhood and fatherhood are not interchangeable. I grew my son inside my body. At the appointed time—unknown and undecided by us—my body birthed him, with strength I didn't know I possessed. My body bled for weeks while it healed the rupture of our union. My body made sweet milk for him. I spent hours marooned in the rocking chair, sometimes enraptured, sometimes bored out of my mind, feeding him from myself. Michael was there, too, caring for him in his way, but our experiences were not, cannot, be interchanged. Before parenthood, our domestic division of labor was equitable, fluid—but now we were at the mercy of biological facticity beyond our control.

While I was experiencing the full force of my femaleness, I was simultaneously realizing how much my wellbeing had become entwined with the males in my life, with my son and his father. Early in my pregnancy, I'd been sure I'd have a daughter; that aligned more neatly with my feminist sensibilities. Once I became a mother to a son, I found it more difficult to maintain a one-sided preoccupation with the female sphere of humankind. Ostensibly, feminism is concerned with the good of all people, but there is admittedly a focus on women's situations and experiences, and a tacit assumption that women are worse off than men, that most social ills can be credited to male power run amok. There's some truth in that narrative, but I began to wonder if that formula was too easily and simplistically applied to all social phenomena. I started to contemplate the unique joys and hardships my son would face, as a boy, then as a man.

His arrival unmasked so many of my illusions. The illusion of my own autonomy. The illusion that my life belongs only to me. The illusion that happiness is found by pursuing my own desires. The illusion that an unborn human being is not a human being. The illusion that maleness and femaleness are incidental to human existence, rather than a powerful and purposeful reality that tethers us to the created order. The illusion that I have it all figured out.

I wasn't prepared for the *I* to become *We*. I wasn't prepared for the wild motherlove that would pull me out of myself. I wasn't prepared for the pain on the underside of that love.

And a sword shall pierce your heart also . . .

Sometimes, in the depth of night, my infant son would stir, begin to cry himself awake, and I would put my hand on his chest to calm him back into sleep. My hand easily covered his torso, and I could feel his tiny heart against my palm, fluttering like a hummingbird. Not so long ago, this heart was beating inside me; our twin organs shared body and blood. Now I swore I could feel both hearts there, beneath his matchstick ribs, mine echoing in the beats between his, a desperate murmur, a plea: *don't stop, don't stop, don't stop . . .*

The Hollow Tomb

The burial of Jesus, the last of the Seven Sorrows on the *Via Matris*. For years, almost a decade, I'd been stranded in that sorrow, unable to move on, either by abandoning Jesus altogether, or by moving forward into the Resurrection. I was like Mary Magdalene who arrives at the tomb to find only murk and echo, stuck in that instant when her heart sinks and she feels sick to her stomach and she wonders *what have they done with his body?* I was suspended in that silent moment before the resurrection, my voice echoing back to me in the stillness of a tomb that has been emptied of God. *Where is he? What have they done with his body?*

At first, the freedom of abandoning creed and dogma was exhilarating. I was able to play. I was able to make Christianity accommodate any belief or desire that sprouted in my young mind. With the Jesus of my childhood dead and buried, I could conjure any version of him that I wished.

There were moments when this Christianity o' mine seemed real enough. My upbringing had primed me to associate powerful, positive emotions with the presence of God. That is when God seemed alive to me, during these rootless years—whenever I was overcome with wonder, or brushed against transcendence. Whenever an unexpected beauty broke into the ordinary to capture my awe: the roar of the ocean at night on a deserted beach; a spider web crystallized with frost and lit up by the morning; low-lying storm clouds trapping the sun in an eerie, glowing calm—a sublime blend of beauty and doom.

Oh! Oh! I'd catch my breath and think, there's God. I'm on the right track. I've found her. And I'd continue playing in the mud, building and flattening pies and castles, fashioning and refashioning whatever I liked, with the zeal of a child who doesn't realize her parent is watching.

But by the end of my twenties, the exhilaration of that freedom had worn thin. The emptiness of the tomb no longer signaled unbridled potential—just emptiness. I'd grown tired of waiting. Tired of trying to keep old words by filling them with new meaning. Tired of romanticizing my doubt into faith.

* * *

And there I was, working at a Christian college—inconvenient circumstances for a girl with an escalating spiritual crisis. This was an environment where faith was omnipresent, where faculty were expected to positively shape the souls of their students and asked regularly to give a spiritual account of themselves. People talked about their faith. A lot. We prayed before faculty meetings and sang worship songs together. The "integration of faith and learning" was a campus mantra. As a junior faculty member, I was required to write a faith essay for my third-year review—ten pages of personal testimony. I wrote it reluctantly and with ample eye-rolls, trying to disguise how much the project terrified me. I groped around for Christian thinkers who were postmodern enough for my tastes and yet orthodox enough to bridge the gap between myself and my institution. But my naiveté was wearing thin. I was becoming increasingly aware of the contortionist moves I had to make to convince myself, and others, that I still inhabited the realm of orthodoxy. *You are a fraud*, whispered a still small voice that I pushed away, that daily grew less still, less small.

One day in early October, I was scurrying across the quad, hurrying toward a ladies' luncheon. I wasn't sure where it was, or what it was for, but I was invited by our campus pastor and doing my best to show up. I was running ten minutes behind, as had become usual, now that I only slept in short bursts between breastfeeding sessions. Not yet a year into motherhood, I still fumbled with the sacred scales of work-life balance, that elusive idol of working motherhood. I seemed always on the verge of forgetting one commitment or another.

When I arrived, sweaty and breathless, trying to squeeze unobtrusively into a chair at the corner of the table, there was already an introductory conversation going, popcorn-style, around the table. It took me a couple of minutes to realize two things: we were there to host a chapel speaker, someone I knew nothing about, because I'd missed her chapel speech, and we were each supposed to introduce ourselves and share something we love about church.

Oh fuck. Such was my succinct internal monologue as I scrambled to come up with something to say. What if I decided to be honest? I flirted with this possibility. *I hate going to church*, I imagined saying to this circle of respectable, non-sweaty women, many of whom I admired. *I rarely go, and when I do, I leave depressed and frustrated, and I'm not totally sure why. So most of the time I sleep in. Who's next?*

In truth, I didn't have a church home. I was intermittently, perennially church shopping, unable to land anywhere. I tried the Episcopal route, sure than I could survive in the Anglican in-between, that middle ground that is not quite Protestant or Catholic, but somehow tries to be both. I went to the local Episcopal church a few times, finding myself temporarily rejuvenated by the liturgy. One Sunday I attended, and there was a guest priest who was raucously irreverent. "Let's stand together now and recite the Creed," he said with a wink, "and keep our fingers crossed behind our backs." At the time, I found this amusing, even refreshing—the very moment in the liturgy for asserting faith had suddenly become an affirmation of my unbelief. This church should have been the perfect place for me; creeds were optional, metaphorical. I could revel in doubt, guilt-free. Maybe it's true, maybe it's not—who knows? One could be an Episcopalian and pretty much believe whatever. Appealing though I found this unabashed ambiguity, this winsome shrug—I did not feel motivated to sacrifice my Sundays in order to gather with fellow doubters in a communal charade of belief.

Plus, there were no children in that church. Motherhood had complicated things. I no longer had my individual spiritual angst to carry; I'd lately begun to wonder: what will I teach my children? How can I give them a spiritual home? So I tried visiting the Episcopalian church one town over. A lovely building, a female priest—both things I loved, but there was only one other family with small children amidst a sea of half-filled pews and graying hair. They were so friendly, feeding us cake afterward, and Michael and I looked at each other as we walked back to our car, shrugging hopefully, "That was great. Let's come here again." We never did.

After this, I returned to sleeping late three Sundays a month, cuddling with my baby and my atheist husband. On the remaining Sunday, I would attend one of the local Quaker churches, where I encountered an inverse phenomenon—a vibrant community with a wide range of ages, scores of little kids. The congregation was wonderful, but the service itself felt hollow, too like the evangelical churches of my upbringing: a handful of songs to stir the emotions, a sermon to quicken the mind. But I missed the Eucharist, and its mysterious consolations.

I'd become the Goldilocks of churchgoers. With a long list of ideological demands and desires, I tried all the beds and tasted all the porridge, yet I was still restless, restless. Nothing quite fit, and I jokingly began referring to myself as a "Quanglican"—an apt term, in a way, as it names nothing that actually exists, nothing but my fractured, made-up spirituality.

Back at the luncheon, the church conversation had rounded the corner, and it was the chapel speaker's turn, so I tuned in, curious about her. "Well, I'm Catholic," she said, "And whenever I don't go to Mass regularly, I find that I miss it."

I was instantly annoyed, like she'd somehow cheated the game. *Yeah, well,* I griped to myself, *if I had to go to Mass instead of church, I'd probably have an easier time answering this question, too.* Listening to her simple response, one free from both angst and manufactured enthusiasm, I felt something akin to envy. I was not inspired or convicted by her words; rather, her presence taunted me, reminding me of my own malaise. I resented where she was, never consciously considering that I could go there, too.

I made some lame excuse and left the luncheon early. I'd sat through many such gatherings before, swallowing hard my discomfort, but this was one too many. I was sick of this endless midnight struggle with God, wrestling for a new spiritual name. I didn't want to wait for a blessing any longer. I wanted to get the hell away.

The Perfect Storm

Autumn. A season of transition, when one extreme ebbs into another, heat and sun yielding to growing darkness and looming rains. In the rhythm of the academic year, autumn seems full of fresh starts, unbridled potential. Things are on the wane—daylight, the green of trees—but it feels the opposite, like things are revving up, churning with possibility. This is the season to make a change. And so I did: a radical, unanticipated move. At the beginning of October, I was a disaffected post-evangelical feminist on the brink of atheism. One month later, I was on the phone with a Mexican nun inquiring about joining the Roman Catholic Church.

After that ladies' luncheon in early October, I grew antsy, convinced I'd had a revelation, long time coming: I couldn't keep working at this university, where I was expected to form young souls, when my own was in such bad shape. I loved my job. I loved the students, the colleagues, the classes I taught. There was part of me that even liked the praying, the God-talk, as if I was listening to a language I once knew but had forgotten, aside from a few scattered words here and there. What had become unbearable, however, was hiding from this truth: I'd been hemorrhaging belief for years and was just about bled out.

In one of my classes that fall, we'd been reading a little Flannery O'Connor, and I came across this passage from one of her letters, where she describes an awkward experience at a dinner party:

> The conversation turned on the Eucharist, which I, being the Catholic, was obviously supposed to defend. Mrs. Broadwater said when she was a child and received the Host, she thought of it as the Holy Ghost, He being the "most portable" person of the Trinity; now she thought of it as a symbol and implied that it was a pretty good one. I then said, in a very shaky voice, "Well, if it's a symbol, to hell with it." That was all the defense I was capable of but I realize now that this is all I will ever be able

to say about it, outside of a story, except that it is the center of existence for me; all the rest of life is expendable.[2]

If it's just a symbol, to hell with it. Those words burrowed into me like ticks. One sentence, and my pseudo-Christianity was unmasked for what it was. The realm of "symbol" was where I'd set up shop, forging a religion with theoretical jargon, using words like *nuance* and *ambiguity* to profess—to risk—absolutely nothing. Thinking of myself as intellectually sophisticated, I'd reduced Christianity to a nexus of compelling metaphors that connected only to other metaphors, like a house of twisted mirrors. One sentence, and I realized how ridiculous it was to hang my soul on something that was *just* a symbol—not a symbol that discloses something real, but symbol alone. One sentence, and I began to see that all my precious, postmodern equivocation was just a bunch of bullshit.

And I wasn't sure where to take refuge. More than Christianity, feminism was the metanarrative I'd chosen, the sacred canopy under which I found shelter. But over the past year, several disparate experiences had begun to tear small holes in its fabric—not enough to rend it or bring it crashing down, just enough to let some strange light through.

First, there was the upheaval of motherhood itself, the new identity it wrought, a self tangled up with other selves, the illusion of autonomy dispelled. I was now the mother of a son; my eye roved over the world and no longer saw merely the wounds of women and the wrongs of men, but all kinds of human anguish, all kinds of human fault.

Over the summer, I'd been following the news cycle, foraying into online journalism, and I wrote a couple of pieces on male victims of sexual violence, who are often left to the margins or forgotten altogether in feminist accounts of rape culture. I was shocked to discover the high rates of sexual abuse against boys: 1 in 6, not too far from the oft-cited statistic of the 1 in 5 women who have been sexually assaulted.

In the aftermath of those essays, several things happened. One, I was surprised at the criticism from some feminists, who saw this focus on males as a distraction from what really mattered. Two—and this was more astonishing—I fell into an email correspondence with several antifeminist men, whose beloved pastimes include trolling feminist bloggers and spouting misogyny online. These men were Men's Right Activists (MRAs), the ultimate bogeymen in the feminist universe.

Predictably, I found much to disagree with in our email exchanges, but what I didn't expect to encounter, first of all, was courtesy, and second, their humanity. These men shared their stories with me, stories of abuse and abandonment, and I caught a glimpse of the underlying pain that fed the anger they vented online, pain from an unhealed wound. One of the men, a victim of childhood sexual abuse, had attempted to start support groups for male abuse survivors in his community and had faced some opposition from local feminists. He actually told his story on Oprah once and mailed me several DVDs of that episode, asking me to share them with others in the hopes that more male victims would feel permission to talk about their experiences and seek help.

I'm far from an MRA apologist—that's another problem with ideologies, the "if you're not with us, you're against us" logic—and I certainly don't condone the online vitriol. But that experience exposed to me the humanity of these men, men who I'd been primed to hate, and I was realizing that while feminism is purportedly concerned with the dignity of all people, my blind and whole-hearted acceptance of it had ushered me into an us-them dynamic that occluded the dignity of some.

Another small tear in the feminist canopy came that June, when I was months into new motherhood. Wendy Davis, a state senator from Texas, was making headlines during her eleven-hour filibuster on the senate floor that blocked a controversial abortion bill. I remember sitting on my couch, watching the news coverage, feeling inspired. Twitter was exploding with adulation, feminists raising a battle cry in support of Davis and her pink sneakers, and I was caught up in the excitement, watching a woman make history in her defense of other women.

Tweets started flying from women who'd had abortions, proclaiming their choice proudly as a way of support. In the midst of the fray, a fellow writer I knew tweeted her chagrin at never having had an abortion, because she wanted to join in the revelry. I read this tweet, just a string of offhand characters quickly lost in the flurry, and my enthusiasm chilled over. I'd been pro-choice for years, like any good feminist, but this lauding of abortion as some kind of jubilant rite of passage, a cause for celebration, was a sentiment that stopped me cold. My unborn son at twelve weeks, a thriving tiny human on parade—this image rushed into my mind, a courier bearing a message I did not want to hear, but could no longer ignore.

After a year of scattered experiences like these, the resoluteness of my feminist convictions was beginning to erode. Moreover, in my teaching and academic work, I found myself increasingly *bored* with the feminist lens. I started to feel like a one-trick pony, my stale hermeneutics always churning out the same questions, the same conclusions, the same narrative. This was not yet a full-blown ideological crisis—that would be overstating it. I was still hanging onto the feminist label; I'd staked my professional identity to it, after all. But I was becoming, somewhat reluctantly, more aware of the blind spots of a narrative that too simplistically sees the world in terms of autonomy, power, and conflict, a zero-sum game wherein men are always privileged over women. I began to tentatively prod the limits of this totalizing story. I hadn't lost my feminist faith, but I was, for the first time, yielding the floor to questions.

* * *

All of these storm fronts—crises of identity, ideology, spirituality—had been gathering for months, streaming towards one another with startling force and speed. Unbeknownst to me, they were set to collide at the beginning of November, on a quiet Monday afternoon, as I sat alone in my office.

After my revelation that I needed to leave my current position, I'd applied for several new jobs, gravitating toward vacancies at Catholic universities. Unlike my own university, most Catholic institutions do not require faculty to sign a statement of faith and are generally more ecumenical in terms of hiring people with different religions, or no religion at all. I am very skilled at romanticizing other jobs, other places to live—any circumstances that are not my own—and the realm of Catholic academia seemed like the perfect place to land. There, I wouldn't have to struggle to speak evangelical any longer, but I also wouldn't have to completely abandon my preoccupation with Christianity, an interest I could never quite shake, despite my angst. Working in a totally secular academic environment was not appealing—I didn't want to be *afraid* to talk about religion, but I didn't want to be *required* to talk about it either. The Catholic university—not any one in particular, rather the perfect Platonic ideal of a Catholic university— seemed to my delirious mind like a city on a hill, shining a beacon down and beckoning: *Come. Be Free.*

But that ordinary Monday afternoon, looking over the job application materials at my desk, I began to doubt my decision to jump ship. I saw the costs of leaving, the costs to my family especially. Asking my gardener husband to move away from his homeland, away from family, to a northern state with a brief growing season—that was asking him to tear up his roots to assuage my sense of unrest. And, if I was being honest, I had become rooted there as well, a nomad no longer. His land had become my land, his people my people.

I had the uneasy suspicion that this attempt to run away would not solve anything, because the real conflict was not between myself and an external institution. The war was within. My will was split, divided against itself, pulling me simultaneously toward and away from Christianity. Because this conflict had been tangled up with my working life, I'd imagined changing jobs would solve it. Now I wondered if that was naïve.

This was when the epiphany came, at once completely underwhelming yet ultimately life-altering. I was staring listlessly into the dark mirror of my laptop screen and this sentence invaded my thoughts, perhaps welling up from within me, perhaps penetrating from outside: *you don't have to work at a Catholic university to be part of the Catholic Church.*

That was the thought, the boneheaded epiphany that changed my life—boneheaded, because it was so damn obvious. Yet still an epiphany, because I had not yet acknowledged that my longing for that city on a hill was for the Church herself, not a university. Consciously, I had been on the lookout for a better professional fit, for more spiritual freedom. Beneath this conscious thought, I was dead drunk on too much freedom and desperate for something to stop my head from whirling.

Without thinking, without a second guess or moment of analysis, as soon as that sentence became my own thought, I looked up the phone number for the local Catholic parish and dialed it. A woman answered, asked how she could help me. I responded hesitantly, with plenty of noncommittal words to shield me from the enormity of the step I was suddenly taking. "I think I might be interested in becoming Catholic. Or at least learning more about Catholicism."

Almost every time since, when I've dialed my local parish, I end up getting the answering machine, but this first and crucial time I reached Sister Juanita, a Mexican nun in her sixties who also happened to coordinate RCIA—the Rite of Christian Initiation of Adults, a year-long discernment program designed for seekers who are inquiring into the Catholic Church.

"Come to the church," she said. And I did, just after work, in the gray twilight. Sister Juanita greeted me, we sat down, and she asked: "So, why do you want to become Catholic?" Instead of backpedaling and saying the words I'd been rehearsing on the drive over—"Well, I'm just interested in learning more at this point, I'm not sure if I want to become Catholic"—I opened my mouth and all my pent-up spiritual longing poured out like a libation. "The Eucharist," I said, "The sacraments." I was not even sure what these were, exactly, but I knew that I needed them. I knew I was dying without them.

Even now, it's hard for me to understand how this happened, because I didn't see it coming. I've met a lot of Catholic converts, and most of them trod a more methodical path. Even if hesitantly, eyes on the exits, they are aware of venturing toward the Catholic Church. Me? I was flying blind, wheeling around in the dark, one minute grasping with renewed hunger at any remaining scraps of faith, the next thinking *to hell with it* and resigning myself to atheism, then—BAM—an underwhelming epiphany at my desk and I am becoming Catholic instead.

There's this thing in Catholic theology called *actual grace*. I grew up with the ditty that mercy is not receiving something you deserve and grace is receiving something you don't deserve—but grace, for Catholics, isn't merely a disposition of God toward people. Grace is a substance, like supernatural sap, a dose of the life and power of God within us. Grace heals us, makes us whole, cleans us up inside so God's charity can well up in our souls and overflow from us toward others. And *actual grace*—that's grace that makes us *move*, grace that translates into action, action otherwise beyond our ability or control. Actual grace: this is the only thing that enables me to make sense of my sudden, reckless decision to join the Catholic Church. This was a supernatural intervention, perfectly timed at a moment of renunciation, when my world was being upended and what I thought I knew suspended.

I was on the edge, wavering. And in that moment of weakness, all my ideological swords clattering to the ground, the arrow of actual grace found its way into my weary heart and instead of falling forward into unbelief, I was thrown back into the arms of Mother Church—the last place I ever expected to be.

* * *

Although this was the moment that I decided to become Catholic and headed down that road with intention, this was not the climax of my conversion, merely the prelude. During the following five or so months, I went through the process of RCIA, preparing to formally enter the Church and receive my first communion at the Easter Vigil Mass. I gobbled up book after book about Catholicism, most from fairly liberal perspectives, because that was still the vantage point I best understood. I was giddy, like a girl in puppy love with someone she's long admired from afar, but never actually met.

Several features of Catholicism quickly captured my affections, but there were other aspects that seemed alien, even distasteful. I was wary, for example, about the Church's stance against contraception, which seemed more than a little nuts. How could something that helps women avoid unwanted pregnancies, and thus the need for abortions, possibly be bad?

For years, the deal breaker that kept me at arm's length was the male-only priesthood. If I'd now reached the point where I was willing to try and understand the basis for that teaching, I still remained skeptical. And marriage: like many millennials, I'd been swept up in the groundswell support for same-sex marriage, and I wasn't sure why the Catholic Church was holding out.

I didn't feel particularly pressured to immediately resolve my objections. I still had a denominational mindset, a hangover from Protestantism: as long as you agree on the essentials, the peripheral stuff doesn't matter. You can pick and choose, agree to disagree. Some of the few Catholics I knew at the time seemed to take that perspective, too; they were comfortable with dissenting from Church teaching, especially its seemingly regressive sexual ethics. I figured I could always be that kind of Catholic. I assumed my liberal feminism and Catholicism would make happy bedfellows, somehow.

My mindset at the time was this: I wanted to understand *why* the Church affirmed those tenets I found confusing or offensive, and once I understood the why, I would follow the leanings of my conscience, whether it sided with the Church or not. So I suspended my concerns about contraception, the priesthood, and marriage, without actually changing my beliefs. Okay, *Mater*, I said. I'll hear you out. Say what you have to say.

Mostly, though, I was dizzy with excitement, tipsy from the flood of spiritual consolations I received from attending Mass, and the heady intellectual buzz I got from my first real glimpses of the Catholic cosmos. I lapped it all up, like a starved little creature come in from the cold.

It's true: I should have felt more at home in the corners of Anglican and Quaker Protestantism, where my feminist inclinations first led me. That would have made *sense*. After all, I was able to seamlessly connect the dots between my fairly liberal beliefs and the tenets of these denominations. I'd tethered myself to an ethic of social justice and love. *That*, I thought, is where the heart of Christianity can be found. Dogma be damned.

But I'd come to question this. One can find, after all, an ethic of love and justice in any number of places, any number of religions, even secular humanism.

If it's just a symbol, to hell with it.

Venturing into Catholicism, I began to understand that what is most unique about Christianity, most essential, is its strangeness. Its improbable, radical story that confounds the mind and refuses to contract into mere metaphor. The wild mystery of the Incarnation, that holy paradox that rushes past the furthest ends of reason and cuts through the polarities that structure and divide our world. It is not enough to say "be just"; it is not enough to say "love"—not when love and justice are uprooted from the narrative that explains *why* we must love, a narrative that makes the startling claim that every human being burns bright with the spark of God, and this same God self-emptied to gestate in the body of a woman, to be born, to live the life of the body, to die, and to live again.

The Incarnation—ah, a mystery I could never quit. Or perhaps it's the other way round; the Incarnation never let go of me. Even through the desert, I carried it with me, carting it around as a beloved concept through the far-off realms of feminist theory and literary criticism. And now, through Catholicism, the Incarnation came alive again, was made flesh again, mere symbol no more—how, after all, could *incarnation* ever be just a disembodied symbol? It is Catholicism, I realized, more than any other form of Christianity, that fully celebrates this mystery that is the heart of the faith.

In those first months of discernment, I became captivated by the Catholic imagination, with its double vision. My taste for paradox, for mystery, had been an anticipation of this and found new completion there. Metaphors still flourished, but what they revealed was *real*, not simply creative human conjurings. God has etched into the created order echoes and figures that signal a divine reality. Nothing is ever simply itself, but is also a mirror of God. While the Protestant imagination can be said to be dialectical, thinking in terms of either-or and stressing the unlikeness of things, the Catholic imagination is analogical—incarnational—seeing things in terms of likeness and unity, welcoming paradox. There is no schism between faith and reason, between the sacred and secular, between the natural and numinous; God, the ground of all Being, inhabits each of these realms. All of reality is engraced.

Once I took the impulsive step to enter RCIA, a hindsight awareness emerged: for years, I'd hidden from Catholicism, projecting my attraction to it onto others while holding myself at a safe distance. When several students of mine had decided to become Catholic, I was overjoyed for them; we talked excitedly about the richness of the Catholic intellectual tradition, the refreshing emphasis on incarnation and mystery, the life-giving feast of the Eucharist. We also tangled amicably about the male priesthood. When my mom expressed a feeling of being "covered by God" in Catholic Mass— a feeling I recognized, but could never put into words quite so well—I promptly bought her several books about Catholicism and a small rosary. I remember thinking, "My mom would be such a great Catholic!" There's something humorous and so glaringly obvious about these gestures, sincere though they were, as if through them I had been saying: *"I can't be Catholic, but can you be Catholic for me?"*

That had been me, for the past decade: orbiting Catholicism, intermittently wandering into Catholic churches, cathedrals, and abbeys, drawn by something unnamable but too skittish to stay, too unwilling to compromise my feminist principles.

I did not decide to become Catholic from a place of certainty. I moved from a place of desire. And I did not walk steadily toward it. I took a reckless leap.

At the end of my twenties, that's where I found myself. Like Flannery at that dinner party, my voice trembled. I was unsure of so much, but I was sure of this: I was ready to leave the tomb and enter fully into Mystery. I was ready to sink my hands into the hot, medieval heart of a sacramental Christianity that sees the world as it really is—charged with God.

* * *

I complete RCIA and formally enter the Catholic Church on April 19, 2014.

One year later, the inward conversion begins.

An Interlude: On Conversion

―――――――――

"What agonizing birth-pangs tore my heart,
what groans it uttered, O my God!"

- St. Augustine, *The Confessions*

G rowing up evangelical, one develops a certain veneration for the art of
the *testimony*. This is a genre of speech devoted to the event of conversion, that moment of breaking down and inviting, at last, Christ into the
heart. This moment of assent is the euphoric climax, bringing with it sudden
salvation, freedom from sin, shame, anguish in a fell swoop. The new man
springs forth, already wholly formed, like Athena from the head of Zeus.
Born again in an instant.

The steeper the arc from sin to grace, the better. It's hard to beat testi-
monies from addicts, who have tasted hell, or prisoners with blood on their
hands. Against these backdrops, Christ's salvific work is shown in sharp
relief, the drama exposed.

A slightly lesser class of testimony comes from those who narrowly
escaped those traps, without ever being owned by them: the rebel teen who
dabbled in drugs or promiscuity; the committer of petty crimes, not quite a
felon. Or even just a good-old atheist who fumbles in darkness for decades
until swept up into the light—that's always a winner. As long as there's a
distinct before and after, as long as one can truthfully sing *I once was lost,
but now am found*, the testimony has rhetorical power.

For me, saved at age three, there was no *before*, at least not one captured by long-term memory. Around the fire circles at summer Bible camp,
or at open mic during an altar call service, there really wasn't much for me
to tell. You might say I had testimony envy; I longed to feel that drama of
salvation in my own heart and life. I wanted a taste of that euphoria. And

without it, I suffered from recurrent anxiety—was I *really* saved? Without that climactic moment that could be told and retold, how could I be sure?

I had to wait awhile for my own conversion, about three decades. And when it came—the dazzling realization I'd at last met Truth and been scooped up by him—the emotional content of that realization was not what I expected. It did not follow the arc of the testimony. For one thing, it wasn't a single revelation, but a grueling series of them over the course of many months. There was no ecstasy—at least not in the sense of a rapturous culmination when the conversion strikes. There were instances of elation, but nearly always accompanied by what I think of as the *oh, shit* moment. That comma is important; this is not a quickfire exclamation, as from brushing a hot stove. This is the drawn-out utterance of someone facing an awful, hereto hidden truth.

Awful is a good word, because in this case, it is about awe. This springs from an encounter with the awful beauty of God, a beauty that overwhelms you and knocks you back and makes you realize how impossibly small and vulnerable and venal you really are.

If you look hard enough, you can discern this dark underside of the testimony between the lines of that ultimate conversion hymn. *I once was blind, but now I see.* Seems innocuous enough, except the recognition you've been blind—dead wrong—about pretty much everything for a really long time is hardly the grounds for jubilation. In truth, when one finds Truth, there is delight and joy and consolation, sure. But there is also a reckoning.

Dreadful joy, joyful dread—one can find this paradox in the first conversion memoir ever written, St. Augustine's *Confessions.* By the time I finished graduate school, I'd learned to hate Augustine. Along with his beloved Plato, Augustine is the *philosopher non grata* for feminist theologians. He's charged with more or less derailing the entire project of Christianity with his sexual hang-ups, his distaste for the body, his preoccupation with sin, and his misogynist views. If it weren't for Augustine, so the tale goes, Christianity might have developed its full potential as a creation-loving, shame-eschewing, non-dogmatic faith system full of hugs and priestesses. I accepted this reading uncritically, encountering it repeatedly in the feminist tomes I read. I learned to loathe Augustine without ever reading him, aside from strategically spliced excerpts in feminist readers. If I had actually gone to the original source, I would have discovered a man more concerned with grace than sin, who robustly defended the good of the body against Platonist heresies of his time. I would have encountered a man whose greatest spiritual hero was his own mother, whose autobiography is imbued with deep love and respect for her. At least I'd like to think so. In reality, I probably would have focused on the passages that grate against the modern feminist ear and dismissed him as a woman-hating hack.

Whatever my past opinions were or might have been—now, when I read *The Confessions*, Augustine's account of his own conversion, I'm amazed how my experiences have come to echo his. Our disparate lives, separated by continent, ocean, and almost two millennia, nonetheless unfold in parallel patterns.

First of all, we share a somewhat lusty adolescence that stretched a bit too long into adulthood. We found fleeting solace in books and sex, each falling in love with a false worldview. For Augustine, this was Manichaeism, a philosophical hodgepodge of Christianity, paganism and Gnosticism that sees the world in dualistic terms, in a never-ending struggle between the equally powerful forces of good and evil. For me, it was similarly a hodgepodge, one of postmodernism, Christianity, and feminism. These worldviews are not total falsehoods; rather, as Augustine describes, they are distortions of the truth:

> O Truth, Truth, how the deepest and innermost marrow of my mind ached for you, even then while they prattled your name to me unremittingly and in so many ways, though only in words and in their huge and copious tomes! . . . I was hungering and thirsting for you, . . . and all they set before me were dishes of glittering myths. . . . Yet I ate those offerings, believing that I was feeding on you. . . . I derived no nourishment from them, but was left more drained.[3]

We each fell for our glittering myths in roughly the same phase of life, from the ages of 19 to 28. In his late twenties, Augustine's Manichean convictions began to falter after he studied the philosophers, namely Plato. I, too, in my late twenties, really read Plato for the first time, and began to get a glimpse at the wide world beyond a narrow feminist lens. We both struggled with our vocations, his as a call to celibacy, mine as a call to lean more deeply into marriage and motherhood. When we became catechumens, finally moving deliberately toward the Catholic Church, we nonetheless remained uncertain, our wills conflicted. We remained for a time in this in-between, drawing closer while still holding back. Eventually, we both were conquered and had wrenching inner conversions in the thirty-first year of life.

The tipping point of Augustine's conversion, that iconic struggle in the garden, falls in the middle of his book; it is the fulcrum on which the whole text turns. He nests this episode amidst tales of other conversions, including that of an unnamed court official:

Then quite suddenly he was filled with a love of holiness and a realistic sense of shame and disgust with himself; he turned his gaze toward his friend and demanded, "Tell me: where do we hope all our efforts are going to get us? What are we looking for? In whose cause are we striving?" . . . Even as he spoke he was in labor with the new life that was struggling to birth within him. He directed his eyes back to the page, and as he read a change began to occur in that hidden place within him where you alone can see; his mind was being stripped of the world as presently became apparent. The flood tide of his heart leapt on, and at last he broke off his reading with a groan as he discerned the right course and determined to take it. By now he belonged to you.[4]

A realistic sense of shame. Struggling to birth. Stripped of the world. Flood tide of the heart. These words capture, almost uncannily, my own emotional experience of conversion—but for me, this was not a lone episode. Being stripped of the world was grueling, dizzying, disorienting—and still ongoing, even if the initial intensity has ebbed.

With a groan. Yes, a groan.

One can also see this amalgam of emotions in the gospel account of Simon Peter's conversion in Luke 5—a laconic, concentrated narrative that provides a near-perfect distillation of the conversion experience.

While the people pressed upon [Jesus] to hear the word of God, he was standing by the lake of Gennesaret. And he saw two boats by the lake; but the fishermen had gone out of them and were washing their nets. Getting into one of the boats, which was Simon's, he asked him to put out a little from the land. And he sat down and taught the people from the boat. And when he had ceased speaking, he said to Simon, "Put out into the deep and let down your nets for a catch." And Simon answered, "Master, we toiled all night and took nothing! But at your word I will let down the nets." And when they had done this, they enclosed a great shoal of fish; and as their nets were breaking, they beckoned to their partners in the other boat to come and help them. And they came and filled both the boats, so that they began to sink. But when Simon Peter saw it, he fell down at Jesus' knees, saying, "Depart from me, for I am a sinful man, O Lord." For he was astonished, and all that were with him, at the catch of fish which they had taken; and so also were James and John, sons of Zebedee, who were partners with Simon. And Jesus said to Simon, "Do not be afraid; henceforth you will be catching men." And when they had brought their boats to land, they left everything and followed him.

Christ shows up, invades your small, ordinary world. You somehow choose to trust him, rather than your own assumptions. You obey an unlikely command—*Put out into the deep*—even though it seems risky, improbable. And then: abundance. Abundance beyond expectation that unmasks the presence of the divine in your midst, and at once you yourself are unmasked, and you fall to your knees, cowered by awe, overcome with dismay, and you are changed.

The moment of dread: Peter had it. Augustine had it. The unnamed court official had it. I did, too, and not just one. At this point in the tale I'm telling, I've become Catholic, but it's the inner conversion after this outer declaration that is the real story, the messy story, the story that unfolded in my second year of being Catholic. That was my year of upheaval and anguish (the *oh, shit* year), yet also a time of deepening conviction and inner consolation like I've never known. This part of the story didn't happen neatly, chronologically, but hit like a thunderstorm, a sky turned dark with lightning striking here and there, haphazardly. Lightning is a good metaphor—flashes of discovery, but those flashes a shock to the system, disorienting and certainly not painless.

The rest of this book tries to capture the lightning, to somehow describe those jolts of light that changed me. This was a kind of enlightenment, yes, but not a slow, painless dawn; rather, intermittent flares so bright and sudden they obliterated the way I used to see.

PART III

Into the Deep

"At some point we must plunge in to discover a greater expanse; yet when this broader horizon does appear, a new depth will open up at our point of entry."

—St. Teresa Benedicta of the Cross, *Potency and Act*

"Too late have I loved you, O Beauty so ancient, O Beauty so new. Too late have I loved you!"

—St. Augustine, *The Confessions*

"Put out into the deep, and let down your nets for a catch."

—Luke 5:4

Holy Thursday

April 2, 2015

The night was clear and warm, early spring. I was walking home from Mass, alone, aware of the muffled sound of my footfall on the sidewalk, the hushed sound of my breath. My senses were sharp, as if newly awakened, the scent of the incense followed me on my way, an invisible tether stretching back toward the church, connecting me with whatever had begun to reveal itself there. I'd been Catholic for a year, but my conversion was only beginning.

I'd stayed awhile after the Mass was over, sitting in the presence of what looked like a wafer of bread enclosed in a gold monstrance that circled it like tongues of fire, like a ring of solar flares. The white circle stared back at me, silently, an open eye.

This was my first experience with Eucharistic Adoration, and I wasn't sure what I was supposed to be doing exactly, so I dutifully prayed a row of beads on my rosary, then thought about leaving, wondering if I'd been there long enough. I thought of my baby at home, eight weeks old, and just the thought made my breasts tight with milk. What if she's awake now, and hungry? What if she's wondering where I am? Surely I'd sat long enough. A lot of people had left by now.

Just a little while longer, wait with me, said the Eye.

I knew the story, the moment of the Gospel we were entering into on Holy Thursday, the agony in the garden, the night of anticipatory pain. The disciples who slept deep while Christ was sweating blood beside them. *Will you not wait one hour with me?*

Yes, but those men were not lactating. Surely patience is a different thing when one's body has altered itself to become food for a weaker, needier body. Surely twenty minutes is enough. One end of my pew had emptied now, leaving a clear path for a quiet exit.

Just a little longer.

I waited and decided to kneel. I stared hard at the Eye, not blinking, until my vision wavered and the world looked like a shimmering curtain that could be pulled back, if only my fingers could grasp it. And what would be behind the curtain? The monstrance moved with molten energy—until I had to blink and everything resettled, clear and solid again.

If I looked hard enough, could I see through the veil of wheat and oil into that deeper reality? This looked like bread, tasted like bread, felt like bread, but was not bread. This was matter charged with God. How could this be?

I shifted in my seat. I thought about my baby. I wondered how long I'd waited. There were even fewer people there, now. Could I make it an hour? Did I need to?

Wait with me.

I opened the missal and began to read the prayers in the back. This was easier. I idly thumbed my rosary, moving the cool beads across my palm. Multitasking. Over toward my left, I could sense the presence of the monstrance and its silent, steady gaze. Could Christ really be here, a few feet away? Not in that spiritual, nebulous way that Christ is always somehow present, at least in theory, in some sort of technical sense—but *in the flesh*. And not only over there, on the altar, but within my body, because just minutes ago the wafer was on my hand, then in my tongue, then dissolving into me. How could this be? And if that is His Body, over there, why would I rather be at home, nursing my baby, or thumbing through the prayers in the missal, prayers that are supposed to somehow form a bridge to Him, yet it's easier to read the prayers than to look at and speak to and be seen by the Eye on the altar.

And then came the voice of the priest, singing the words of benediction—*tantum ergo sacramentum, veneremur cernui*—and with a rush of surprise and triumph, I realized I'd made it. I'd waited the hour.

On my way home, I walked slowly. My eagerness to return to my baby had abated, now that I was en route, not waiting but on the move. As I walked, a prayer came to me—not a remnant of the Mass, or an invocation newly learned, but an echo from my evangelical childhood.

Create in me a clean heart, O God
And renew a right spirit within me.

I learned these words as a song at summer Bible camp, in the Utah mountains, under a canvas Army tent that functioned as a makeshift meeting hall. The tune is slow and somber, in a minor key, unlike many of the other clap-happy songs we sang at camp, and the simple lyrics fit onto a single poster board, held aloft by one of the counselors. From this memory, the words surfaced, and I sang them quietly to myself on the way home.

I wasn't aware of the song's deeper history, that I was actually singing a fragment of the *Miserere*, Psalm 51, a song of conversion, traditionally prayed in the Ash Wednesday liturgy at the opening of Lent. I was late to Lent that year; I'd all but missed it. On Ash Wednesday, I had stayed at home, still bleeding from childbirth, ensconced in a timeless haze of newborn love. I had missed the call to penance, the sign of black ashes, the inauguration of the forty-day path to Easter.

But Lent came to me that night, on the walk home, through a prayer both from my evangelical past and from the ancient corridors of the Church herself—a prayer I have come to see as a dangerous one, if prayed with desire.

I did not fully know it then, but the world was rearranging itself. For the time being, the stars were mostly stars, charged with their own natural beauty, and only the glimmer of something else. The warm spring air through which I moved was newly animate somehow, newly tangible, but perhaps it merely seemed new because the seasons had turned over again. The trees that lined the sidewalk were ordinary trees, pruned and domesticated, evenly spaced, but were they bending toward me somehow, their budding branches reaching up, at the same time beckoning? Each of these was a messenger, bearing a single word, a fragment of a whole that I was only just piecing together. I heard the words that night, but from a distance, as if they were moving closer, yet on the horizon. Or perhaps it was me who was finally moving.

The Inner Altar

I gave birth to our daughter in February, almost a year after becoming Catholic. She was born on the brink of Lent, just six days before Ash Wednesday, but all that passed me by unawares, lost as I was in the postpartum limbo, where nights swallow days, time flattens out, and everything is upended. At first, there was the euphoria of release and new life, those first couple of days in the hospital, where I was waited on by efficient angels wearing scrubs, and I was able to rest, depleted with joy, nursing and napping in a cocoon of new love. Then the elation ebbed; I went back home, which brought its own kind of comfort, but the milk came in with a vengeance, the hormones hurtled off a cliff, and the sleepless nights yawned and swallowed me. The endless nursing sessions were an uneasy mix of bliss and boredom; at times I was transfixed, gazing at my baby in beatific self-forgetfulness, getting a long draught of the deep charity that holds the cosmos in being. Other times, nipples blistered and raw, breasts aching and grotesquely huge, the repetition of newborn care was stultifying, the long nights relentless.

So Lent began offstage, elsewhere, seemingly a world away from my hovel of fresh motherhood. I was not particularly anxious to get to Mass; I knew the obligation to attend on Sundays is lifted for those too busy caring for infants, and I was content to play that card with liberality. I'm giving up sleep for Lent, I joked to myself, and didn't give it much thought. Back to breastfeeding.

This laidback attitude toward practicing my faith wasn't new. It was a hangover from years of being a half-assed quasi-believer; it was old habit. At this point, months into my Catholic infancy, my faith had been revived, rescued in its death throes, but the pulse was yet weak. I was quite fervent on Sundays, for the most part; before giving birth, I went to Mass willingly and took the sacramental cup, imbibing all the grace I could, hoping it would tide me over until the next Sunday. If Catholicism was a spinning gyre, a planet unto itself, I was whisked into its orbit once a week, much to my consolation—but as the days unfolded, the entropy of ordinary life pulled me away, back out in the void of secularism. So turned the merry-go-round.

One of those gloomy Lenten evenings, I'm not sure when—that time of year, all the days seem the dreary same, even more so in the postpartum fog—I was laying on my mom's couch, no doubt still wearing my pajamas, watching one of those obscure but critically acclaimed foreign films she likes. Baby was asleep downstairs, for the moment anyway, and I was content to be lulled into some other, subtitled world. Despite my mom's enthusiasm, I assumed the film would be boring, but that was okay. I could do boring, as long as it was a different flavor of boredom than my daily ennui.

Although the film, *Fill the Void*, sounded like a sci-fi thriller, which was more my speed, it was anything but—instead an understated portrait of love and marriage in an Orthodox Jewish community. The filmmaker was a convert to Orthodox Judaism, and she captured the inner rhythms of that world with quiet intimacy. The plot was simple and well-told, but it wasn't the story that gripped me so much as the world it opened, a world totally alien to the modern landscape with its sterile disenchantment, where time is ordered to the demands of capitalism, where feast days celebrate things we can buy—it's National Coffee Day!—where God is an optional add-on. In this modern milieu, the sacred is sequestered, cooped up in scattered church buildings, where faithful gather for one or two brief hours a week to glad-hand one another, pay God his due, and return to lives where football and shopping capture the firstfruits of our attention. Not every modern Christian lives like this, of course. But many—too many—do. And, watching this film, l realized I was one of them.

The Jewish characters on the screen inhabited another world entirely, one infused with God. Every aspect of their lives gestured toward a divine reality: the way they clothed their bodies, the way they interacted with one another, the way they ate and drank. Prayer flowed freely, giving structure to the day and making each moment an offering. The self-willed, autonomous individual—that American obsession—was absent. Love and marriage were not simply a matter of choice and desire, but treated as communal concerns. There were stark lines between men and women, and this preservation of difference opened a space that women alone share, and vice versa. Those twofold spheres created a tension, a magnetism made possible by the mysterious distance between them. Mystery: yes, mystery was kept alive and cultivated—mystery between the sexes, and the infinite mystery of God.

The women onscreen, at least the married ones, wore head coverings, turban-like wraps that completely hid their hair. I wondered: what would it be like to adorn my body like this—without concern for the latest trends, but in a way that signaled my relationship to the heavens above and the husband by my side? What would it be like to have a constant physical reminder, cumbersome and awkward as that seems, that I am, at every moment, covered by God? Just two short years ago, I probably would have watched this film and thought, *thank God I don't live in such oppressive, patriarchal society!*—but there I was, feeling downright envious of those characters, of a life woven wholly with the fabric of faith.

I do not intend to romanticize this kind of insular religious community, though the temptation is strong. I mean only to highlight what a glimpse of it revealed to me: it is *damn hard* to be a believer in the modern, secularized world. It is *hard* not to have a faith that functions like tepid sports fandom, where you gather and cheer on game day, slap the decal on your car, and call it good, where religious affiliation is more like a club membership, just one label among many, no more central to one's identity than being an avid NPR listener.

The title of the film began to feel like a directive, a dare, to more actively practice my faith. *Fill the void*—that six-day void, where time loses its sacred heartbeat, flattening out into a monotonous line, where God's presence recedes and the cosmos is silent again. I knew, intellectually, that for the Catholic there should be no strict opposition between the sacred and the secular. The world, though fallen, is still seen as *good*, not something to hide from or guard one's faith against. In the Catholic view, the doors of a church building are not a boundary; the sacramental grace we receive from the Church should flood every area of our lives. But that's not how I was living.

I'd been Catholic for almost a year now, and after that joyous whirlwind of initiation, where everything was so new and exciting and happening so fast, where I was able to dip, at last, into the sacramental life—I'd hit something of a plateau. I was still holding my head above water, struggling with some of the Church's hard teachings, the ones that seemed most at odds with modern notions of progress, like the ban on contraception and the affirmation of traditional marriage. In this film, I could see an apparition of what it might be like to give myself wholeheartedly to the Church, to just let go, to close my eyes and stop kicking, to dive deep and be subsumed.

O, reader, what grave sins against feminism began to flood my mind and heart! The foremost of these? I had the perverse urge to wear a head covering.

I was vaguely aware of a veiling tradition in Catholicism. At my own suburban parish, I'd seen a smattering of old ladies wearing what looked like doilies on their heads, and the occasional nun's habit. My few exploratory jaunts into more traditional parishes revealed a far wider range of veiling women, women of all ages with delicate lace coverings of various shades. They were beautiful, those adorned heads, lowered in devotion—but also unsettling, a spectacle I wasn't used to seeing and didn't quite know how to interpret. What did the veils mean? That these women were subservient to their husbands? But not all the women I saw with veils even had husbands. And one such woman—she was like me, an academic and breadwinner for her family, hardly a poster child for patriarchy.

I can remember the first time I saw her in Mass, wearing a stiff and somewhat severe veil of black lace, the only veiled woman in the room, aside from the few aforementioned old ladies. I felt embarrassed for her and couldn't help joining the collective stare. I assumed she must be some sort of Catholic fundamentalist, some holier-than-thou type, and the display made me feel uncomfortable. I'm all for being devout, I thought, but let's not get *excessive.*

Yet there I was, just months down the road, wondering what it would be like to wear a veil myself.

In secret, by the glow of my smartphone, I began reading about this practice while breastfeeding late into the night. I'm just researching, I told myself. No harm in that. I read various first-person accounts about why some women choose to veil, none of them involving women being under the authority of men. Rather, this seemed to be an individual devotional practice, a way of acknowledging the profundity of being in Christ's sacramental presence during Mass, something akin to Moses removing his sandals when confronted with the burning bush. I learned that veiling was obligatory for women during Mass before the second Vatican Council, but in the 1970s it became an optional practice, no longer normative. Hence the few elderly women who'd maintained the practice, and the small but increasing younger crowd who were trying to revive the tradition. The more I read, the more I felt an inner prompting to veil. Not an overpowering compulsion, but a steady nudge I couldn't ignore.

Eventually, I succumbed to temptation. One night, baby asleep at last, instead of collapsing into bed or watching more British crime drama, I started digging around in my closet. I found an infinity scarf and looped it around my neck like normal. But then, with a quick furtive glance behind me, to ensure I was truly alone, I draped one of the loops over my hair, Mary-style, and knelt beside the bed. I was aware I probably looked like a crazy person, cowering in the dark in plaid pajama pants, a green owl-print scarf on my head, mumbling to myself as the sound of an artificial ocean perpetually looped in the background. At one point I heard Michael coming down the hall, and I quickly yanked off the scarf, playing it cool, until his footsteps faded away and I ducked back under again. I was embarrassed, but also exhilarated. I felt so *naughty.*

When spring break rolled around, I was starting to emerge from the postpartum haze, enough to entertain the idea of going to a midweek Mass, wanting to make the most of the Lent that was left. As I walked the three short blocks to the parish, I harbored the secret thought that this would be the first time I tried covering my head for Mass. I let the prospect idle in my mind without dwelling on it, aware I could easily chicken out. That was one of my motivations for going to a daily Mass—much smaller crowd, less pressure. A roomful of staring eyes during Sunday Mass was still too intimidating.

I was wearing a simple gray scarf around my neck, nothing special, standard fare for late winter. Or was it early spring? I wasn't sure. I only knew that it was overcast outside, raining halfheartedly, so I walked briskly, assuming it was just an ordinary day on the liturgical calendar.

Far from it. It was March 25, as it turns out. Nine months from Christmas. The Feast of the Annunciation. This is the day the Church celebrates the advent of the Incarnation, when the angel Gabriel appears to an unwitting Jewish girl, hailing her as full of grace, with the impossible message that she will be the mother of the messiah. And she responds—first, with wonder: *How can this be?* Then, with perfect trust: *Be it done unto me according to thy word.* Yes, she says, assenting with her whole being. She is not bowled over by God, but gives herself freely. *Fiat mihi.*

I had no idea, as I scurried along, thinking and not thinking about veiling during Mass, that this was such an important feast day, and not just any feast day, but the Annunciation, a mysterious event that had captivated me for years, even when I saw it as merely a lovely symbol. Providence is always at work around us, most often beyond our awareness—but there are moments when a shaft of light hits the web just so, and for a instant we can glimpse the subtle workings of God that somehow gather up all threads for our ultimate good. This was one such moment, a gift of liturgical providence, that I would show up at Mass unknowingly on the Feast of the Annunciation, all the while planning to veil for the first time as a silent assent to that still small voice that I was beginning to trust, even if I did not yet understand.

* * *

Praying and veiling—two practices that unfolded together for me. During that Lent, for perhaps the first time in my life, I felt a deep desire to pray, and veiling was an expression of that desire, an outward posture that was, unbeknownst to me, teaching me the inner posture of prayer. The body calling forth the heart.

Over a year prior, when I was just beginning RCIA, I had politely informed Sr. Juanita that I was an *intellectual*, and thus needed some hefty reading material to aid my discernment process. She took one look at me and said, "You don't need to read more; you need to pray more." She was right, of course, but I just nodded and scuttled back to my protective realm of theological tomes and papal encyclicals.

Private prayer was intimidating. I'd never been good at it, never really understood what it was for. Liturgical, communal prayer—that was different. That kind of prayer was a river endlessly running, propelled onward by voices around the globe, voices stretching back through time, all these echoing in concert with the eternal prayers of the saints. The river was always there; I didn't have to conjure up the right words or gestures, I only had to step into it, let my voice join the chorus, and step out again, while it continued to flow.

But private prayer? And, God forbid, *extemporaneous* prayer? I was too skittish, still on the lam from my evangelical past, to try it. Spontaneous prayer conjured memories of those "popcorn prayer" circles, where you take requests and pray for them, one-by-one—I could still feel the pooled palm sweat of joined hands, barely listening to what's being said, too busy rehearsing my part so it would sound sufficiently pious. Or the infamous sermon prayer, meant more for people's ears than God's, to passively aggressively goad them in one direction or another.

At one point, in college, I became hyper-aware of the crutch word "just," how it punctuated nearly every other word in the evangelical prayer vernacular, e.g., *Lord, we just come before you and just ask that you would just . . .* I resolved to eradicate it from my own prayers, which made me even more self-conscious. I remember one particular instance during my freshman year: the professor asked for prayer requests at the beginning of class, and I volunteered to pray for a friend's bike that had been stolen. I launched in, meticulously making sure to avoid the word "just"—so much that I wasn't sure what I *was* saying. Before I knew it, I was on a retributive tangent, asking God to unmask the perpetrators of this heinous crime and "bring them to justice," inwardly panicking all the while, *what the hell am I even saying?*

During my post-evangelical years, I gave up private prayer altogether. By the time I landed on Catholicism's shore, I carried only a simplistic, juvenile notion of prayer with me, prayer in Girl Scout mode—knocking on God's door and asking him for stuff, trying to charm him into buying your cookies. There are many problems with this model, the foremost being that it doesn't demand any sort of change in me, only a change on the part of God. And this gives a weak, wavering sense of divine providence, as if God's ultimate divine plan is subject to our whims.

So what is prayer, if not this? In the words of Pope Benedict XVI, "prayer, properly understood, is nothing other than becoming a longing for God."[5] The true purpose of prayer is the inversion of the cookie shill: I pray not to bring God's heart around to my desires, but to bring my heart around to his.

There's sort of a sickness of our age that treats our desires as god-like, infallible, one that confuses desire with conscience, what I *ought* to do with what I *want* to do. Our entire economic engine runs on the fuel of unquenchable human desire, peddling the myth that doing and buying and consuming whatever you want is the way to find happiness. Keeping us wanting, rather than content, is the goal. Humans are creatures of desire, so it goes, and to deny or suppress our desires cripples our True Self.

There's a sense in which that is true, from the Christian perspective. Most compelling lies are not whole-cloth fictions, but distortions of truth. Christianity does not go as far down the road as Buddhism, for example, by asking us to purge ourselves of desire altogether. Rather, in the Christian view, human desire is a purposeful force that, when channeled toward the right things, brings us closer to God and thereby to our own wellbeing. Desire is an inner magnetism that is meant to draw us somewhere in particular, toward that which alone can fulfill. Most people, even when going awry, are driven by desire toward some kind of good, but if we mistake finite, temporary goods as ends in themselves, our desire is never sated, always churning, keeping us forever restless. Christianity asserts that we are made *for* something—union with God—and to desire anything other than what leads to this ultimate end will be inherently dissatisfying.

If conversion is an about-face, away from the road of restless desire back toward God, prayer is the turning. St. Thérèse of Lisieux describes prayer as "a surge of the heart." For St. John of Damascus, prayer is "the raising of one's mind and heart to God." Each of these descriptions[6] captures a dimension of prayer—sometimes it is a movement of desire itself, sometimes the heart surges, able to cry out in love and longing. Sometimes it is more difficult, an act of will rather than wanting, a furrow painstakingly plowed for desire to follow. Whatever the emotional content, prayer is meant to transform us from the inner being outward, to shape our desire towards the only hope of fulfillment, to make us a "longing for God."

There's a place, of course, for prayers of petitions, intercessions—we are supposed to bring our needs and desires to God. But when this kind of prayer is unaccompanied by a spirit of sacrifice, the supplicant remains cut off from real transformation.

Sacrifice: a bloody, ancient word. A word plucked from the Books of the Law, those dull, legalistic tomes that drag down the fat half of the Bible, for seemingly no other purpose than to remind us what Christ rescued us from. Or so I used to think. But the sacrifice of Christ only has meaning against the backdrop of this strange, ritualistic world. The old covenant notion of true worship *as* sacrifice—that ideal still stands, though given new meaning through the covenant of grace.

Christ did not come to save us from making offerings; he did not come to jettison the sacrificial dynamic between God and man altogether. No, he came to fulfill and complete, rather than replace and abolish. In fact, he extends it. He raises the stakes. Christ is concerned, above all, with the inmost being; those who nurture lustful thoughts are just as culpable as adulterers. To give one's interior life over to sin is as destructive as external actions. So too with worship. We are still asked to make offerings—and not merely of our prized possessions. We are to be living sacrifices, to put our lives and hearts on the altar and give them up into God's keeping. Prayer, then, is precisely this: the inner movement of offering oneself.

Today, as I'm writing the end of this chapter, there happens to be a selection from a homily by St. Ambrose in the Office of Readings—one of the seven "hours" or sessions in the Church's daily liturgy of prayer. This homily is on prayer and includes the following passage—a small gift of liturgical providence:

> The apostle teaches us to pray anywhere, while the Saviour says *Go into your room*—but you must understand that this "room" is not the room with four walls that confines your body when you are in it, but the secret space within you in which your thoughts are enclosed and where your sensations arrive. That is your prayer-room, always with you wherever you are, always secret wherever you are, with your only witness being God.[7]

This is the inner altar, the place where true prayer happens, where we can come, again and again, to renew our humble offerings and be changed.

I did not know all this when I began to pray during that Lent, in the dark, under the veil. I was taught slowly how to pray by the words of the Church herself, words echoing through her ancient halls, home to so many voices. As I read and listened, like a wide-eyed infant studying the contours of this unfamiliar world, fragments of language, simple strings of words, found their way to me. Those words became vehicles for my desires, giving shape to them. I took the words in, harnessed them with my attention, filled them with longing, and offered them back.

These proved to be dangerous words, dangerous prayers, when prayed with desire and attention. Dangerous because they prompted a sea change—a sweeping, maddening, disorienting shift in worldview. This is where it began, that real conversion, the wrenching and inward revolution. Not all at once, but hour by grinding hour, month by grueling month.

This upheaval began unwittingly when I first entered the Church and began to be nourished by her sacraments. Those sacraments are not just lovely symbols after all; they are *efficacious* symbols, they impart what they represent. And the sacred liturgy began to teach me true worship, not merely through its ancient words, but also its gentle demands on my body, that I kneel and bow and genuflect and through those motions be reminded of who I am—and who He is. Fed on this steady diet of grace, tutored in the school of liturgy, I began to learn reverence, obedience, restraint.

Yet it is when I began to pray privately that the birth pangs quickened. Not because I was *making* it happen—I was finally *letting* it happen.

> *Create in me a clean heart, O God. Renew within me a steadfast spirit.*
>
> *You desire truth in the inward being. Teach me wisdom in my secret heart.*
>
> *O blood and water, which gushed forth from the heart of Jesus, as a fountain of mercy for us, I trust you.*
>
> *Domine, ut videam.*

These are the dangerous prayers that ransomed my mind and heart. Each of these prayers, at its root, is a prayer of submission. Surrender. Not surrender wrought by violent conquest, but surrender freely given. God is not Orwell's Big Brother, who pummels us into obedience, extracting our love, our devotion, by obliterating our individuality. That is an evil inversion of the Trinitarian love that woos us with grace, but never compromises our freedom, and wants nothing other than to make us fully ourselves, fully alive. This is surrender as trust, the way a bird trusts the wind. Surrender as *yes, I will, yes.*

I trust you. Change me. O Lord, I long to see.

For years, my feminist convictions led me to resist the idea of submission. It was a dirty word, one to be rejected, rewritten. And, to be fair, in my religious upbringing, the word "submission" was mostly trotted out as a scriptural mandate that wives should submit to husbands. This directive was typically interpreted in a one-sided way, often broadened to mean the general submission of women to men in all spheres. The corresponding verses that demand self-sacrifice from husbands and mutual submission between all believers were rarely brought to the foreground. "Submission," then, was a bludgeon word used against women, and in that limited sense, the feminist is right to resist it. But rather than trying to understand the wider scriptural meaning of submission, I jettisoned the idea altogether—and in doing so, I hobbled myself spiritually. I chose instead a path of arrogance and self-rule. If after my feminist "awakening" I felt like God was disappearing behind a wall, I now know that wall was not patriarchy; it was my own hardened will.

In truth, submission should be the spiritual posture of every Christian. Receptivity, obedience, surrender—these are not weaker, delicate traits best left to the ladies. These are the lifeblood of spiritual vitality. Mary, in her *yes* to God that broke open our world, her *yes* that became an eternal bridge between God and humankind—in this self-abandonment to the divine will, we find the pinnacle of human becoming, the perfect response of creature to Creator. This surrendering of the will does not obliterate it, making us some kind of automaton—no, it sharpens it, heightens it, by redirecting it toward the good, the beautiful, the true.

Wearing the veil isn't a spiritual mandate for all women; that's not what I believe, and that's not what the Church herself teaches. It's a personal devotion, a longstanding tradition that perhaps holds as many meanings as wearers. Not all women need the veil, but I did. I needed to break the feminist thrall on my unbending knees and stubborn will, and this happened, through the gentle promptings of the Spirit, by taking upon my own person a symbol of submission—not to men, but to God.

This is the first of many paradoxes that I encountered in my Catholic conversion, the first of many exquisite surprises: I discovered spiritual life and true freedom by surrendering to a patient Love beyond myself, by offering up my will and desires in prayer, night by night, at the inner altar.

O Hidden God

I was fifteen the first time I attended a Catholic Mass, a freshman in high school. My first-ever boyfriend was Catholic, a kind, geeky boy with a lovely French name. I'll call him Etienne. Etienne lived in another tiny Idaho hamlet about three hours away. We attended rival schools, and I met him on the speech and debate circuit. Our first interaction involved him holding forth at length about *The Lord of The Rings*, while I listened politely and thought about his pretty eyes. Our short-lived relationship was an innocent and giddy fling that never flamed into love. We went to prom together, as young folks do, and because he lived far away, I stayed the night in town and went to Mass with his family the next morning.

The church was a tiny, one-room building from the pioneer era, twinned with the schoolhouse from *Little House on the Prairie*, but with a plain cross on its prow. At the time, I thought of Catholics as strange, distant cousins of true, Bible-believing Christians, for whom salvation was ambiguous. There was something foreign, un-American about Catholicism; they seemed to have a lot of extra stuff going on—saints, candles, feasts, rosaries, Mary. Doesn't all that just get in the way? And those crosses with Jesus still attached—don't they know he's *risen* already?

Like many a good Christian teen, I had a healthy judgmental streak, and went into Mass with my defenses on alert, ready to resist any affronts to my *sola scriptura* sensibilities. The basic structure of the liturgy itself was sort of familiar, not unlike the Lutheran service I was attending at the time. But I didn't know any of the responses as I scrambled to follow along in the missal, too caught up in what I was supposed to be doing to pay any real attention to what was happening around me. Whatever *was* happening, the Lutheran version seemed a little toned down, more palatable, not quite so extravagant.

The greatest affront occurred when it came time for communion—the word "Eucharist" was not yet a part of my religious vocabulary. Etienne leaned over with a whisper, directing me to fold my arms across my chest like a sleeping vampire, so the priest would know not to give me communion. I would get a simple blessing instead.

So I filed along with my vampire arms, watching the small crowd of faithful eat the bread and drink the wine without me, feeling like a middle schooler who's arrived at school and realized it is her week to be ostracized by all the other girls. The tandem gestures, the prayers known by heart and spoken as one, the Eucharistic table closed to outsiders: all this sent the very clear message that there was a communal body present, and I was not a part of it.

Looking back on this memory as a Catholic, an "insider," I am relieved that Etienne gently directed me away from taking communion, because I absolutely should not have been partaking. My sense of not being fully part of the body was accurate, but I had neither the understanding nor the humility to accept that gracefully. I had no idea what was happening in that tiny clapboard church, there before my eyes, without the faith and tradition of the Church to reveal that to me. I had no idea that the cup I passed was Christ, the bread his body, and I was in no way prepared to receive it.

* * *

In the Catholic understanding, the ultimate end or purpose of human life is union with God, union made possible only through the incarnate bridge of Christ. Salvation is not simply a matter of being let off the hook for our sins, because Christ paid our debt. Salvation, for the Catholic, involves actual transformation, an ongoing process of sanctification, so the love of God, which has been poured into our hearts by faith, can be kept alive and continually refine us. Since salvation ultimately culminates in union with the triune God, the soul must be purged from sin altogether, not merely freed from sin's consequences. Contrary to popular misconceptions, this process is not something we accomplish on our own, through our own works and merits—that would be Pelagianism, a heresy rejected by the Church in the fifth century. No, sanctification is only possible through supernatural aid— divine grace—and our active participation with that grace.

Protestantism, with its *sola* sensibility (*sola fides*, *sola scriptura*), might be described as having a dialectical outlook, wherein faith is pitted against works, belief against reason, science against religion—but Catholicism upholds a resolute both-and. We are saved by faith, absolutely, but not faith *alone*. Justification is a cooperative effort of divine grace in participation with human free will. God reaches out to us with grace, we respond by faith, and the link thus established is kept alive not just by faith, but also by *caritas*: love. If God is love, as taught by Scripture, when we act against charity by sinning, we weaken and damage the divine life within us. Our actions do matter. As St. Paul writes in his epistles, we are saved by grace through faith, and our faith must express itself in love. Grace, faith, free will, love—these are all forces collaborating in our sanctification.

For the Catholic, faith creates a real, substantial link between the believer and Christ. To use the words of Dom Anscar Vonier, a Thomist theologian, faith is "the first grafting of man on Christ which underlies all other fruitfulness."[8] This harmonizes with my evangelical upbringing, where salvation was presented as inviting Christ into one's heart through the assent of faith, creating an unbreakable salvific bond.

But within the expansive both-and of Catholicism, faith is not the sole means of union with Christ. There is another tie that binds us to our savior and his passion, in an actual and not merely metaphorical sense: the sacraments. Some Christians seem to manage, somehow, through faith alone, cut off from the sustaining flood of sacramental grace that still flows in the ancient Church. But my faith couldn't survive without it. I'm too weak, too wayward for that. I need that golden cord to bind myself to the mast. Without it, I wander.

We humans are embodied beings, creatures of spirit and bone, crafted from the soil and animated by divine breath, as that first story teaches us. This is why the Word becomes flesh in order to dwell among us, to descend fully into our sensible reality. The sacraments are best understood in this context, as an extension of the Incarnation. In fact, the sacraments make no sense without it; they are deeply incarnational, deeply christological. Christ himself is a sacrament, *the* sacrament: he is the image of the invisible God, as Colossians tell us—but he is not merely an image, merely a sign, but God truly with us. Just as Christ, in his nature, is fully human and fully God, so are the sacraments both material and divine.

The sacramental principle holds that God can take hold of external things just as he can take hold of the human soul, and the Catholic Church teaches that he does this. God takes hold of and transfigures the waters of baptism, so that they *actually*, not just symbolically, cleanse the soul of original sin. God takes hold of the bread and the wine on the altar, altering them at their deepest level of reality, so that they become charged with Christ himself and enable a tangible, mystical union with him that draws us together as his body.

Sacraments and the rituals surrounding them are not harsh burdens placed on humans by God—rather, they are manifestations of God's abundant grace. To put it simply, the sacraments are not for God; they are for us. Sacramental worship exhibits a deep understanding of our nature as human beings: our dependence on the senses, on food and water for sustenance, our need for tangible signs. What better way for God to supply us with sanctifying grace than through these signs made alive?

In contrast to the onerous rites of the Old Testament, which signified a divine reality without actually transmitting it, the Christian sacraments are *signs that effect what they signify*. We can discern, in a shadowy, inchoate form, the body of Christ's church in the people of Israel, just as we can see in Israel's sacrificial worship an anticipation of our sacramental worship—but the sacraments, as extensions of the Incarnation, are not just symbols. They are alive with Christ's power, which is Life itself. To quote Vonier once more: "Sacraments are, then, truly an energy that comes from Christ in person, a radiation from the charity of the Cross; a stream of grace from the pierced side of Christ."[9]

If one primary force drew me to Catholicism from afar, it was a thirst for the sacraments. Or, to be more precise, God's grace was the force, and it worked patiently, gently, creating a growing hunger for the Eucharist. Even though I didn't yet have an intellectual or theological understanding of the sacraments, I nonetheless had a visceral longing for them, especially the Sacrament of the Altar.

I can see a nascent devotion to the Eucharist even in my childhood. The Bible church we attended in Utah served communion once a month, and it was always a welcome deviation from the standard service. The pastor would wrap up his lengthy sermon a bit early, and around would come the shiny platter of cubed white bread and plastic thimbles of grape juice. White bread and juice, both luxuries rarely served in my house, so I'd sneak several cubes of bread, down a few extra sips of juice. There was never much explanation for why we took communion; I only knew that it was a memorial, like a truncated mystery play, a short and sweet reenactment of Christ supping with his disciples. Still, even in this pared down form, there was something different, something set apart about this minimalistic ritual. For a moment, the past was drawn into the present, and my body and its senses were invited into a non-verbal act of worship. Even stripped of its context, its sacramental power, there was in this communion a foretaste of Eucharistic fullness.

Understanding this fullness requires a backward look into the Pentateuch, into those strange books of the law, to provide the necessary backdrop. Exodus 12 describes the institution of the Passover, the culmination of God's persistent efforts to free his people from slavery. During the final plague, the judgment of Yahweh came upon Egypt in a wave of destruction. Only the sacrifice of a lamb protected the Israelite households: the blood of the lamb, spread on the doorposts, and the body of the lamb, eaten with unleavened bread.

The Eucharistic parallels are potent: a sacrificial lamb, whose blood has saving power; a sacrificial meal, wherein the body of the lamb is eaten with unleavened bread. The commemoration of the Passover is a stark foreshadowing of the Eucharist, which is why Christ institutes this sacrament during a Passover meal. He makes clear through his words—*This is my body, this is my blood*—that he is the new Paschal lamb. His coming crucifixion will complete the imperfect sacrifices of the old covenant and save us not from earthly bondage, but slavery to sin.

The Eucharist, then, is the Passover meal of the New Covenant. It is a memorial, yes, but specifically a memorial *sacrifice*, like its Jewish antecedent. In every Catholic Mass, Christ's sacrifice on the cross is once again offered to the Father for the sake of our salvation.

Behold the Lamb of God, who takes away the sins of the world! This is the antiphon that introduces Christ in John's gospel, which has its fullest meaning only in the context of the Eucharist. The entire gospel of John, in fact, is deeply Eucharistic in its imagery and content, particularly chapter 6, in which Christ insists emphatically and repeatedly that unless we eat his flesh and drink his blood, we have no life in us. Six times he asserts this teaching, even though many are repelled by it. The Catholic takes Christ at his word here: each Mass, we eat his flesh, we drink his blood, and this gives us sanctifying grace, a share in the divine life of the Trinity.

The Catholic Mass is a liturgical drama of the history of salvation, tracing a trajectory from the old covenant to the fulfillment of the new covenant through Christ. The first half of the Mass is the Liturgy of the Word, in which four pieces of Scripture are proclaimed: a passage from the Old Testament, a psalm, a passage from the New Testament, and, lastly, a passage from one of the Gospels. Ordinarily, these texts evoke a shared theme, showing the work and fidelity of God from the time of the Israelites into our era, the era of the Church. This portion of the Mass hearkens back to Jewish worship in the synagogue, in which believing Jews gathered to hear the Hebrew Scriptures proclaimed. We see Jesus participating in this form of worship in Luke 4, when he reads a prophecy from Isaiah and announces to the people that the prophecy has been fulfilled in their hearing. The Catholic Mass carries this Jewish mode of worship in its Liturgy of the Word, but it does not culminate there. That is only the beginning, the prelude that prepares us to ascend to the summit of worship, to the Liturgy of the Eucharist, in which the mysteries of the Incarnation, Crucifixion, and Resurrection are staged and presented anew to the people.

The Liturgy of the Eucharist begins with a procession bringing forth ordinary goods that will be transfigured and offered back to God: unleavened bread and wine. These goods are both *fruit of the earth* and *work of human hands*, as the priestly prayer tells us. They are gifts from God's natural abundance—wheat, grapes—that have, in a smaller sense, been transformed by human work and ingenuity into bread and wine. This is an anticipatory shadow of the miracle the Triune God will perform.

Indeed, the Catholic Eucharist is intensely Trinitarian—all persons of the Godhead are active: the priest, serving *in persona Christi* as an icon of Jesus, offers the gifts of bread and wine. At the heart of the ancient Eucharistic prayer, Christ's own words from the Last Supper are recited by the priest to consecrate the bread and wine: *take this, all of you, and eat of it; this is my body.* . . . Christ's words bring forth the moment of *epiclesis*, when bells ring out and the Holy Spirit descends to change the elements into the sacramental Body and Blood of Christ. The divine elements are then offered back to the Father, through a commemorative meal, as a perfect sacrifice.

The Catholic Church maintains the original teaching of the Eucharist as a sacrifice—the only sacrifice that can merit our salvation, because what is offered *is Christ himself*, the Lamb of God. In every Mass, God provides the only offering that could possibly reconcile us to him. Recall the iconic story of Abraham and Isaac from Genesis 22, a story that prefigures the sacrifice of Christ. In that story, as here, Abraham trusts that *God will provide the sacrifice*. And so it is in the Mass. God gives us a gift, and we offer it back to him. Charging the bread and wine with his sacramental presence, while leaving the outward sign intact, Christ enables us to give a worthy sacrifice to the Father. This does not mean Christ's death on the cross wasn't complete—it was. This is the re-presentation of that one, original, perfect sacrifice that occurred at Golgotha. Through the Mass, the crucifixion and resurrection are made present again; they become eternal moments, and we enter into these eternal moments through the sacramental door of the Eucharist.

What the Eucharist *is* and *does* can explain why one must be part of the Catholic Church to take communion during Mass. Understanding this requires entering, as reformed theologian Karl Barth called it, "the damnable Catholic 'and.'" The Eucharist is not just a symbol. As sacrament, it is symbol *and* reality. It is an efficacious symbol, which transmits the reality it represents. If it is just a symbol, Flannery O'Connor is right: to hell with it. Celebrate it however you want—or not at all! Pass the bread and juice around to whomever and throw the leftovers in the trash, or sneakily eat them, as my child-self recommends.

But if the Catholic Church is right about her Eucharist, if the outward appearances of bread and wine carry within them the sacramental Body and Blood of Christ, we must proceed with caution, with a healthy, reverent dread. As St. Paul warns in 1 Corinthians, we must "examine ourselves" and "discern the body," lest we "eat and drink judgment" on our heads.[10]

Discerning the body. There's a dual meaning there, revealing a double ignorance of mine when I attended that first Mass as a teenager. I was blind to the body in both senses: the Body of Christ, hidden within what appeared to be ordinary bread and wine, and also the Body of Christ *qua* Church. Had I taken communion then, I would have been completely unaware that the wafer I took into my body was full of Christ himself. I probably would have laughed at the prospect. How ridiculous! Even as an Anglican, when I experienced a Eucharistic liturgy for the first time, I had a profound sense that what was happening was sacred, set apart, that Christ was among us in a unique way—but it was still sort of nebulous, still mostly symbolic, even if the symbols were far richer, and more potent, than what I'd known before.

* * *

Adorote devote, latens Deitas. So begins one of St. Thomas's Eucharistic hymns: I adore you devoutly, O hidden God. The Christ who comes to us under the veil of bread. Why this hiddenness? Why is such a profound divine reality so obscured, accessible only to the eyes of faith? Even after becoming Catholic, it took me awhile to discern the body of Christ in the Eucharist. Exactly a year, in fact—after my daughter's birth, during that latter half of Lent, as I began to practice my faith more intentionally, praying dangerous prayers each night by candlelight.

One of those prayers was a fragment of Scripture from Mark's gospel, the story of the blind cripple, Bartimaeus, who calls out to Jesus for mercy and healing. The blind man's outcry became something of a mantra for me: *Domine, ut videam.* I prayed this, over and over: O Lord, that I might see! I saw in this weak, broken man a mirror of myself, blinded from years of dormant faith and a godless habit of thinking, spiritually lame. I longed for Christ, but couldn't yet *see* him, at least in nothing more than flashes on the periphery, which I doubted as soon as they disappeared. And I was too weak to follow him anywhere. I'd trained myself, often passively and unknowingly, to see the world through a lens that had little to do with traditional Christianity. So this prayer was a plea to reshape my horizons, my intuitions, my desires, to unsee what had become familiar, and to see anew through a strange, ancient light. *Domine, ut videam.*

That Easter, the prayer was answered. But not quite in the way I'd hoped, not with a cryptic, ecstatic vision in which Christ hands me his bleeding heart, or the consecrated host starts to glow and levitate over the altar. I wanted something like that; I wanted Jesus to put on a show for me, to do some tricks, flaunt his power a little; I wanted something more than this gentle, unobtrusive God.

Instead, I got something in between. No swoons, no fireworks. Just a sudden, dawning realization in the middle of Mass that *Oh my God, this is Jesus.* That Sunday, Easter Sunday, they were short of volunteers to distribute the Eucharist, and since I'd been trained how to do it months earlier, I agreed to help. I'd done it before, no sweat. After the prayer of consecration, when the people turned to one another and gave the kiss of peace, I went up to the altar with the other Eucharistic ministers and waited to receive. The priest finished his silent prayers and held the cup and the host aloft. "Behold the Lamb of God," he said, looking not at the people, but at the small, sacred circle in his hand. "Behold him who takes away the sins of the world. Blessed are those called to the supper of the Lamb."

"Lord, I am not worthy that you should enter under my roof," I prayed the response quietly to myself. "Only say the word, and my soul shall be healed." The words of the faithful centurion from Matthew's Gospel, in that moment, became my own. And it hit me, the quiet, crushing truth that *this is Christ*, his very body and blood, in sacramental form, given for me.

The priest loomed over, with Christ in his hands. He reached out, "The Body of Christ," and put Christ into my hands. He handed me the cup, "The Blood of Christ." I was supposed to take it, drink from it, and then carry it over to the corner, by the choir, and offer it to each person who approached. I took the cup, my hands trembling, suddenly aware that I was standing in front of two hundred parishioners. I looked like a lunatic, I realized, with my disheveled veil and ill-fitting clothes that strained against the abundance of my postpartum body, a body that was starting to noticeably sweat.

You'd have thought this realization of Christ's sacramental presence would give me a spiritual thrill, or an overwhelming sense of peace. Instead, I started to panic. What am I doing here, in this ridiculous head covering and these effing stretch pants that don't even fit? Why am I in front of all these people? Why on earth did I think I was prepared to do something like this, to take hold of Christ himself and distribute him to the masses? I wanted to dissolve into the blue carpet. I wanted to run.

As each parishioner ambled up, unaware of my inner terror, I wasn't sure where to look. I had the urge to avert my eyes away entirely, away from the intimate moment of Christ being poured into each thirsty soul. But I couldn't look away, because I was even more terrified of accidentally slosh- ing the precious blood on the terrible carpet, or—God in heaven forbid— dropping the cup altogether. "The Blood of Christ," I was saying. I heard myself saying it, somehow keeping my voice steady, while channeling most of my energy into calming my shaking hands.

Christ is here, in my hands. I couldn't escape the thought. *When I re- ceive communion, I touch him, he enters under my roof, and my soul is healed.*

I thought of the transfiguration, when Christ revealed his full divinity to his close disciples. They fell on their faces, as I now longed to do, as Moses did, before the burning bush, as Simon Peter did on that faraway shore. In the transfiguration, it was not Christ who was changed, but the disciples. They were given, in that moment, the power of seeing Christ as he truly is; what was hidden in the ordinary was suddenly unveiled.

Christ is truly and actually present in the Eucharist, not in his natural mode, but in a way appropriate to the sacrament—a sacramental mode, one accessible only through eyes that have been transfigured. *What people has a God so near as the Lord our God is to us?* And still nearer now, to us, through the Incarnation, that engine of all sacraments, particularly the Eucharist. After experiencing such fullness, the church services of my upbringing now seemed hollowed out. How could I ever go back? Those services were cen- tered on *the word*, yes, but not the *Word Made Flesh*, who, in the Mass, is tangibly among us again.

That Easter morning, I came to know this. It is now the ground on which I stake my life. But it still takes effort to see it. Grace, yes, and rapt attention—an attention that I usually don't have the patience or reserves to summon, especially while wrangling small children. Luckily, I know that my attention, or lack thereof, doesn't alter what happens during each Mass. Whether I feel it or not, whether I see it or not, Christ comes.

* * *

There's another body that must be discerned at the Lord's table. Christ's body is sacramentally present through the Eucharist, and also mystically present, through the people themselves. And not just the people gathered in that particular place, that particular time, but the worldwide Catholic Church—the word "catholic," after all, simply means "universal."

The Mass awakens us to another realm, the burning furnace of charity that is the Trinity, our God who bestows upon the universe its being, in each moment. Picture bright light flooding through an open door, and millions of these doors, all over the darkened globe, opening and closing, flashing like fireflies. Of course, God is with us in all places, at all times—our ongoing existence, life itself, depends upon this—but the Mass awakens us to this enduring reality. Each Mass in this global dance of light is a discrete celebration, a single node, in the communal worship of the universal Church, which continually offers the sacrifice of Christ on behalf of the whole world. To partake of the Eucharist binds us closer to Christ through the mystery of his Body, the Church.

The Christianity of my youth was all but divested of sacramental realities. There, the faith of the individual was all that mattered, not communion with an actual, concrete ecclesial body, and the sacraments were contracted into mere symbols. From this perspective, why not have an open, buffet table with self-serve juice and bread, like many churches do these days? No wonder many are perplexed and offended by the exclusionary Catholic Mass, as I once was.

In actuality, the notion of the Eucharist being "a banquet of the reconciled," to use Pope Benedict's term, stretches back to the beginning of the Church. Jesus ate many meals, with many people, but the Last Supper was limited to an intimate circle of his apostles, those chosen to give birth to the Church on earth. St. Paul, too, speaks of the Eucharist as gathering the believers into one body in 1 Corinthians 10.

In the first year of my conversion, I began to read some of the early Church fathers, and I was shocked to discover that their theology and worship was thoroughly Catholic from the beginning—something I wouldn't have been able to recognize before becoming familiar with the Mass myself. Justin Martyr, a convert writing mere decades after the deaths of the apostles, gives a detailed picture of the worship of the early Church in his *First Apology*. As he writes, only the person who has been "washed" through baptism and has "assented to our teaching" is invited to the Eucharist:

> And this food is called among us the Eucharist, of which no one is allowed to partake but the man who believes that the things which we teach are true, and who has been washed with the washing that is for the remission of sins, and unto regeneration, and who is so living as Christ has enjoined. For not as common bread and common drink do we receive these; but in like manner as Jesus Christ our Saviour, having been made flesh by the Word of God, had both flesh and blood for our salvation, so likewise have we been taught that the food which is blessed by the prayer of His word, and from which our blood and flesh by transmutation are nourished, is the flesh and blood of that Jesus who was made flesh.[11]

This was written in 155 AD, the earliest days of Christianity, the first generation after the apostles, and it reflects the current practice and theology of the Catholic Church. The Eucharist is not mere symbol, not "common bread," but is an extension of the Incarnation, the "flesh and blood of that Jesus who was made flesh." And admittance to this sacred meal requires conversion; regeneration through baptism and assent to the teachings of the Church. This harmonizes with St. Paul's account that one must first examine oneself and discern the body before approaching the Lord's table.

In truth, the table is not closed, in that any person is welcome to enter into full communion with the Church and participate in her sacraments. But those two things are connected, inseparable. It does not make sense, from the Catholic perspective, for someone to ask to receive her sacraments without first receiving her. The table is waiting; it simply sits *inside the Church*, as it has from the beginning. And the doors are open. The Church longs to embrace all of her children. This notion of a closed table is all backwards, upside down. It is not the Church who rejects; it is the Church who is rejected.

* * *

Sixteen years after that first Mass in rural Idaho, in another church building, another state, I am again in Mass, again excluded from taking communion. I am filing up to the front with vampire arms, bowing my head for a blessing from the priest, passing by the raised host and gilded cup. But this time is different; I'm a catechumen in RCIA, preparing to receive the Catholic sacraments in just a few weeks. I do not yet belong to the Church, but soon.

This time, the exclusion is not an affront. Through it the Church is teaching me the sacredness of what is happening at Mass, opening my eyes to the quiet miracle of the Eucharist. She is teaching me patience, reminding this laidback American that some things are important enough, holy enough, to require careful formation on my part. She is making me keenly aware of my thirst, my need for the grace she offers.

Back in my pew, I kneel, but don't bow my head. I keep my eyes open, anticipating. I watch the people milling forward toward the priest with outstretched hands, open lips. I see mothers carrying babies, I see men in their prime, I see restless children, I see a man who can barely walk shuffling forward, I see a girl in a wheelchair who can't speak, I see a woman reaching out with gnarled, useless hands, I see the old, the young, the fat, the poor, the clean, the weary, the grimy, the keen, all bent, all broken, in one way or another—all hungry and weak.

All of these bodies, like a river rushing up, like a tide of human frailty and beauty and need, I watch them and long to be one of them, to enter the current with my thirst and my wounds, to be buoyed up—not moving, but being moved.

One day, soon enough, I will drink from the fountain. I know this. For now, I wait.

Mater Ecclesia

When I look back at my decade of doubt, a desolate image surfaces, one that captures my spiritual state during that time. The image is this: I am floating in the middle of an unnamed sea, an ocean that seems infinite, stretching ruthlessly to the horizon in every direction. I am a mere speck on that watery landscape, only afloat because I'm clutching a makeshift raft of discarded wood. I'm hanging on with my arms, the rest of my body suspended in the darkness below. I am utterly alone, just sort of bobbing along listlessly, in no particular direction. I am unmoored.[12]

I invoked this image in an earlier chapter, and I want to lean into it here, interrogate it a bit more, press it for answers. What is this ocean, this unforgiving sea? Water can be nourishing, cleansing, a symbol of abundance, profundity, sustenance, yes—but it can also represent death, nothingness. That's what it is here: an abyss. A faceless, meaningless void, utterly impersonal, utterly detached. There is no life teeming in its depth, only darkness.

The water is undrinkable; it would kill me steadily if I used it to dowse my thirst. Not because of malice; it is entirely indifferent to my existence, to all existence. I am simply not made to live here. I cannot thrive here. The more I drink, the more I need. Rather than replenishing me, its salt withers me from within.

Somehow, I'm keeping afloat. The abyss hasn't swallowed me—yet. But I am gradually being enveloped; the ocean fills my vision, everywhere I turn, and its waters lap against my chest. If I think I see something on the horizon, some interruption of the relentless gray line, I feel hope flare up. But nothing seems to fully materialize.

Still, I am holding on. To what? The makeshift raft. I'm clutching it, my piece of hard, solid ground, the fragment of stability I've brought with me to sea. It's made of wood, dismembered branches long ago separated from their roots and hollowed out now by the saltwater. The raft is small, suited just for me. It is, in fact, exactly the size of myself.

This is my faith, what's left of it. It is a fragment of something far bigger, far older, some distant tree that is still alive and growing. I've refashioned it to suit my needs, my whims, only to discover that what once seemed secure is now hopelessly fragile against the sea.

Every person in modernity, believer or not, has to face and contend with this ocean. It is the specter of life without God, a universe in which our existence is an absurd accident, and the only meaning that exists is what we carve out for ourselves. In this universe, love is transient, mere spurious, chemical happenstance, and it will die a human death. Meaning and memory will die a human death. Life itself will eventually flicker out.

What if none of this is real? The believer must ask himself this, looking nervously over his shoulder, glimpsing the void. And this is the thought that plagues the atheist, who has learned to abide the abyss, when she catches sight of a religious landscape: *What if that is true?*

Such is the modern human condition: none of us is spared, at least no one with a penchant for asking why. We all must reckon with truth and its absence; we all must reckon with doubt.

And that is where I was, indefinitely suspended in an abyss that had become more real to me than God, grasping the debris of a disintegrating faith. That is where I was, and would still be, had I not found the Catholic Church. You could say, *had I not found Christ*, because those have become inseparable for me. I did not come to truly know and love Christ outside of his Church. I entered the Church, washed up on her shores, and there I found him, learned how to see him, to recognize that he had been closer than I knew.

* * *

As a child, my nascent faith was nourished under the protective canopy of my believing parents, who taught me to anchor myself in the authority of the Bible. The tradition of my upbringing was thoroughly *sola scriptura*, and all the gaps, the blank spaces left by the absence of sacraments, tradition, saints, and ecclesial authority were filled by the Bible alone. At times, this became an unhealthy extreme, almost a bibliolatry. I remember as a child, in multiple settings—church camp, AWANA, Sunday school, VBS—reciting a pledge of allegiance to the Bible, hand over my heart, in front of a Christian flag. The Bible was seen as God's mouthpiece, the guardian of absolute truth, and given almost sacramental power.

In this light, the Bible, which is really more of a dazzling and diverse anthology than a monolithic text, was viewed as self-interpreting, sort of like a cosmic car manual, a guide with clear, unambiguous answers to any questions or difficulties that might arise. There was no sense that the Bible needed to be *interpreted*; it need only be *read*. The language of "the word"—traditionally and within Scripture applied to Jesus Christ, the Word made flesh—was instead shorthand for the Bible. And the Bible, at times, seemed to function as a Christ-like intermediary, as the primary bridge between humankind and God.

Ironically, this view of the Bible has more akin with the function of the Qur'an in Islam than with the understanding of sacred Scripture for the first fifteen hundred years of Christianity's existence. Muslims believe the Qur'an to be the exact words of God dictated to Mohammed via a divine messenger. There is nothing human about the Qur'an; it is entirely of divine origin, and revealed in one fell swoop to a single person. As the direct words of God, spoken in Arabic, translations of the Qur'an into other languages are not possible—or, at least, these translations are seen as something other than God's actual words.

The churches of my youth often treated the Bible as divine dictation, à la Qur'an, rather than a book of both divine and human origin, with a complex history of transmission, reception, and canonization. It never occurred to me, as a child, to wonder how the Bible came to be, and, until college, I never heard that question raised. I just had a vague sense that the Bible had always been with us, since the time of Christ, that it had descended from God into our hands like manna.

The most glaring inconsistency with the *sola scriptura* view is that it is self-refuting: the doctrine does not appear in Scripture itself. And it couldn't—the various texts that comprise the New Testament were written centuries before the Church settled on a consistent canon of sacred Scripture. In short: the Church long predates the Bible as we think of it. Jesus, when he ascended, did not leave behind a book; he left behind a Church, a community of believers built on the rock of Peter and guided by the Holy Spirit, whose descent at Pentecost marks the Church's birth.

This is not to say that the Bible is somehow discounted in Catholic tradition. Hardly. We've just circled around, once again, to that Catholic both-and. Authority in Catholicism is twofold: sacred Scripture *and* sacred tradition. Sacred Scripture is seen as divinely inspired and infallible on matters of faith, and it plays a central and vibrant role in the life of the Church, especially in its prayer. Listening carefully to the words of the Mass, for example, one can hear the words of Scripture woven throughout—as Catholics we do not simply read Scripture; we hear it proclaimed, we sing its Psalms, we reenact its drama through the liturgical seasons, we let it infuse our prayers. That was something I never learned to do until I became a

Catholic—*praying* sacred Scripture. Most of my conversion prayers, those dangerous prayers, come from the Bible itself. As a Catholic, I am exposed to more Scripture on a weekly basis than I was as an evangelical, through praying the Liturgy of the Hours, through attending Mass, through praying the rosary—all of which are almost entirely composed of Scripture.

The Bible is a vital part of my spiritual life, likely more than it's ever been, because now it is rightfully situated within the life of the Church. I have a much greater understanding of the continuity of Scripture, of its echoes and resonances, its dramatic arc, the way the New Testament is pre-figured in the Old, and the Old fulfilled in the New. I have a sense of the scope of the whole, its mysterious yet harmonious synergy.

Now, when I take the time to read the Bible privately, I do so within the context of an authoritative interpretive tradition. I am not alone, but a single mind joining a concert of minds who have been grappling with this divine book for millennia. And this, I have to say, is *so comforting.* No longer am I left to my own devices in trying to interpret a book so dizzying in its variety and complexity. I have somewhere to take my difficulties, my perplexity—not always to get easy answers, but also better questions and enigmas that never fully disclose themselves, but nonetheless satisfy. No longer can I make the Bible my marionette, speaking in the voice I think best, saying the words I want it to say.

That was, once, exactly where I found myself, after college, at the dead end of a long road where *sola scriptura* ultimately took me. Once I embraced feminism, especially as an evangelical, the Bible presented a problem. While there were passages that clearly affirmed women's dignity and celebrated female heroism, there were also passages that, at best, cut against modern feminist sensibilities, and, at worst, seemed to demean women. A straight-forward, wholehearted acceptance of the Bible was no longer possible. It became an antagonist, a wild horse that needed to be broken and brought under rein.

In essence, my Bible-alone evangelicalism and my newfound feminist faith were at odds, and I tried to make peace through the magical art of *hermeneutics,* which I first encountered in college. I carefully researched the problem passages, most in Paul's epistles, that seemed to affirm a strict hierarchy between men and women, particularly in the Church. I looked up words in the original Greek, researched their connotations, and drew on other passages in order to make thorough, well-reasoned interpreta-tions that resisted an easy patriarchal reading. For a while, the Bible be-came safe again, believable as a divine authority; my Christianity and my feminism were allies. But something significant happened in this foray into hermeneutics, a substantial shift had occurred, even though I remained, for a time, unaware of the implications.

I remember once, as a college sophomore, sitting in a "Women in the Bible" class during a lecture on the Pauline household codes in Ephesians and Colossians. The course was taught by one of my favorite professors, the lone woman in the Department of Bible and Religion. She was a committed feminist and reformer, sort of like an academic Norma Rae, and I greatly admired her. There's a journal entry from that time in which I envision myself as her disciple.

I was excited for the lecture; these were two passages I knew well. I'd worked them over with my evangelical feminist hermeneutics, and I firmly believed that, rightly interpreted, they were no threat to a feminist perspective and, in fact, affirmed one. I expected the professor to tread familiar ground, to discuss the original Greek terms and their meaning, to show the relevance of the surrounding context. I expected her to show how the text was both Christian and feminist.

Instead, she went in an entirely different direction, circling around to the conclusion that the text is just as patriarchal as it appears to be, but because Paul seems to contradict Christ's egalitarian spirit here, we can disregard it. We are not beholden to its authority. I remember feeling surprised, annoyed; many of the other women in the class were still holdouts on feminist matters, and I knew that her approach would alienate them. She was taking the hermeneutical game to another level, which at the time seemed to me too radical, too dismissive of Biblical authority. But soon enough, I followed suit.

The shift that was happening was in one sense necessary, inevitable. It was important for me, in a time of intellectual growth, to realize that the Bible is not self-interpreting, and that the question of hermeneutics is essential: whether or not we are aware, everyone reads the Bible through a specific lens. As a student of mine once observed, one can cherry-pick verses to make the Bible sound sexist, and one can cherry-pick verses to make the Bible sound feminist; what really matters are the assumptions you begin with that guide your interpretation. That is the Protestant predicament: once the naiveté of a self-interpreting Scripture dissipates, one is left to consciously decide which hermeneutical choices to make, which assumptions to import into the text that guide its interpretation. This demystifies the Bible as self-interpreting and alters the dynamic of its authority, which now rests upon a correct interpretation. It's not enough to simply read what the Bible *says*; one must understand what it *means*. But whose interpretation is true? Without a connection to sacred tradition or the teaching authority of the Church, this crucial interpretive role is ultimately filled by the individual. I become the guardian of the Bible's meaning.

In medieval philosophy, there is a concept called "voluntarism," first peddled by William of Ockham and Duns Scotus, which addressed the theological quandary of God's will and its relation to reality. Is something good because God wills it so, or is something good because it is inherently good, grounded in the very nature of God? The voluntarist puts all his chips down on God's will. This leads to a sort of moral arbitrariness; anything, even what we consider the most heinous evil, could be deemed good by God, if he so willed it. God's *will*, rather than God's *nature*, creates all moral categories, according to voluntarism.

This perspective contrasts with that of Thomas Aquinas, which is the Catholic position. For Aquinas, all moral categories, our very sense of good and evil, stem from God's nature, which is the source of the Good. God is Love itself, and his will cannot violate his nature by turning an evil into good. Robert Barron, Catholic Bishop and theologian, has spoken of a "new voluntarism" in our day, one that shifts the power of will from God to the self.[13] In this new voluntarism, good and evil, even reality itself, are subject to our will. I decide what is real. I decide what is true. I decide what is good. *Truth is what I will*. This philosophy seems clearly at odds with a Christian outlook. But the *sola scriptura* faith of my youth that emphasized an individualistic, emotional relationship to God did not protect me from the New Voluntarism. In fact, it became a gateway. The authority of the Bible, cut off from the Church that birthed it and safeguards its meaning, became a tool of my will, the instrument by which I remade Christianity in my own image.

This does not mean my biblical interpretations were always misguided or heretical. I continue to believe that the Bible, rightly interpreted, does not devalue women or enslave them to men. But, as a Catholic, I have had to temper my impulse to filter Scripture through a narrow, twenty-first-century lens, making it a mouthpiece for one contemporary ideology or another.

Most heretical distortions of Christianity emerge in an attempt to erase or resolve one of the many paradoxes that animate the faith. Take Gnosticism, an age-old heresy perennially cropping up in varying forms, which tries to escape the complexity of the Incarnation by positing Christ's humanity as illusory. An inversion of that heresy casts Jesus as only a human. Left to our own devices, our own hermeneutics, most will read the Bible in a heretical trajectory, one that explains away the disconcerting paradoxes that the text itself demands we hold in tension. Without the guiding beacon of an interpretive tradition, the Bible can be easily adapted to any ideology, becoming, e.g., a manifesto for egalitarianism, or conversely, for patriarchal power.

And this happens, often, with the best of intentions. I had no inkling, once I started interpreting the Bible through a feminist lens, that I would eventually conclude, like my beloved professor, that the Bible is simply, glaringly *wrong* about some things, and you didn't have to listen to those parts. I did not know that the playful, seemingly wide-open world of hermeneutics would create a de facto situation where I was functioning, as a Christian, outside the boundaries of any religious authority at all, aside from some nebulous sense of an always-affirming Spirit, which amazingly never seemed to ask any sacrifices from me, or urge any real transformation.

Recently, over Christmas, I was listening to my brother and mother banter amicably about this question of authority. My brother is Protestant, and my mother has recently become Catholic. My brother was speaking honestly about feeling pulled, in some ways, toward Catholicism, but that the central obstacle for him is the Church's assertion of authority. This makes him skittish, that he would somehow be beholden to sacred tradition, especially to the Church's magisterium, to whom the safekeeping and interpretation of Scripture and tradition has been entrusted.

I remember feeling shocked by this idea, and then surprised at my own shock, which indicated how instinctually Catholic I'd become. I was surprised by my brother's aversion, because I see the problem of authority as the Achilles heel of Protestantism. What keeps him from becoming Catholic is a central reason why I could never again be a Protestant. Without an authoritative interpretive guide to Scripture, *I* become the magisterium—a magisterium of one. And there is no way to discern whether my version of Christianity, my reading of Scripture, is truer than anyone else's.

In the Catholic perspective, God's revelation comes to us through sacred tradition and sacred Scripture, which together make up the *depositum fidei*, the Deposit of Faith. From the dawning of Christianity, the gospel was proclaimed by the apostles through both spoken word and writing. Even before the composition of the texts of the New Testament, the apostolic ministry was thriving, and with the aid of the Holy Spirit, sacred tradition was being formed.

The apostles established churches, and there was quickly an emergent but distinct hierarchical structure, visible in the Church's first ecumenical council, the council of Jerusalem, which convened to decide whether circumcision would be required for new converts. This was a crucial decision, one that would shape the trajectory of Christianity and define its distinctiveness from Judaism, and it was decided by an authoritative gathering. This council, described in Acts 15, shows the development of sacred tradition and how, from its infancy, Christianity has been guided and shaped by apostolic authority. This authority has been preserved and handed down through the Church via apostolic succession, and today, the Church's bishops, in union with one another, serve a similar function as those early leaders in the Council of Jerusalem.

What guides our interpretations of Scripture? How do we navigate and resolve conflicts that divide Christians against one another? How do we know what the proper Christian response should be to contemporary problems? How do we translate the gospel anew for each generation, while preserving its discomfiting truths? Protestantism, with its rejection of the visible reality and authority of the Church, has ambiguous and dissatisfying answers to these questions. G. K. Chesterton, in his own conversion narrative, writes that the Catholic Church "is the only thing which saves a man from the degrading slavery of being a child of his age."[14] Without a connectedness to Christian tradition, to the Church through time, we too easily dilute its strangeness, succumbing to the tyranny of the present. We make Christianity comfortable, palatable, adorn it in the fashions of our day. While the Church must always work to make her truth alive and heard in the present age—which is difficult, if the Church is not a coherent entity—she must also preserve it from being harnessed by the zeitgeist and made to serve its ends. When this happens, Christianity loses its countercultural witness, its prophetic voice, which will always, in one way or another, be at odds with the surrounding society.

* * *

I grew up with a concept of the Body of Christ *qua* universal church—it was presented as a mystical, invisible bond between all Christians everywhere. This gave me a sense of solidarity with other Christians, a nebulous kind of connection, but nothing more than that. This conception of the church is little more than a loose affiliation; this is not a church you can see, this is not a church that speaks clearly and boldly on the earthly plane, and, certainly, this is not a tangible entity that you can come to trust, as one might trust a mother.

Even while I was in the process of becoming Catholic, the unity and actuality of the Church wasn't part of my attraction. At least, not directly. I was enamored with the ancient prayers of Catholicism, the rich and primal symbolism, the depth of its intellectual tradition. I was drawn by delight toward its potent, archaic splendor, and only later did I come to appreciate, even love, the visible Church that has enabled this beauty to endure.

Too late have I loved you, O Beauty so ancient, O Beauty so new, too late have I loved you! These words of St. Augustine's capture the sense of elation

and awe I experienced as a newly initiated Catholic. The ancient beauty of
Christ's Church entranced me, hooked me, reeled me in—but once inside its
halls, I had to reckon, honestly, with its authority, which I did not yet fully
trust. The smells and bells were easy to love, but its hard teachings? Not so
much. Would I continue to use contraception, as I had since I was a teenager? Would I come to adopt its view of marriage, which excluded same-sex
unions? Would I be able to accept that only men can be priests? On these
issues, I was still wary, eyeing the Church from afar, arms crossed dubiously.

I will delve into the agony and the ecstasy of how I came to trust the
Church on those specific questions in subsequent chapters. It was a hard-
won battle, but, as is typical in the upside-down world of Christianity, this
loss became a gain. I will describe—I promise—*how* I came to trust the
Church. Here, however, I want to first consider *what* it is that I came to trust.
Who is she, this *mater ecclesia*, this Body of Christ, this Bride?

During the postpartum Lent after my daughter's birth, I developed a
nightly ritual of taking a hot bath while drinking a beer, a way to help my
body relax and heal. While soaking, I slowly read a book given to me by
my friend Stephen, a former student who was now a spiritual mentor to
me and godfather to my children. The book was *The Wellspring of Worship*,
a dazzling, lyrical initiation into the meaning behind the Catholic liturgy.
It was written by Father Jean Corbon, an Eastern rite Catholic priest and
theologian from Beirut, and his words brought alive for me the mysterious,
divine reality of the Church's worship, as well as the Church herself.

Father Corbon describes the Church as a "visible, present, accessible
fountainhead that is given to men in order that they may be able to see, hear,
and touch the Word of life."[15] The three adjectives he uses there—visible,
present, accessible—underscore the stark difference between the reality of
the Church as I now experience it, and the vague sense of a universal church
that I was given as a child. The mystery of this visible Church depends upon
several interconnected tensions, pairs of apparent opposites that must be
held together by the damnable Catholic "and."

Human and Divine. Corbon characterizes the Church as synergistic,
incarnational. She is fortified by the Holy Spirit, the Advocate that Christ
bestowed to us, but is peopled by mortals: "The sacramentality of the
Church means that in her everything is the joint energy of the Spirit and the
humanity he transfigures."[16] Like Christ himself, like the Bible, the Church
is both human and divine. The parallel with the Incarnation is not perfect,
however, because the human dimension of the Church is not sinless—not
even close. The Church exists *for sinners* and consists *of sinners*; as Pope
Francis has remarked, the Church is a "field hospital," there to treat our

wounds and brokenness, to restore us to life in Christ. The divine nature of the Church can be glimpsed in her extraordinary longevity and unity; she has endured since Pentecost and continues to safeguard the Deposit of Faith against heresy. She is also the fountainhead of the sacraments on earth; her liturgy dispenses grace to her children, drawing them together in charity, in the divine life of the Trinity. This grace strengthens us, enables us to struggle against the recurring sin in our lives, even though it is understood that we are imperfect, that we will stumble and fall in our attempts to follow Christ along the Way.

Yet there is always the possibility that, as free human beings, we will resist this grace and choose to turn away from Christ. Even those within the Church, with access to her abundance, can decide to embrace evil instead. Thus, we can see, within the Church on earth, the full range of human activity: extraordinary feats of love, courage, and self-sacrifice, and also terrific human evil. It's important to realize that the evil within the Catholic Church (or any Christian church) is always at odds with her teaching, with the truth she proclaims. There was a Judas in the earliest inner circle of believers, and there are Judases still. Judas's actions were not somehow reflective of Christ and the gospel but represented a complete rejection of them. Similarly, those who try to use the Church's power for their own ends betray her and show contempt for her teachings.

The Church, in her human dimension, will always be battling sin; there will be schisms, scandals, abuses of power until the fullness of time, in the hierarchy, and among the laity. But the divine dimension of the Church, and her fortification by the Holy Spirit, ensures that she won't be overthrown. When Christ gave St. Peter the keys to the kingdom of heaven in Matthew 16, naming him as the foundation of the Church, he also promised that the gates of hell shall not prevail against it. Human sin won't win.

Heaven and Earth. The Church, properly understood, encompasses the faithful already in heaven, and those still in pilgrimage on earth. Death separates them physically, temporarily, but these two outposts of the Church nonetheless remain united through prayer. The Mass on earth opens a door into heaven, bridging the gulf between these two realms. Our sacred liturgy reflects and anticipates the heavenly banquet, the wedding feast of the Lamb, when the Church will be wholly reconciled and presented to Christ as his Bride.

Past and Future. The Church exists in the present, but not blindly. She looks forward to the future, toward the renewal of all creation; her pilgrimage has a destination. The Church lives according to the rhythms of sacred time, which maps the drama of our redemption. We live in the age of the Church, the age following the historical events of the Incarnation, Crucifixion, and

Resurrection, and this age will culminate in a new heaven, and a new earth. The sufferings of the Church on earth are birth pangs—not meaningless or fruitless, but bringing rebirth, both in our lives as individuals, and in our communal body. This labor is productive, anticipatory, charged with hope of the promises to come.

Yet the Church is also backward-looking, rooted in the past. She keeps alive the revelations of God and the collective wisdom that springs from the contemplation of that revelation for two millennia. The Church is always, in her rich intellectual and theological tradition, pondering the mysteries of Christ, entering into them more deeply, translating the ancient truths for the current age. She likewise keeps vibrant the symbols and rituals of Christian worship, symbols that make present an eternal reality.

This brings us to a related tension: change and stability. The Church is not dormant. Her connection to the past is not a source of paralysis. She is continually changing—but in a specific way. She is changing in the same way that a tree changes, by becoming more and more itself. She is Christ's Body, and behaves as a body should, by growing outward and upward, but also remaining herself. She cannot change what she has already declared to be true, but that truth can always be more deeply understood and more profoundly realized. It is forgetting the past and forsaking its wisdom—wisdom that has taken centuries to unfold—that leads to paralysis, growth that is stunted or ceases altogether.

Unity and individuality. We can see even in the New Testament the organic beginnings of an ecclesial hierarchy. The apostles are clearly tasked with the authority of teaching the gospel, protecting it from corruption, and interpreting its truths as unexpected problems arise, as happened at the Council of Jerusalem. The original twelve expanded to include other apostles, like St. Paul, who appointed local church leaders to guide the new believers. By the beginning of the second century, mere decades after the martyrdom of St. Paul and St. Peter in Rome, a visible and catholic Christian Church exists, one governed by an organizational structure of bishops, presbyters, and deacons.

St. Ignatius of Antioch, one of those early fathers whose writings shocked me, because of their Catholicity, was a disciple of the apostle John and appointed as the Bishop of Antioch. He wrote a series of epistles to his fellow Christians that urged them to "maintain union" with their local bishops, because "apart from these, there is no Church." His letters show a keen emphasis on unity, a unity made possible by obedience to church elders, and one that protects them from false doctrine, a particularly potent threat in the precarious days of Christianity's infancy. Ignatius' Epistle to the Smyrnaeans provides the first record we have of the word "catholic" (*katholikos*) being applied to the Church, indicating that even in the apostolic era, the Christian Church was conceived as a universal whole, with a hierarchal structure that ensured unity of doctrine and worship:

> See that ye all follow the bishop, even as Jesus Christ does the Father, and the presbytery as ye would the apostles; and reverence the deacons, as being the institution of God. Let no man do anything connected with the Church without the bishop. Let that be deemed a proper Eucharist, which is [administered] either by the bishop, or by one to whom he has entrusted it. Wherever the bishop shall appear, there let the multitude [of the people] also be; even as, wherever Jesus Christ is, there is the Catholic Church. (Chapter VIII)

This letter dates from the end of the first century, written around the same time as the biblical book of Revelation.

Yet the unity of the Catholic Church, either in the days of Ignatius or our own time, is not an oppressive, monolithic collectivism, one that seeks to subdue or obliterate the individual. Christianity is an intensely personal religion, one that celebrates the uniqueness and dignity of every single human person. God desires a relationship with us as a communal body, yes—but he also longs to inhabit our hearts. The evangelicalism of my youth preserves this latter dynamic of Christianity in a wholehearted, enthusiastic way. And many cradle Catholics who have been poorly formed—never taught the profound meaning of the sacred liturgy, never taught the reality that a personal relationship with Christ is precisely what the Eucharist celebrates and cultivates—many of those folks have found refuge in the individualistic fervor of evangelical Protestantism.

Catholicism, rightly understood, preserves both dynamics: union with Christ on the level of the individual, and union with Christ as a communal body. While Catholic worship has clearly corporate elements, as the gathered body prays, sings, kneels, and moves in unison, there is also something intensely private about the Mass. Each person brings the prayers and intentions of her hidden heart before the altar, communing intimately with Christ through the Eucharist, a Christ who descends into and nourishes the solitary soul.

* * *

Sacred tradition and sacred Scripture give us three primary metaphors for the phenomenon of the Church: Body, Bride, and Mother. Held in tension, the dual symbols of Bride and Body show how the Church is both one with

Christ, and yet distinct from him. The Bride metaphor depends upon a biblical understanding of conjugal union: the man and the woman become one
flesh, a union made possible by their differences, a union driven by mutual
love, a union that is synergistic, procreative, that carries within it the potential for new life. The metaphor of Christ's body evokes the Church's calling
to function as an extension of Christ on earth, to make the love of God
present through works of charity and self-sacrifice, to draw together our
diverse personalities, abilities, and proclivities into a functioning, harmo-
nizing whole that makes present the Kingdom of God in the here-and-now.

And mother? How is the Church our mother?

This was a new one for me. Bride, body—I'd heard that language, but
never "mother." The symbolism of motherhood was absent in the faith of my
youth. There was no room for maternal imagery for God; Mary was a minor
figure, on stage for a bit part during December, before vanishing again into
the wings. And the Church as a visible, accessible entity was not present at
all. How could something so inchoate and invisible be a mother?

There's a canticle from Isaiah 66 that appears in the Morning Prayer
liturgy of the Divine Office, and every time it cycles around, the language
delights and surprises me anew:

> Rejoice with Jerusalem and be glad because of her,
> all you who love her;
> Exult, exult with her,
> all you who were mourning over her!

> Oh, that you may suck fully
> of the milk of her comfort,
> That you may nurse with delight
> at her abundant breasts!

> For thus says the Lord:
> Lo, I will spread prosperity over her like a river,
> and the wealth of the nations like an overflowing torrent.

> As nurslings, you shall be carried in her arms,
> and fondled in her lap;
> As a mother comforts her son,
> so will I comfort you;
> in Jerusalem you shall find your comfort.

> When you see this, your heart shall rejoice,
> and your bodies flourish like the grass.

In a Catholic reading of Scripture, which stresses a hermeneutics of
continuity between the Old and New Testaments, Jerusalem is a *typos* or

prefiguring symbol of the Church. So, whenever I read this passage, I imagine the Church. I think of how she has comforted me, drawing me out of spiritual desolation. Her unwavering faith carries me through seasons of doubt. When my heart and mind wander too far, she coaxes me back with her maternal wisdom. Every time I stumble into Mass hardened and dried up and weary, I leave somehow sated, nourished by her merciful, sacramental abundance. I have entrusted my children to her. *You must be born of water and Spirit.* And so we are: through the saving waters of baptism, I've seen the babies I birthed reborn.

When I first began to take the Eucharist, I received the host in my hand, as I'd been taught to do in RCIA. I noticed, however, that a few parishioners chose to have the Body of Christ placed directly into their gaping mouths. I thought it was a bit strange, at first, to be honest. There was something a little too vulnerable about it, too intimate. But not long into the conversion after my conversion, the one that began during my first Lent as a Catholic, I began to wonder what it would be like to receive communion on the tongue, rather than in the hand. I decided to try it—and why not? I was already wearing a veil to Mass, for Pete's sake. Things couldn't get any weirder.

From the first moment I tried this mode of reception, the gesture felt natural, but I didn't understand why. The insight came later, during a quiet, ordinary moment as I was nursing my daughter. I cradled her in one arm and pulled up my shirt with the other. She rushed at my breast with her mouth open wildly and latched on, her hands cupped against my skin as she drank and drank and drank. That's it, I realized, that's the gesture. The instinctive, primal movement of an infant toward its mother.

In Jerusalem shall you find your comfort. And so I have. At her banquet, I am a nursling again, hungry and trusting, wriggling in for a taste of sweet milk.

The Totality

For over a decade, the maleness of the priesthood kept me away from the Catholic Church. By the time I was a junior in college, my feminism was in full swing, and the ordination of women had become my litmus test for whether or not I could be part of a particular church or denomination.

Once, in college, I was chatting with a fellow student about his decision to become Catholic. Listening to him describe the feast he'd found there—sacraments, Eucharist, saints—I sighed with something like despondent resignation, "Oh, I think I'd be Catholic, too, but they don't ordain women." I was sort of wistfully fatalistic about this, as if I wasn't actually making a choice to reject Catholicism; rather, it was Catholicism that had eliminated itself from the menu of legitimate church options. Already, the beauty of Rome was beckoning, but I stood mournfully on a far shore, like a marooned castaway, unaware I'd rowed there with the strength of my own will, stroke by stroke.

It never occurred to me that there might be compelling reasons for a male-only priesthood—how could there be? I took as an unquestioned premise that all forms of ministry should be open to both men and women. I'd adopted the eschatology of the progressive: century after slow century, Christ was leading his mulish, plodding church out of the gloom of patriarchy and into the beige radiance of egalitarianism. The Catholic Church, weighed down by male bureaucracy, was simply having a hard time relenting to the inexorable tides of justice. Even if I could enter the Church myself, as a conscientious objector, how could I justify raising my hypothetical daughters in a tradition that denies them access to the priesthood? So I reasoned, steering clear.

Years later, after I began teaching, one of my students decided to convert to Catholicism. I remember him telling me this in the living room of my small rental house, where I'd been hosting a Christmas gathering. My reaction to his news was unbridled joy; I remember gasping and saying,

"Oh, Stephen, that's so wonderful," and my effusiveness was genuine. I understood, and even felt to a degree, that magnetic pull toward the Catholic Church, and when people around me followed its call, I cheered enthusiastically from the sidelines, as if the presence of those crossing the Tiber was somehow comforting, even though I was unwilling to make the swim myself.

My enthusiasm for Stephen's conversion noticeably chilled, however, when it came to his shifting views on gender and sexuality. Prior to his conversion, Stephen was a devoted evangelical, and he'd embraced progressive views over his first year of college. I saw in him, to use the buzzword, an "ally" like myself, someone who championed the full inclusion of women in the life of the church. So when his perspective on women's ordination began to change, I took this as a personal affront. I was fine with Stephen becoming a Catholic, but not one of *those* Catholics.

I remember one instance when we wrangled over the issue. I was coaching the university debate team at the time, and travel to and from tournaments created ample opportunity for substantive, energetic discussions. The team had stopped to eat at a Red Robin, and before long the conversation turned toward the issue of female ordination. Stephen explained the multiple reasons for a male priesthood, but none of them seemed compelling. Not that I was really listening; my conviction was so deeply held that I did not entertain the possibility that I could be wrong. But even if I *had* been willing to listen, I'm not sure I could have understood, because I was looking at the issue from outside of Catholicism, rather than from within.

To a post-evangelical feminist, appeals to the constant tradition of the Church are easily dismissed. I respected tradition, vaguely construed, but only its endowments, its gifts from which I felt free to glean. A little Mary here, a little sacramental theology there. I did not see tradition as authoritative, as something to which I was accountable. There were parts to be preserved, and parts to be discarded, and I thought myself in a position to discern the difference. And, from my progressive bias, the longevity of a particular teaching might even be a detriment, rather than an indication of truth.

I was similarly dismissive of the apostolic argument—that Jesus chose only men to be his Apostles. Despite my tenure as an Anglican, I never really understood the importance of apostolic succession. When I glanced at Scripture, I did not see a meaningful difference between the role of an apostle and the role of any follower of Jesus. I latched onto the passages that described women's participation in the ministry of Jesus and the early life of the Church, overlooking those that seemed to give the twelve apostles a unique commission and authority, including the power to forgive sins.

"Just look at the many times Jesus empowers women to proclaim the gospel," I argued, "like the Samaritan woman at the well, and Mary Magdalene, who first brings word to the other disciples about the Resurrection." I probably added the counterargument that Jesus was constrained by the patriarchy of the time, and his choice to send out only male apostles was an expedient one, not meant to be a precedent for the Church that they would establish. Of course, these two assertions subtly contradict one another— I was pointing out that Jesus clearly has no qualms about violating social norms, especially when it comes to women, while also appealing to those same social norms as a reason for his selection of only male apostles.

You can imagine how our discussion unfolded, circling around and around, our assertions flying past each other, because we were speaking from different premises. Stephen was working from an understanding of the unique role of the priest, whereas I was thinking of the non-priestly role of the Protestant pastor; Stephen was appealing to the authority of sacred tradition and Scripture, while I was playing an adept feminist game of *sola scriptura* cherry-picking.

Our conversation ended in an aporia of mutual defeat. We were standing in the parking lot of the Red Robin, outside the university van, while the rest of the team loaded up. "You have to understand," I said to him, my voice cracking with emotion, "That for men this is just an intellectual discussion. There is nothing at stake. But for a woman, it's personal. This is my dignity, my value as a person that's being called into question." Stephen looked pained, his face signaling both empathy and frustration. He seemed to understand, in that moment, that there was nothing he could say, no argument he could make, that I would be able to hear. At its core, my resistance to his position, the Catholic position, was an emotional one. It was not my mind that needed to be persuaded, but my heart.

Eventually, several years hence, my desire for Catholicism overwhelmed my feminist resistance. By this time, Stephen was a seminarian, on the road to becoming a priest himself—as it turns out, this question of the priesthood *was* deeply personal for him. He became my primary spiritual advisor when I went through RCIA. Teacher and student swapped places. During that year of discernment, my qualms about the priesthood were still unresolved, but they had receded to the background. Although I was not yet persuaded by the Catholic position, I was willing to suspend my disbelief.

After I became Catholic, I returned to the various arguments given by the Church for the male priesthood. I understood them all, in a rational sense, and was able to accept them in my newfound trust for the Church and her authority. But none of those reasons were able to enter my heart and alter my sentiments—save one: the argument from sacramental theology, the idea that the priest serves as an icon of Christ during the Mass.

Stephen had tried to explain this all those years ago, but standing as I was outside the sacramental Catholic cosmos, I didn't understand it. "Why essentialize Christ's maleness and not his Jewishness?" I argued. "Saying only men can be priests is like saying only Jewish men can be priests, since Jesus was also Jewish." The argument was unintelligible to me, and remained so, until I had a better understanding of how the Mass differs meaningfully from a Protestant worship service, and a priest from a Protestant pastor.

The Mass, as I've mentioned before, is a liturgical staging of a cosmic drama. All the central mysteries that beat at the heart of Christianity are made present: the Trinity, the Incarnation, the Crucifixion, the Resurrection, the mystical union of Christ and his Church. The Mass re-presents Christ's sacrifice, his gift of self to humanity, and through that sacrifice, in a literal and symbolic sense, we become one flesh with Christ in communion. If this sounds like conjugal language, it is. The conjugal metaphor is the primary metaphor given to us to understand the relationship between God and humankind, and this metaphor animates the sacred liturgy, because the Mass is also a wedding, a consummation of the marriage between Christ and his Bride—us.

This conjugal language is not a projection from the realm of the human, a convenient illustration gleaned from the reality of human sexual dimorphism. Rather, *sexual difference exists to carry this metaphor*, to reveal this divine reality, as well as to facilitate marital union and the transmission of human existence. The conjugal metaphor is etched into the fabric of our embodiment, and whether we realize it or not, whether we accept it or not, we are living icons of this cosmic marriage between God and his beloved.

This is why priests must be male; not because men are smarter, or better leaders, or more spiritual, or fill-in-the-blank, but because of the iconography of the male body. This is not something earned or chosen but *given*. There is a givenness to our bodies that makes present the realities of God, and the intricate nexus of these images, that sacred web, has become far more precious to me, far more beautiful than a flattened, bland gesture toward earthly equality. Sacrificing the embodiment of these metaphors to satisfy some modern egalitarian sensibility would be, to me, a tragic desecration, a calamitous loss.

It is difficult, perhaps impossible, to make a comparison between a Catholic Mass and the evangelical church services of my upbringing. Stripped of the Eucharist, there is no divine drama being staged. There is merely the word, and words about the word, but *the* Word never becomes flesh for his people to touch and taste. There is no altar, no one standing *in persona Christi* to signify Christ as bridegroom and eternal high priest, offering the only sacrifice that is pleasing to the Father: himself. There is no wedding banquet of the lamb. The preacher is not a direct corollary to a priest, and in Protestant worship, the sacred iconography is not preserved. So when it comes to the debate about women's roles in Protestant circles, the justifications tend to revolve around women's capacities (or lack thereof) for ministry, devolving into cartoonish understandings of the sexes and selective interpretations of Scripture—justifications my younger feminist self was right to find dubious.

As a Catholic, the entire debate has been reframed in a sacramental light. I've come to not merely tolerate the tradition of a male-only priesthood; I have developed a deep gratitude and love for it, and I hope the Church protects this tradition with *matrem ursus* ferocity, especially as it becomes increasingly countercultural. This feature of the Catholic Church that once kept me away from her has become a mark of beauty—a sign not of patriarchy, but of the divine iconography that all sexed bodies carry.

* * *

This newfound understanding of the priesthood became a key for me that opened an entirely new—and thoroughly ancient—way of thinking about manhood and womanhood. In the Protestantism of my youth and the feminism that followed, debates surrounding gender tended to focus more on *doing* than *being*. What differing capacities do men and women have? And how do these translate into roles? The tacit assumption in these debates was that sexual difference and sex-specific roles go hand-in-hand, so a rejection of the latter entailed a suspicion of the former.

What led me to feminism in the first place was an intense need to have my dignity *as a woman* affirmed. I had an intuition that being a woman was meaningful, that it carried some kind of significance—one that had been overlooked, even distorted, in the fundamentalist evangelicalism of my childhood. I seized onto feminism as an affirmation of that intuition, and for a time, it gave me the language I needed to begin to express and understand what I felt to be true.

Quickly, though, as I foraged more deeply into the categories and concepts of contemporary feminism, I also fell prey to its internal contradictions. The central of these is that modern American feminism, at its core, valorizes the masculine, affirming the key virtues of autonomy, success, and power.

In college, when my evangelical feminism was at its height, the question I dreaded most was this: doesn't feminism have an undue emphasis on power, and isn't that antithetical to the gospel? I had an answer to this of course, which I kept ready in the holster, just in case—but the reason I dreaded the question was because I didn't think my answer was a good one. Even then, I saw a tension between the Christian virtues of self-giving love, humility, obedience, and the virtues of feminism, which were preoccupied with power imbalances, with making sure everyone gets an equal slice of the pie. But instead of listening to that tension, my response was to find a way to bury it. This signals to me how, even then, my feminist commitments had subtly supplanted my Christian ones.

Feminism's masculine bias is most evident in its championing of abortion. Rather than seeking to change social structures to accommodate the realities of female biology, the feminist movement, since its second wave, has continually and firmly fought instead for women to alter their biology, even through violence, so that it functions more like a man's. Tellingly, the legal right for a woman to kill a child in her womb was won *before* the legal right for a woman not to be fired for being pregnant. This transmits the message that women must become like men to be free.

There's another central contradiction in contemporary feminism. The movement itself is built upon the premise that women exist, that "womankind" is a meaningful category, and despite vast diversity among women, there is nonetheless a commonality that unites them. Yet feminism, both in its academic and popular forms, is resolutely anti-essentialist: it denies that women are essentially different from men, asserting instead that differences between them are largely or exclusively cultural fictions.

To be sure, essentialism has sometimes been used as a tool of oppression against women throughout history. Simplistic appeals to women's nature and abilities were used to deny women access to education and the right to vote, for example. But in countering the misuse of essentialism, feminism has opted to reject it altogether, which makes "feminism" itself something of an irony.

I have to confess that, even as a feminist, I was a closet essentialist. I would have denied the term, of course, because it violates a central dogma— but I never fully rejected the idea that women are actually and meaningfully different than men. Not in a simplistic way, not in a way that can be expressed by a trite list of attributes or dispositions, but at the level of *being*.

But I was hamstrung as a feminist academic; even if I wanted to appeal to some objective ground for womanhood, I was being trained to think in a strictly secular, postmodern mode—a mode that favors the particular over the universal, that denies the existence of any objective ground from

which to approach this question. In this understanding, all of our conceptual categories, our entire sense of reality, is fundamentally created through
language—our words make the world, rather than express it. Any meaning
we ascribe to bodily realities is arbitrary and ultimately fictitious.

There is no room in this worldview for a sacramental understanding of
maleness and femaleness. The cosmos has been flattened; there are no natural signs of divine realities, because there are no divine realities. There is no
givenness to our bodily nature at all, no grand order to which we belong and
through which we come to understand ourselves. Sexual difference itself is
reduced to mere biology, something we can manipulate at will, rather than
something that is intrinsic to our being, that concerns the *whole person*, not
merely chromosomes or body parts. I turned to feminism to discover the
significance of my womanness, and I was initiated into an ideology where
womanness itself is ultimately renounced.

What I was unknowingly seeking, and unable to find in either secular
or evangelical feminism, was the understanding of woman as a *sign*. It is not
merely the priest who serves as an icon during the Mass; every man and
every woman is a living icon, carrying in his or her body a divine sign that
reveals the sacred bond between God and humankind.

In the midst of my interior conversion, I came across a little book
called *The Eternal Woman*, by Gertrud von le Fort, a German writer and
Catholic convert who was active in the early twentieth century. In just over
a hundred pages, she articulates a Catholic understanding of womanhood
that is more beautiful and profound than anything I have ever read on the
topic. She describes a vision of womanhood that pulls my gaze upward,
away from the endless, banal squabbling over roles and power dynamics
that, in comparison, seems hopelessly trivial. She writes from within a world
that has been all but forgotten in Protestantism and secularism—two points
on a shared trajectory that moves away from a sacramental understanding
of the cosmos.

Von le Fort begins by describing what it means to consider *woman*
under her symbolic, rather than historical or social, aspect:

> Symbols are signs or images through which ultimate metaphysi-
> cal realities and modes of being are apprehended, not in an ab-
> stract manner but by way of a likeness. Symbols are therefore
> the language of an invisible reality becoming articulate in the
> realm of the visible. This concept of the symbol springs from
> the conviction that in all beings and things there is an intelligent
> order that, through these very beings and things, reveals itself as
> a divine order by means of the language of its symbols.[17]

The significance and value of a woman lies not in what she *does*, but in who she *is*. She carries and embodies a metaphor that illuminates the ultimate purpose of the human being: to be fully united to its Creator. This is another reason I choose to wear a veil during Mass. I am calling attention to the sacramental character of my femaleness, which represents the Church as Bride. Woman is an icon of humanity itself, vis-à-vis God. And man is an icon of God vis-à-vis humanity.

One could quickly protest—doesn't this imply a difference in value, if man signifies God and woman signifies humanity? No, because these are not signs that point to humanity and God in isolation, but rather toward the relation between them. Maleness and femaleness represent the same relationship from two different angles. The bodily receptivity and fecundity of the woman is an emblem of humanity's greatest power: the capacity to be receptive to divine love, to assent to that love and invite God into one's inmost being, where divine love flowers into new life.

This symbolic significance is carried, embodied, by every woman—whether or not she is aware of it, regardless of whether she is celibate or married, fertile or barren. The inborn capacity for motherhood is that "essence" that unites all women, even if it is never actualized in a biological way in the life of an individual woman.

The significance of manhood and womanhood is grounded in the objective reality of how human existence is transmitted, and that biological facticity, to which we all owe our existence, points toward a spiritual reality that is even more vital, one that concerns the eternal, and not merely the temporal. This shifts the discussion about sex and gender to another plane entirely, away from *doing* to *being*. Whatever the individual personality of a woman, whatever her sense of vocation or profession, she brings her feminine genius with her, a genius that springs from her connection to the divine order. To quote Von le Fort again: "Be truly a woman, and do what you will."[18]

I hope to live a long life. I hope to grow old, even if that means experiencing the gradual deterioration of my body—the withering of my skin, the gnarling of my bones, the clouding over of my eyes. Even then, as an old, weak woman with sunken breasts and a dormant womb, long past any hope of professional success, fully purged of the fantasy of autonomy—I will be a divine image. Even as it falls apart, my body will remain a sign, pointing upward and outward toward the wedding feast to come.

* * *

Entering into a sacramental understanding of the cosmos likewise resolved another feminist quibble I had with Christianity: the preponderance of masculine language for God. When I was a feminist, this language bothered me, even though my attempts to replace it were less than successful. Either I switched entirely into a feminine mode, calling God "she" and praying to God as mother, or I tried performing the grammatical gymnastics of avoiding pronouns altogether, using only the terms "God" and "Godself." Both of these efforts, however, seemed forced and awkward, and diverted my attention away from God as a person toward God as a concept. I was too preoccupied with linguistic games to enter into an orientation of prayer.

Despite these obstacles at the level of praxis, I remained convinced that the masculine language for God was a distortion of the truth, something from which God needed to be rehabilitated. I scanned the vernacular of evangelical worship and preaching and detected what I saw as hypocrisy, a welcoming of all biblical divine metaphors *except* those that were explicitly feminine. It was fine to talk and sing about God as a rock, or a lamb, or a king, but not as a nursing mother, or a hen sheltering her brood. Or take the set of three interrelated parables from Luke: the faithful shepherd, the woman with the lost coin, and the prodigal son. I regularly heard the first and last metaphors used for God, but not the middle. The image of the searching woman was referenced far less frequently, and even when it was, the woman was sometimes read as the church, rather than God. Even now, I think I was right to be suspicious of this selective use of metaphors that warily avoided anything feminine. I still get a thrill whenever one of those biblical passages cycles through the lectionary during Mass, when I get to hear those beautiful feminine metaphors proclaimed in the assembly.

Wanting to reclaim and embrace all of the rich imagery we are given to describe God is laudable, but my deep-seated feminist suspicion didn't ultimately lead me to a diversity of divine metaphors, both masculine and feminine. It led me to despise the Father metaphor altogether.

Even when I first entered the Catholic Church, I modified my individual responses in the liturgy, putting myself out of step with the gathered body and the language of the Church. I dodged any male pronouns, saying "God" instead, and skipped the word "men" in this line of the Creed: *for us men and for our salvation, he came down from heaven.* This line, I now know, is not making a distinction between men and women, but between humankind and angelic beings; it became part of the creed to combat a heresy that Christ also came to redeem demons. But the *reason* behind such language didn't matter to me at the time. I saw only a word that seemed gender-exclusive and so I stepped over it, displaying by that very movement that I still saw myself as the ultimate authority. It wasn't until my subsequent internal conversion that I began to purge those feminist suspicions that kept God at a distance, and my Protestant individualism that was holding me apart from the Church.

I was right to conclude as a feminist that God is not *actually* male, that such language is metaphorical—something that, honestly, was not made entirely clear in the churches of my youth. But I was wrong to assume that the masculine language could then be brushed aside, as something archaic and arbitrary. Underneath this angst lurks an instinct I now find troubling: the idea that God should be expressed in language that helps me identify with him, to see God in my image, rather than the other way around. Taken too far, this blurs the distinction between Creator and creature. We are not primarily meant to *identify with* God, but to worship him.

This is precisely why the Father metaphor is meaningful, and why it holds prime of place among the various metaphors given to us in Scripture and tradition. Again, it is not meant to disclose God in himself, but our relationship to him. A human father creates by endowing new life while remaining distinct from it. This differs from the human mother, whose personhood is not initially separate from her child's, but rather envelops it. In this way, fatherhood is *more* analogous to the relationship God has with his creation. We are made in his image, but he remains Other in his nature. This does not mean motherhood is not analogous at all, which is why we do have feminine metaphors for God in both Scripture and sacred tradition, metaphors that typically highlight God's nurturing and protective love for his people.

This insight about the significance of the Father metaphor came to me more recently; it was not the original reason I began to accept, and even appreciate, this language for God. That happened gradually over the first year after I entered the Church. There was no sudden epiphany, no blindfold abruptly whisked away. Rather, I was steadily adjusting to a new way of seeing, as if I'd been living in a dark room, and someone was pulling back the curtains, letting in shafts of light, one by one, until the whole space was illuminated. I was experiencing, for the first time, a full restoration of the Christian cosmos.

When I look back at my birthright evangelicalism, it's as if the feminine aspects of the faith have been lopped off: there's no Mary, no genealogy of heroic female saints, no visible Church as our mother, no Mass with its iconography of the bridegroom and bride, no sacramental understanding of our bodies as sacred signs. I rightly sensed that something was amiss in this version of Christianity, that it was too monolithically masculine, that anything feminine was sidelined and relegated. In that religious context, the masculine metaphors, in isolation from their female counterparts, were harsh and unremitting, like banging out a melody using only the lower keys on a piano. When I finally encountered the totality of the Christian sacramental cosmos, and pitched my tent under its sacred canopy, my feminist angst faded away—as did my need for feminism itself. The yearning that initially drove me to feminism was fulfilled, at last, in Catholicism.

* * *

Years before I was Catholic, I went on a trip to Ireland with a group of students and two colleagues. While in Dublin, we had the opportunity to attend evening prayer at a Church of Ireland cathedral. Remembering with fondness the Anglican prayer gatherings of my college years, I looked forward to this, assuming it would draw me into a sense of fullness, give me a taste of the transcendent, something I hadn't felt in years. We arrived a little early, filing into pews of dark wood. The first thing I noticed was that the church was empty, except for us, a rag-tag group of American tourists. I glanced around, surprised to see no iconography whatsoever, just a contrasting interplay between light shades and dark, some abstract embellishments here and there.

Then a convoy of men marched up the center aisle, all dressed in black and white, faces grimly set. They processed ahead in silence, carrying a lone metal staff, raised aloft with nothing on it—no crucifix, not even a cross, just a blank, phallic rod.

That image captures the spirit of the prayer service itself: disincarnate, dreary, and resolutely masculine, fully shorn of anything bodily or feminine. Rather than pulled into a sense of God, I was repelled, my feminist suspicions confirmed. I was suddenly hyperaware of my womanhood—not in a positive sense, but as a spiritual defect, an aberration that expelled me from the holy of holies, as if I'd come to pray and been caught trespassing on masculine ground.

Days later, on a Sunday, we are in Galway, attending Mass at the Catholic Cathedral. After my experience in Dublin, I am pessimistic. The Church of Ireland ordains women, after all, yet their Cathedral and prayer service had been dismally masculine—how much worse, then, will a Catholic Mass be?

I enter the Cathedral and immediately feel as though I am no longer inside a building at all. The space is cruciform, like a body itself, and rows of arches draw my eye up and up and up. Stained glass colors the light that funnels in through the many windows; the heart of the space, above the altar, opens into a basilica overhead that is filled with blue light, as if it's not an additional chamber, but a portal into the sky.

Beyond the altar, I see an icon of the crucified Christ gazing down at his mother, who is staring up at him from the foot of the cross, alongside the apostle whom Jesus loved. Looking at them looking at each other, I am pulled into their tender sorrow.

Alongside me, down the long end of the cruciform, flanking the rows of pews, is a series of archways within archways that evokes a sense of infinity, of doors opening into other doors opening. I am a body, surrounded by other bodies, and together we are within this larger body, which is both a Cathedral in Galway and something else entirely—not that we've been lifted to another realm; instead, that other realm has come to us.

As I sit, transfixed by the space, something wells up behind and above me, so instantly omnipresent that I cannot trace the source. It seems to come from everywhere: music. Music made by voices alone, male and female intertwined, a synergy of harmony made possible only by the different registers, the highs and lows that plow over the earth and curve along the underside of heaven, gathering together all that lies between into a tremulous golden cord.

Absolution

When I was eight or nine, my parents called my brother and me into our living room to have a talk. I had been playing outside, a game of make-believe based on one of my favorite books at the time, *The Farthest Away Mountain*. This was a magical book, full of gargoyles and charms, tracing the journey of an ordinary young girl who is one day called forth from her home to travel to a mysterious mountain in the distance. It is the mountain itself that calls her. In my backyard reenactments, I was the girl, and my imagination filled out the rest of the cast.

I remember I was wearing one of my favorite dresses—this was not a church dress. It was too otherworldly for that. This was distinctly a make-believe dress, a frock capable of transforming me into someone else, and my backyard into somewhere else. It was cream-colored, with long sleeves and a high collar, both of which were fringed with stiff lace. Thin white ribbons and tiny pearled buttons ran vertically down the bodice, and the skirt flared out slightly on the way down to my ankles, moving freely when I walked or climbed. The ivory fabric was dotted with intricate red-pink flowers. I kept this dress close at hand, even taking it on camping trips, so I could be prepared for those moments when the ordinary world collapses into two dimensions, turns sideways and disappears, revealing an enchanted world that is always hiding behind it. Whenever this happens, it is best to be dressed appropriately.

I was still wearing the dress when my parents called us in. One glance at their faces told me this would not be a happy conversation. There seemed to be an excess of gravity in the room. I sank into the couch, hands in my lap, feeling my heart pound in my chest, and not just because I'd been frisking about outside. We must have done something wrong, I thought, and my mind began racing through possible transgressions.

But we hadn't transgressed, as it turns out. We weren't the ones in trouble. My parents gently explained to us that our pastor's daughter was pregnant. She was in high school, still a kid, really, although to my young self she seemed infinitely older, prettier, and more sophisticated than I could ever hope to be. I don't remember what my parents said exactly, only that they gingerly conveyed the following information: Claire was pregnant, and she would be making a public confession to the congregation tomorrow during church, and my parents thought it best for us to stay home, since we were still a bit young to handle something like that. While I don't remember their specific words, the emotional content of that memory remains palpable, even to this day. There was a pit in my stomach that broke open as I listened to them, blooming into waves of hot shame that made my hands sweat, my cheeks burn red.

I came away with the sense that Claire had done the *worst possible thing*, so bad that I myself had been contaminated by it. My gaze was fixed downward; I avoided looking at my parents' faces, looking instead at my body, which seemed no longer to belong to me. It was like an alien entity, something I couldn't control that might one day betray me. I stared at the make-believe dress I was wearing and suddenly felt embarrassed. I saw now how ugly it was, how ridiculous. Why hadn't I noticed before? Just like that, the dress lost its power. It was only a cheap hand-me-down; it couldn't take me anywhere, or make me anyone.

There is much about the religion of my youth that I am grateful for; much was planted in those years that, after a period of dormancy, led to an abundant harvest. But there are also some things that require forgiveness, certain elements that distorted the truths of Christianity, rather than faithfully carrying them. This seemingly trivial episode calls forth those things, which is perhaps why it remains so emotionally charged.

When I think of this memory, several passageways of thought open. I recognize, immediately, how this anticipates my own fall as a teenager, into precisely the same kind of sin. The vicarious shame I experienced then, as a child, is a foretaste of the shame that will later cripple me. The sense I had of her sin as my own now seems eerily prescient, like phantom pain from a future wound.

Being Catholic has provided another angle from which to interpret this memory. On the one hand, I'm just as disturbed now as I was then at the idea of making a teenaged girl confess her sins to a large group of people, in a gesture that is entirely unrequited. I spent my childhood in that church, and I never saw an adult publicly confess his transgressions like that. No one else was required to wrench open their deeds in a similar way, though there were plenty of sins to go around. It's difficult for me not to feel angered, even now, at the flagrant double standard. It is no wonder that I came away with the impression that having sex was the apex of depravity, the queen of all sin, because that is precisely the message conveyed by an ad hoc ritual like that. I'm grateful my parents didn't let me witness it.

But when I push past that anger and tell myself to be more charitable, I recognize that this ordeal nonetheless expresses a genuine desire to be purged from sin, to be free of it, to restore the self and community to wholeness. This is a good and thoroughly Christian impulse, even if the application was misguided. This episode exemplifies a wider problem that the evangelicalism of my childhood was never able to efficiently answer: how does one deal with personal sin, and the damage it leaves behind?

* * *

Before I was Catholic, the biblical book of Leviticus seemed like a vestigial organ in the body of Scripture. I took several glances into its strange pages, which seemed both bloody and hopelessly boring. I never read it in depth, or heard it preached from the pulpit. There seemed to be no purpose to this book, other than to demonstrate the ritualistic legalism from which we'd all been freed.

As a Catholic, the bizarre terrain of Leviticus feels much more familiar. There are priests, after all, who offer sacrifices to God on behalf of the people, much like a priest offering up the Lamb of God in the sacrifice of the Mass. Yes, it's true that these obscure books demonstrate the need for a new covenant, a covenant of grace. But this new covenant was not a radical break from the old. The sacrifice of Christ does not eradicate a sacrificial economy between human beings and God, but completes it. The burden temporarily and imperfectly borne by the animals in the old covenant has been taken up and fulfilled by Jesus.

Leviticus and the other books of the law also show, in often horrific detail, the magnitude of sin and its destructive effects on the individual and the people as a whole. The old covenant displays the persistent pedagogy of God, who is trying to teach us something we still have a hard time believing: *spiritual death is worse than physical death*. Sin is death. Sin contaminates. Sin compromises the integrity of the person, both the individual and the collective body of the people. In Leviticus, sin is presented as substantial, metaphysically real, something that interacts powerfully with the physical world and must be purged for that world to heal.

In the Old Testament, physical death is often used as an illustration of spiritual death; episodes that seem ruthless to us demonstrate that one cannot take a half-hearted, indulgent attitude toward sin, because what is not eradicated will spread and grow and maim the health of the whole. This is ultimately what happens to the people of Israel in the book of Judges. Against God's commands, they've intermingled with the idolatrous peoples of the land, and as a result, the people succumb to a downward spiral of increasing confusion, chaos, and sinfulness, one that culminates in perhaps the most violent and disturbing episode of the Bible, the rape and dismemberment of the unnamed concubine in Judges 19. That is where sin leads: destruction, disorder, disintegration, death.

What I now see prefigured in Leviticus, and fulfilled in Catholicism, is something I did not experience in the Christianity of my youth. Between the lines of the repetitive priestly code—use grain for this kind of offering, a dove for this—I see a religious sensibility that recognizes the reality of sin, both its devastating power and pervasiveness, and the need to provide the people with a tangible means of reconciliation, of healing.

When I think about how the churches of my upbringing dealt with sin, I am faced with a number of inconsistencies. On the one hand, sin was presented as something that did not actually endanger my soul. Because I was "saved" already, once and for all, there was no way my sins could harm me in any lasting way. Yet I struggled with persistent guilt, because committing sin was simultaneously treated as a serious offense. While I often heard the maxim that all are sinners, I also had the sense that this was supposed to be the "before" picture, a prelude to salvation, and since I'd been saved at such a young age, I should know better. I was without excuse. Despite the emphasis on salvation by faith alone, there was an oddly puritanical streak in many of the churches I attended, and I felt as though my actions were under a microscope. Even by wearing the wrong things, or listening to the wrong music, I could stray too far into "the world" and be corrupted. Sin, then, was paradoxically a big deal, but also not a big deal.

All this made sin seem more *extrinsically* harmful than *intrinsically* harmful. I did not see sin as a kind of self-poisoning, partaking of something inherently bad for me. Rather, sin was wrong primarily because it violated the mandates of Scripture, or the norms of the community. In other words, all sin could be distilled down to one underlying infraction: disobedience. This introduced a subtly arbitrary character to sin; I could know a particular action was bad, because the Bible said so, but I didn't have a deeper sense of *why*.

Once I got older and, like many young adults, developed a flippant attitude toward authority, sin lost its sense of gravity. Even during those phases when I was contrite and anxious about my sins, it was never clear exactly what I should do to be free of them. I was taught that I should turn to prayer and ask for forgiveness, but this led to a dizzying loop: I was saved

and thus already forgiven for my sins, freed from their penalty, yet I needed
to ask for forgiveness for new sins I committed, from which I'd already been
forgiven, because I was saved. And when I did make the effort to ask for
forgiveness (which, frankly, was never something I regularly did), I felt the
uncertainty that plagued me about my salvation in general: how do I *know*
I'm forgiven? How do I *know* I'm saved?

While my tradition did emphasize the need for forgiveness, I was never taught that sin leaves behind wounds that also require healing, a kind of
restoration that goes beyond forgiveness. This accentuated the notion that
sin was just a matter of transgressing God's commands, since pardon alone
was required. But if sin is intrinsically destructive, we don't merely need
God to let us off the hook; we need to be made whole.

Catholicism takes sin more seriously, while also being much less
shocked by the existence of sinners. In the Catholic understanding, salvation is an ongoing process of sanctification, a process spurred on by our
continued participation with God's grace. Sin, then, is a real danger, because
we always have the freedom to reject that grace. And grave sins, when entered into willingly, in full knowledge that one is betraying God, actually
snuff out the life of divine charity within us. St. John, in his first epistle,
distinguishes these kinds of sins as "mortal," because, without repentance,
they lead to spiritual death.

There is also, within Catholicism, the open understanding that our
struggles with sin will be life-long; we are in dire and continual need of the
supernatural grace of God. There never comes, in this life, a point when we
can say we're done with sin. The Church exists for sinners and is teeming
with them. There is thus a special sacrament precisely for dealing with our
sin, as well as a clear expectation that *everyone* needs it. Sitting in line for
confession has been a revelatory experience for me, seeing everyone from
children, grown men, and little old grannies go through the door to receive
absolution, providing a concrete illustration that we all mess up, and we all
can be healed, through the plentiful grace of God.

The sacrament of confession, like all sacraments, recognizes the nature of the human being as both incarnate and relational. The Israelites who
lined up outside the temple with their goats and their doves were able to feel,
in a palpable way, both the cost of their sins and the release of repentance.
We need tangible signs. We need to encounter the reality of God with our
whole selves, body and mind and spirit. We need the voice and presence of
another human being, one charged with divine authority who can serve, in
a specific way, as an icon of Christ. We need to hear, with our ears and not
just with our hearts, that we have been given God's pardon and peace. And

unlike the rituals of the Israelites, our tangible signs, through Christ, have become sacraments; they make real that which they represent. The words spoken by the priest and his sign of the cross do not just portray absolution; they make it happen.

Some might balk at the idea of confessing one's sins to another human being, rather than directly to God. And sure, it's not as if God *needs* to work through a human being. But he has chosen to do so, because that is the way he has always chosen to work—God works through his people. The mystical reality of the Body of Christ shows us that Christ has included us in his saving work. While he can forgive and heal on his own just fine, he nonetheless entrusted that power to his disciples, when he breathed his Spirit upon them: *If you forgive the sins of any, they are forgiven; if you retain the sins of any, they are retained.* Christ has opened his saving work on earth to the Church, which is guided by the Holy Spirit, our Advocate and Comforter. The priest, in giving absolution, works not from his own power, but the power of Christ. He makes Christ present. The sacrament provides a channel for this divine power to invade our lives, our souls. Confession is not for God's benefit; it's for ours. We not only need forgiveness; we need to *know* we are forgiven, and we need grace to mend the marks left behind by our sin.

* * *

If I had to pinpoint the most damaging aspect of my evangelical upbringing, it would be its treatment of sexual sin. This is one instance where sin *is* considered to be intrinsically harmful—and to the extreme, to a point beyond restoration. Essentially, my tradition told me that healing from this sin was not possible. Fornication is something that you can't quite come back from, not fully. At least for women. You can be forgiven, but you'll always be tainted, because something has been lost that remains lost forever. Someday you might get married, but that white dress will be a lie; you will walk down the aisle, but you'll be a maimed bride.

There were isolated moments, growing up, when I was able to feel free from sin, able to feel its burden lift and vanish. This tended to happen at youth group or summer camp, in the context of an improvised ritual, like writing down a sin on a piece of paper and laying it at the foot of a wooden cross. Being able to make a tangible gesture of repentance, and receive a sign of forgiveness, helped me to believe the biblical promise that our sins are flung away from us, as far as the east is from the west.

But these moments were few and far between, and the language surrounding sexual sin made it clear that this kind of fall was in a different category. The word "purity," which in the New Testament has an expansive meaning of holiness, Christ-likeness, was reduced to mean sexual purity. "Purity," in this usage, was more or less synonymous with "virginity," so rather than something continually being pursued and cultivated, it was a default status that could be permanently lost by a single decision. Once I made that decision, and others that followed, I felt like a pariah in my religious community. All the sex talks at youth group and my Christian college seemed designed to dissuade people from becoming like me, damaged goods.

As I look back and search my past, I wonder how much of my flight from orthodox Christianity, as I knew it then, was actually a flight from this pain. The wounds from my sin, the intrinsic harm I'd brought upon myself, were now tangled up and amplified with the anguish of becoming anathema. During and after college, I sought refuge in a more progressive, therapeutic version of Christianity, one that distanced itself from the language of sin, preferring instead to focus on God's love. In an attempt to escape the pain of sin, and disgrace in the eyes of my community, I walked away from the concept of sin altogether.

Even then, I brought my wounds with me, because denying they existed did not mean they'd been healed. I remember once talking to a lecture hall full of students about the spiritual dangers of evangelical purity culture. I shared my story and assured the women present that they did not need to be defined by their sexual histories, that such an idea is antithetical to a gospel of grace. I tried to speak persuasively, confidently, brave-facing it until the panel was over, and I ended up sobbing in the parking lot while a friend put her arms around me. "I think I'm over it," I said to her, "But whenever I talk about it again, I stumble into this deep well of shame that's still there, that's been there all along."

This shame did not magically disappear the first time I went to confession, at the tail end of Lent after my year in RCIA. I would be joining the Church at Easter, just a couple of weeks away, and finally receiving the Eucharist after months of anticipation. First, I had to prepare myself spiritually by going to confession.

Despite the gothic glamour of TV confessions—the half-lit, cavernous cathedral, the ornate wooden confessionals with screens that slam open to reveal the shadowy form of a faceless priest who apparently just hangs out in there all day, waiting to hear the juicy sins of penitents—my first confession was nothing like this. My home parish was built in the 1990s and doesn't even have confessional booths (to my chagrin, I'll admit). I made an appointment and met with the priest in his office; we sat face to face at a small brown table. I'd been given no real advice on how to prepare for my first confession. "Just go in, and the priest will guide you through it," they said.

"So," I began awkwardly, after we exchanged pleasantries. "What exactly do I need to confess? Do I need to go into my past, or just confess the sins from my life right now. . .?"

The priest smiled kindly at me. "Just confess whatever is weighing on your conscience."

Ah ha. There was ample ambiguity in that statement, which gave me the out I needed. I kept the skeletons tucked tightly away and confessed the sins I could remember from the past few weeks, like a lie I'd told to cover my ass at work, some anger and resentment I'd been feeling toward a former friend, and so on.

The priest listened patiently, we prayed together, I expressed my contrition to God in my own words, haltingly, then the priest said the words of absolution and made the sign of the cross over me. I left his office with a lightweight penance to perform and a spring in my step. That had been awkward, but relatively painless, I thought, and I felt the weight of my resentment toward that friend lift.

I wasn't intentionally being deceptive by leaving the stones of my past unturned. I honestly figured that those old sins, committed so long ago, were best forgotten. I was a married woman now, living an ordinary married life—those sins were no longer a problem for me, so why dredge it up? The priest urged me to follow the leadings of my conscience, which might have been helpful advice, except my conscience was pretty impotent in those days, dulled from years of me telling myself that sin didn't exist. I hadn't yet learned that one can find healing from sin, as well as forgiveness. By leaving my most painful transgressions unspoken, however distant I tried to convince myself that they were, I was guarding those wounds from the only salve that could cure them.

I remained in this condition for over two years, intermittently going to confession, but never approaching that locked door within me. I might still be there, hiding from my history, had I not read a book that encouraged me to open it.

This was not a theology tome, but a work of fiction, one I cracked open while visiting my parents in Idaho. Night by night, I read by the narrow beam of a clip-on book light, trying not to disturb my three year-old son, who was sleeping next to me. I was reading the Kristin Lavransdatter trilogy, written by the Norwegian Nobel laureate Sigrid Undset, also a Catholic convert. The novels are set in medieval Norway and trace the life of the heroine from childhood to her death. The world crafted by Undset is rich and compelling, everything unfolding under the sacred canopy of a Catholic cosmos.

Kristin's story gripped me; I stayed up late each night to devour as much as I could before succumbing to sleep. The pattern of her life mirrored many of my own experiences. Like Kristin, I fell in love as a teenager and lost my innocence, rebelling against my parents and our shared religious beliefs. For years, Kristin wrestles with the consequences of her choices, both shouldering and resisting a hefty burden of guilt. For a long time, she refuses to admit that she did anything wrong. How could following a deep love be wicked?

Reading her story led me toward that darkened inner door, and I peeked inside my sexual past to find a tangled mess: there was genuine love there, but also abuse. I began to see how I was, at times, used and misled by men years older than myself. Yet I also saw those actions that were not coerced, when I chose poorly out of passion, or spite, or self-loathing. Would I have made those mistakes if I hadn't first been mistreated? It is impossible to know. Yes, I was wounded by my religious community, taught to see myself as irreparably damaged, which abetted more bad decisions. But it is also true that I put my family through hell; I acted selfishly and callously, and I harmed myself by rejecting the norms that were there to protect me. The common denominator here, the underlying culprit, was sin—sometimes my own, sometimes someone else's. That is what sin does: it breaks bonds between people; it masquerades as something benign, even something good and true; it infects the soul, twisting it away from what it was created to be.

In the second novel, after Kristin has married her illicit love and birthed the child they secretly conceived, she goes on a pilgrimage up the length of Norway to the cathedral in Nidaros. Once there, she has a series of prayerful, mystical encounters that allow her to face the reality of her sin—especially how she has hurt her father—and at last be free of it. As I absorbed the story of Kristin coming to terms with her own sin, I realized that was something I had never done. I had ruminated on the damage done *to* me, while hiding from the damage I had caused.

For almost half of my life, I'd been deceived by two lies—first, the lie that I couldn't be healed, and then, the lie that my sin didn't matter. The truth was between those two lies, and within this mirage of medieval Norway, I was finally able to see it: my sin *had* wounded me, and I *could* be healed.

* * *

I returned to Oregon with a mandate from my conscience, which had bounced back from those years of entropy to become a thriving gadfly again: I needed to make a full confession, and I needed to do it ASAP. I arrived home on Sunday afternoon, the day before the 4th of July, and there wasn't another Mass scheduled until Wednesday. Unfortunately, I would have to wait a few days to speak to the priest.

This is when things started to get a little weird.

I feel the need to preface this part of the story with a disclaimer. I am not particularly attuned to the activities of angelic and demonic forces; until fairly recently, in fact, I didn't believe in them at all. After growing up on a steady diet of Frank Peretti novels, and experiencing the paranoid fear that demons would, for example, stream into my room through the radio if I listened to secular music, I dismissed all that stuff as superstitious nonsense when I reached the enlightenment of adulthood. Sure, I played around with a Ouija board a few times, and saw some odd things happen, but that could be explained away by something science-y, no doubt. In graduate school, I even took a part-time job at a New Age shop that shilled magic crystals and hosted Tarot readings in the backroom, assuming it was all just a bunch of sparkly bullshit. Just for fun, I bought some Tarot cards and made a half-hearted attempt to learn how to read them. It was a silly game, I thought, a mode of creative storytelling.

So I'm not, historically speaking, someone who sees demons in every shadow or flickering light bulb. Most of the time, for good or ill, I have a default skepticism that kicks in when someone starts talking about demonic forces. Even now, I'm hesitant to tell this part of the story because I know how ridiculous it sounds. I can still feel the cynicism with which my former self would regard these words, responding with a smug scoff, maybe an eye-roll. But I'll tell it nonetheless, because this is what happened.

When I got back from Idaho, I paid a visit to some Catholic friends who'd just moved to the area. I was hungry for Catholic community, and I regarded this couple with a mix of awe and curiosity. They were seasoned Catholics; they knew the ins and outs of how to live the faith, something I was still—am still—figuring out how to do. The first thing I noticed in their small living room was a giant crucifix and a makeshift altar with missals and prayer cards. "These guys are hardcore," I thought, with approval, maybe even a tinge of envy. I was a greedy baby Catholic. I wanted all the things.

So I stopped by their house to say hello, to catch up, and before I left, they gave me a tiny plastic pouch filled with blessed salt. They'd just had their house blessed by a priest, who used the salt and gave them extra. "This is high-octane stuff," they said. "A powerful exorcism prayer has been prayed over it."

"Oh wow, okay." The pouch had a tiny hole in it, so I cupped my hand to keep the grains from escaping. They gave me some holy water, too, so I could bless my own house, which had never been done.

That night, I went through our house singing a medieval Benedictine exorcism prayer I'd recently learned. The acronym of this prayer is engraved on every St. Benedict medal, and it goes like this:

Crux sacra sit mihi lux	[Let the Holy Cross be my light]
Non draco sit mihi dux	[Let not the dragon be my guide]
Vade retro Satana	[Get back, Satan]
Nonquam suade mihi vana	[Never tempt me with your vanities]
Sunt malo quae libas	[What you offer me is evil]
Ipse venana bibas	[Drink the poison yourself]

As I sang, I sprinkled the exorcised salt and holy water around the edges of each room and in each doorway. I tried to do this furtively, waiting until a room was empty before I blessed it, trying to steer clear of Michael, who would no doubt think I'd gone batshit. I felt energized and emboldened while I performed this little ritual, and also a little ridiculous. What can a little salt and water possibly do? My inner skeptic was dubious. But I pushed those doubts aside, and one by one, I blessed all the rooms, except for my bedroom, where my daughter was sleeping.

The next night, when everyone else was asleep, I sat at our kitchen table, teaching myself the *Salve Regina*, a Marian hymn that is usually sung at the end of night prayer in the Liturgy of the Hours. I alternated between playing the song and singing it myself, trying to memorize the Latin words, as well as the melody. It is a beautiful, powerful prayer invoking Mary's protection and intercession. We sing it almost daily as a family now, but this was the first night it was ever sung in our house.

After awhile, I made sure the house was locked up and headed to bed—but was stopped short at my bedroom. There are two doors in my bedroom, one leading into the adjacent bathroom, one into the hallway, and both of them were open. This startled me, because I had made sure the bedroom was closed tight, like I always did, after I put my daughter to sleep in her crib, and no one else had gone down the hallway since. I was confused, a little unnerved, but I shrugged it off and went to bed.

In the morning, I was the first one awake. I walked out of the hallway and into the kitchen, only to see that our front door was wide open—not cracked, not ajar, but flung back on its hinges as far as it could go. I could see through it to the street outside, a fairly busy stretch of road with cars and pedestrians constantly going by. I rushed upstairs to make sure my son was still in his bed—he was, asleep—and went back downstairs. The door to our mudroom was closed, but when I walked through it, I discovered to my confusion and dismay that the back door to house was also completely open. I suddenly felt vulnerable and exposed, like our house had been violated somehow, infiltrated.

When Michael woke up, he casually told me, while grinding the coffee, that he'd had demonic dreams all night about a menacing presence in the house. Mind you, this is my diehard skeptic husband speaking. Neither of us had a plausible explanation for both entrances of our house being splayed open like this. There was nothing missing, my laptop was still sitting on the table in full view, easy pickings. We wondered if maybe it was our three year-old son, but this also seemed unlikely. When he wakes up at night, he screams like a banshee until Michael comes to get him. He's afraid of the dark, always sleeps with a light on; he's not one to go traipsing around the house at night, quietly opening doors into the darkness outside. And, to boot, our back door is extremely difficult to use. Even an adult has to tug, and our son needs help in order to pry it open.

Michael seemed bemused by the whole thing, but I was freaked out. I went over to the house of my wise Catholic friends, hoping they'd have some sage advice to share, but when I arrived they seemed antsy, unsettled—and completely unsurprised by what I told them. Turns out they'd been experiencing what they called "demonic oppression" all night. I didn't ask what that entailed. I wasn't sure I wanted to know. As we talked, I mentioned that I'd once worked in that New Age occult shop, years ago, and my friend asked if I'd kept any physical items from that shop that might still be in the house. Well, sir, indeed I did.

I went back to my house in full-blown purge mode. I'd kept some jewelry and a handful of crystals from the occult shop—not because I thought they were magic, but because I like pretty rocks. Even as I gathered them up and threw them in my trash bag, I was unconvinced that they were somehow tainted with evil, just because they were unfortunate enough to end up in an occult shop in Scotland. Nevertheless, into the trash they went. As I combed through every room, on the lookout for anything that might have ties to the demonic, I prayed to St. Anthony, the patron of lost things, for his intercession: "Help me find whatever it is that I need to find."

I ended up in the disaster zone of our attic, a sea of boxes and furniture and suitcases. At this point, I wasn't even sure what I was looking for anymore. I only had a vague sense that I'd know it when I saw it. And finally, I did. In a box within a box within a box, in the back corner of the attic, I found it: the deck of Tarot cards.

I gasped when I opened the lid and saw what was inside, as if I'd found a coiled up snake, because, until that moment, I was absolutely positive I'd gotten rid of them years ago. Even as I was combing through my house, *looking for occult things from that shop*, the Tarot cards never crossed my mind. It was as if a cloak had been thrown over that little slice of my memory, as if within an entire row of colored lights, only a single one—the most glaring one—had been snuffed out.

By now it was twilight, on the edge of night. I pulled out our rusty old wheelbarrow and found a lighter. The cards were glossy, laminated with a sheer coat of plastic, and hard to burn. I had to light them on fire one at a time. Before long I was working in the dark, so I turned on the outside light to see what I was doing. It was a motion-sensor light, and I was well within its range, but it started flickering on and off erratically, entirely unrelated to my movement. Eventually, the light cut out altogether, not turning back on until I went back inside and physically flipped the switch. I had to do this about seven times while I was burning the cards. I've never seen our backyard light behave this way before, and haven't since, but I was more exasperated than frightened—these cheap horror movie antics seemed so cliché.

The next day, I went to an evening Mass in Portland with my Catholic friends. They introduced me to the priest who had given them the exorcised salt, and I told him I used it to bless my house. "That's powerful stuff," he said, and when I explained the subsequent events that led to my discovery of the Tarot cards, he smiled and nodded, as if hearing the answer to a riddle. "Some things can't be blessed," he said.

When I first saw the doors of my house flung wide, I had assumed that our home had been invaded, that the doors were open because something, or someone, wanted to get in. But perhaps I had it backwards. Perhaps the doors were open because something was being driven out.

* * *

The next morning was Wednesday, at last, so I went to daily Mass at my home parish, hoping to speak to the priest afterward to set up an appointment for confession. I didn't want to crash the scheduled confession times, because I knew I'd need a good amount of time. Everything that had happened over the past 48 hours had only increased my sense of urgency; I needed to do with my own soul what I had now done with my home.

Every few years, priests are sometimes rotated to serve a new parish, and while I was in Idaho, we had been assigned a new priest, Father Marcos, a middle-aged Mexican man, short and dignified, who moved around the altar with reverence, seeming to disappear into the Mass. I liked him immediately. This was my first time meeting him, walking up after Mass, asking him when I could make a full confession. It crossed my mind that this would make a hell of a first impression—"Hi, I'm Abby, nice to meet you. Can we set up a time for me to recount all the worst things I've ever done?"

Remarkably, I didn't care, which was a small miracle in itself. After all, I was the person who once sought out a priest I didn't know to confess a sexual sin, just to avoid the anxiety of my own priest knowing I'd done it. But that wasn't important to me, not anymore. I was a woman on a mission, the devil at my heels, and all I cared about was getting to the other end of that confession, so I could experience the full force of the sacramental grace. *Vade retro, Satana!*

I made an appointment for the next day, Thursday, to give myself time to prepare, to pray and search the dark recesses of my conscience. I rifled through my life, opening doors I'd barred shut and chests I'd buried, finding inside not dust and dried bones but throbbing memories that still bled when I prodded them. I began to make a list in a tiny red notebook.

I showed up a little early at the church and went straight into the small reconciliation room in the left corner of the sanctuary. Inside, just to the right, there is a thick curtain with a kneeler in front, a chair for the priest hidden on the other side. For those who prefer face-to-face confessions, there's another chair, facing the priest's, just past the curtain. I surprised myself by choosing the latter.

I was alone for a moment before Father Marcos walked in. Who knows what he first thought of me, sitting grim-faced in that chair, shrouded under a brown lace mantilla. Miraculously, I barely cared. This was my pilgrimage: not across Norway, but three blocks from my house. I came not to a cathedral, but a simple parish church, to bare my soul to a priest I'd just met. There was no stained glass to color the light, no stone floor, hard on the knees and cool to the touch. There were only makeshift walls of acoustic paneling, a purple curtain, and two wooden chairs facing each other, with cushy upholstered seats. But none of that mattered, because I knew that Christ, in his Eucharistic body, was waiting in the tabernacle on the other side of that wall, and the next time I walked past him, I would be whole again.

So I launched in. *Bless me, Father, for I have sinned.* I confessed all the sins that I could remember, all the ones that still troubled my conscience, from my childhood to the present day. It must have taken over an hour, and I wept almost the entire time. Father Marcos listened patiently to me, dispensing tissues at appropriate intervals. He did not seem disturbed or impressed by my revelations; there was never a hint of disapproval, nor any fawning attempts to make me feel at ease. His manner was gentle and quiet, like a clear pond of water, translucent and perfectly still.

When I was finished and had prayed the Act of Contrition, funneling all my angst and shame into those words given to me by the Church, he took some time to speak with me, to give me spiritual direction. He urged me to draw close to Mary, to learn how to better love her Son. For my penance, he told me to pray a rosary, and then he said the words of absolution, words that opened up into pools of supernatural grace that flowed down into each and every one of my wounds, so that they brimmed over like jars of new wine.

* * *

I returned home and made my second bonfire of the week. I tore the long list of sins from the little notebook and tossed them in the wheelbarrow. One, two, three lit matches and the pages were aflame. I watched them curl inward as the fire grew, as if shrinking away from the power of the light. The letters on the paper, the marks of all my sins, turned black and disintegrated, disappearing altogether, until there was nothing left but fire.

The Language of the Body

I got pregnant three weeks after becoming Catholic. This was not planned. (Insert joke about Catholic fecundity here.) In fact, I'd been struggling valiantly over the past few months to learn Natural Family Planning, the Church-approved way to plan and space pregnancies. There are a variety of specific NFP methods, all of which involve monitoring the signs of a woman's fertility to either achieve or avoid conception.

This fertility-awareness approach to birth control was not totally new to me. I learned the basics long before I became Catholic, when Michael and I decided to start a family, six years into our marriage. I went off the pill so my cycles could regulate, and I started to track them, triangulating the data to pinpoint ovulation. I figured it would take a few months for my reproductive system to normalize after years of chemical disruption—but by using fertility awareness, I got pregnant quickly. In just those few weeks of reading my body's fertility signs, I caught a glimpse of a fascinating interior world. Even as a committed feminist who was very much concerned with women's bodies, I had never taken the time to actually understand how mine worked. I just swallowed a pill and made sure it didn't.

I was reluctant to go back on the pill after my son was born—not for any theological or philosophical reasons, just intuitively. I'd finally experienced the raw power of my femaleness, the incredible feats my body could accomplish. I had a newfound sense of awe and respect for my body, and it felt strange to intentionally make it malfunction. More viscerally, I hated the idea of complicating the already tumultuous postpartum period by ingesting excess hormones. Something didn't seem healthy about that—my hormones were already easing back to normal after childbirth, and here I was preparing to disrupt the balance again. Still, I trusted my doctor, and I didn't want to get pregnant right away, so I went back on the pill.

When I started RCIA, my son was almost a year old. Even though I did not yet understand or agree with the Catholic Church's stance against contraception, I decided to try and live in accord with it, so I ditched the pills. This might sound like a faithful, sacrificial act—choosing to trust the Church and live by her teachings, even before I'd totally accepted them. And perhaps that was part of it, a desire to live a fully Catholic life, to step off the pick-and-choose Protestant carousel. However: there were other aspects of Catholic sexual morality that I was *not* so quick to embrace in my choices and habits. Why, then, did I readily decide to practice this teaching?

I think, on some level, I was tired of being at war with my body. Even though I was on the pill for much of my adulthood, and the first six years of my marriage, I remained ambivalent about it. My maternal grandmother died at a fairly young age from breast cancer, and I was always vaguely aware that pumping my body full of synthetic hormones was increasing my own risk of cancer. But that risk seemed more distant than the risk of pregnancy, so I took the pill and tried not to think about it.

Somewhere along the way, artificial birth control had become compulsory in my mind, a mandatory feature of female health. It's simply what women were expected to do. Our fertility is pathological, something that needs to be treated, controlled. I followed this norm unquestioningly, assuming it was for my benefit, consciously believing and asserting—to quote my former self—that birth control was the lynchpin of female freedom.

Deep down, though, I wasn't so sure, and when the Catholic Church came along and gave me permission to rebel against this conventional wisdom, I took it—without yet knowing why. I remember throwing those pills in the bathroom trash, only halfway through that month's pack, and I felt relieved: not fearful or reluctant, but free. I returned eagerly to the work of tracking my fertility, charting my cycles, regaining that sense of discovery and self-knowledge that I'd experienced when I first began to understand my fertility.

This enthusiasm lasted for about a month. I expected my cycle to quickly resume, like it once had. But it didn't. As it turns out, my use of hormonal contraceptives had been totally superfluous. My body takes a long time to resume fertility when I'm lactating; I had been needlessly trying to force my body to do something it was already doing naturally.

I soon found, to my dismay, that monitoring fertility during this anovulatory postpartum phase is *really hard*, especially if you're just learning how to do it. My body, which once seemed so easy to read, was now constantly giving mixed signals. I had no idea if I was on the brink of ovulation, or still months away from it. I didn't know when I would become fertile again. Since we were trying to avoid pregnancy, this meant refraining from sex on days that I might be fertile—which was almost every day. This translated into long stretches of abstinence, punctuated by furtive couplings under a shroud of anxiety.

I was intensely frustrated to discover that, although I had ditched contraception, I was still at odds with my body. I felt torn apart by impossibly conflicting expectations. Some of these I had absorbed from secular culture, such as the expectation that women should be sexually available while never getting pregnant, or the notion that frequency of copulation is the barometer of marital health—or even the idea that it is unhealthy not to act on sexual desire, lest we curdle in our pent-up juices. Funnily enough, I had received similar messages within evangelicalism, where married sex is dangled like a ripe carrot in front of chaste singles: just make it through this time of abstinence, and then you can enter the marital wonderland of sex-on-demand, where all your desires will be met, and all your fantasies come true! Now I had a new expectation to pile on top, courtesy of the Catholic Church: that I would somehow meet all these ideals without using contraception.

Finally, after months of ambiguity, I saw the glorious egg symbol pop up on my fertility monitor. I had ovulated! I felt a rush of relief: now that my fertility had returned, I would be able to read the signs more clearly. Getting to that first postpartum egg was the big hurdle. I felt the pressure ease and geared up for my first menses after childbirth, which I'd heard could be quite torrential.

But after two weeks, Aunt Flo still hadn't come, and I found myself needing to eat every ninety minutes and wanting to yell at everyone, at which point the awful thought dawned, so I peed on a stick and sure enough: I was pregnant. That longed-for ovulation symbol had been a lie; the monitor was not detecting the Lh hormone of ovulation, but the almost identical hcG hormone of pregnancy. The real ovulation had come a couple of weeks earlier. That first postpartum egg? My monitor missed it, and her name is Margot.

* * *

After I found out I was pregnant, I fell into a kind of spiritual depression. Not something intense and melancholic, more like sluggish apathy. Already, I was awakening to love the child growing under my heart, but the fact that I hadn't *chosen* this pregnancy, that it had happened against my intentions— this began to fuel a sense of anger toward the Church. Mixed up in that anger was shame, as if an unplanned pregnancy was a personal failing on my part, an embarrassing oversight.

Even though I was a newly minted Catholic, I had little desire to go to Mass. I avoided confession altogether and found myself slipping into old habits, sleeping late on Sundays, avoiding thoughts of God. When I did think of him, I felt an inner hardening that was all too familiar—a buried, bitter stone of quiet resentment. I'd stepped out in faith, followed the Church's teaching, and look at what happened. I'd done everything right, like a good little Catholic, and still ended up pregnant.

Reflexively, I slouched back into the posture of the feminist critic: I thought of the Pope, all those bishops and cardinals, with their gleaming robes and fancy hats. What did they know about tracking fertility while lactating? Did they have any idea how difficult that is? I perseverated on their maleness, losing sight of the Church as mother, falling instead into a more comfortable trope—the Church as a masculine entity, at odds with my experience as a woman. So much for the convert's honeymoon phase.

Eventually, after several months in this state, I took my anger to confession. By this time I was visibly pregnant, well into my second trimester. This was only my second time ever going to confession, the first since I joined the Church almost six months ago, and I was not coming with an especially contrite spirit. Rather, my defenses were up. Through the priest, I was putting the Church on trial—would he react dismissively? Judgmentally? Would my feminist suspicions of male authority be confirmed?

We sat down in his office, and I disclosed my frustration, my anger, my sense that the Church had betrayed my trust. I can remember feeling, at the time, as if becoming pregnant was something unnatural that had happened *to* me, against my volition. Despite my best efforts, my body had revolted. The priest listened to me with patience and compassion—so much that I decided to spare him some of the details I'd been prepared to share, like the intricacies of cervical mucus and estrogen production.

Then he said something that surprised me. Invoking Thomas Aquinas, the priest explained that following one's conscience is of utmost importance. If I've made a good-faith effort to understand and follow Church teaching, but my conscience leads me elsewhere, I am free to use contraception, and I don't have to confess that as a sin.

Sometimes, you have to be given what you ask for to realize you don't actually want it. I'd come in with my feminist defenses primed, ready for the male priest to tell me to blindly follow the male hierarchy. Instead, he told me to follow myself.

Rather than feeling vindicated by this, I was dissatisfied. Apparently I didn't actually believe my knee-jerk dismissal of Catholic teaching as some kind of patriarchal conspiracy, because as soon as the priest said I could ignore it, I wanted to retort: *but there's something meaningful there.* I thought the Church's stance on contraception was frustrating and difficult, to be sure—but I was not convinced that it was wrong. Here was a priest telling me I didn't have to follow the dictates of the Church, if my conscience said otherwise—and here was my conscience chiming in to tell me to ignore the priest, rather than the Church.

* * *

This confession brought to mind another recent conversation—one with Stephen, my former student, who had become something of an advisor and confidant through my process of joining the Church. It was to Stephen that I brought my hardest questions, knowing I would get a straight, if sometimes unappealing, answer.

I'd been encountering this notion of conscience as a trump card in some of the books I'd been reading; it was often played by Catholics who dissented from teachings of the Church. Initially, I found this conscientious objection comforting. It seemed to clear a space for me to join the Church, even though I was still unsure about her stance on contraception and gay marriage. I could always be one of those dissenting Catholics, I figured, if need be.

Stephen, however, burst my shiny liberal bubble, by explaining the Catholic view of conscience in more detail. Conscience is not a free-floating entity, something within the confines of my interior life that directs me toward one thing or another—conscience, to function properly, must be anchored in something outside of myself, in the steady ground of truth. My conscience is meant to direct me *toward* something, something beyond my sensibilities and intuitions, something objectively true. Without such grounding, conscience becomes a broken compass, a madly spinning needle unable to find true North. Stephen explained to me that conscience needs to be *formed*, oriented, aligned toward the truth of Christ that has been entrusted to his Church and safeguarded from human distortions. If the Church is true, then my conscience should harmonize with its teachings. If the Church is not true, well, then, what's the point of being Catholic?

I was a little confused, a little dubious after Stephen's tutorial. For years, I'd allowed my emotional convictions to serve as a barometer for truth. It didn't make sense to me that my conscience could somehow be other than, or even at odds with, those deep feelings. Still, this idea that conscience must be formed in order to function stuck with me, and when the priest gave me the pass to follow my conscience and use contraception, I knew that I had to make a good-faith effort to shape my conscience first.

I began a steady regimen of study. I read *Humanae Vitae*, the 1968 encyclical that reaffirmed the traditional stance against contraception, even while the rest of Christendom was abandoning it. In it, Pope Paul VI makes several predictions of the fallout of contraception's widespread acceptance, predictions that now seem prophetic. I was particularly haunted by his claim that respect for women as whole persons would plummet, and their sexual objectification would become pervasive. Even a cursory glance at our culture reveals this to be true.

I also read John Paul II's *Love and Responsibility* and his series of catechetical homilies known as the Theology of the Body. These texts illuminated an entirely new understanding of the body and sexuality. I was glimpsing, for the first time, that Catholic Totality, an understanding of reality as a divinely ordered and sacramental whole. The question of sexuality and embodiment was not tangential to this whole, but integral. I began to suspect that opting out of the Church's hard teachings on sexuality would create a rupture in this cosmos, by extracting the human person out of its scope.

I came to recognize that the anger I felt after becoming pregnant—anger toward the Church, toward God, toward myself—exposed something crucial: I had ditched contraception, while retaining a contraceptive mindset. I'd been following the Church in practice, but not in my understanding, because I had never internalized the reality that sex is intrinsically linked to procreation. *That* is why I was continually at war with my body. I should not have been angry with the Church, whose teaching recognizes and respects the life-giving reality of sex. I should have been angry at our culture, which insists I live at odds with it.

For all of my adult life, I had been living behind a shroud of ignorance, only vaguely aware that I was a fertile being. At the level of ordinary living, I implicitly thought of myself—and sex—as sterile. When I was in graduate school, I participated in a week-long colloquium with a number of other doctoral students. We were all from different fields, each of us employing the work of a prominent feminist philosopher, Luce Irigaray, in our dissertation work. One of the other participants was a British physician, whose research was an attempt to understand why so many of her patients had unplanned pregnancies. These women were all prescribed birth control and told how to use it. Most of them had even had children before and were intimately aware of the realities of reproduction. Despite this, these women kept ending up pregnant. I was fascinated by her work, myself on birth control at the time, and in our conversations we kicked around various theories. Not once, however, did anyone suggest that the contraception itself might be the problem.

Now, through the lens of Catholic theology, I began to see how using contraception—and living in a contraceptive culture—had shaped my understanding of sex as having little to do with procreation. Even though I'd understood, intellectually, where babies come from, this had seemed almost like a tertiary function of sex, an optional add-on—or even, in certain circumstances, an outright *malfunction*, sex gone wrong. This creates a fascinating irony: a contraceptive mentality can lead to riskier sexual behavior and incorrect use of birth control, and thus more unexpected pregnancies, because the possibility of pregnancy seems far removed. There's sound research to support the existence of this irony: when a society first becomes contraceptive, unplanned pregnancies and abortions actually *increase*.

An understanding of sex as recreational, and only procreative if you *want* it to be, had thoroughly shaped my self-understanding and my relationships. In one of his essays, agrarian philosopher and cultural critic Wendell Berry describes how the sexual revolution, made possible by contraception, has altered our understanding of sex:

> In fact, our "sexual revolution" is mostly an industrial phenomenon, in which the body is used as an idea of pleasure or a pleasure machine with the aim of "freeing" natural pleasure from natural consequence. Like any other industrial enterprise, industrial sexuality seeks to conquer nature by exploiting it and ignoring the consequences, by denying any connection between nature and spirit or body and soul, and by evading social responsibility. The spiritual, physical, and economic costs of this "freedom" are immense, and are characteristically belittled or ignored. The diseases of sexual irresponsibility are regarded as a technological problem and an affront to liberty. Industrial sex, characteristically, establishes its freeness and goodness by an industrial accounting, dutifully toting up numbers of "sexual partners," orgasms, and so on, with the inevitable industrial implication that the body is somehow a limit on the idea of sex, which will be a great deal more abundant as soon as it can be done by robots.[19]

When I read this now, I feel a sense of sadness, because I spent so many years with that understanding of sex, of my body as a pleasure machine that needed to be divested of its procreative power in order to properly function, to provide as many gratifying hits as possible.

In the "sex-positive" realm of popular feminism, where I once sought refuge to escape condemnation for my past, pleasure is the ruling paradigm. I was reminded of this recently, when I attended a feminist panel on sex and theology at the national convention for the American Academy of Religion.

In the entire ninety minutes of discussion, with multiple scholars presenting and an audience of female academics actively engaging, *not once* did anyone mention the fact that sex can result in pregnancy. It was as if we were operating within a world where that no longer happens, where new human beings emerge out of cabbage patches, or spring from men's thighs, like Dionysus from Zeus.

Unfortunately, it is women who pay the price when this fantasy skids into reality. I remember seeing a heart-wrenching Facebook post in the midst of my conversion, in which a woman I don't personally know was explaining her decision to have an abortion. She begins the post by revealing that this is the second time she's gotten pregnant on long-term hormonal birth control, and she concludes by making a pitch for access to abortion, because "bodily autonomy exists and it exists for a reason." There's a basic logical problem if we can't see the contradiction there: the very fact that she is in such a difficult and painful situation is because, in fact, bodily autonomy does not exist for women as it does for men. Men can have sex until their eyes pop out; they will never get pregnant. This is not true for women—just ask my husband, who was conceived after a tubal ligation. The myth of complete sexual freedom, complete autonomy, is based on male biology, and women can only pursue that ideal by doing violence to themselves. Feminists, of all people, should be attuned to this, but they believe and propagate the myth as much as anyone. As I once did, wholeheartedly.

The crucial first step for me, in embracing a Catholic view, was reinstating sexuality in the context of the created order. Through my graduate studies, and rote cultural osmosis, I had lost sense of any meaning of sex beyond an intimate, pleasurable activity to be shared with a person one trusts and loves. I had no concept of teleology—of the ultimate purpose of sex—beyond the orgasm. In this light, there was no meaningful difference among the assorted menu of sexual acts, since they all ideally led to an orgasm. I didn't have a sense that male-female conjugal union was an altogether different kind of act than, say, oral sex between any two partners. Yet this perspective completely overlooks a glaring reality: sex is how human beings come to be.

Even though I'd been having sex since I was a teenager, the biological facticity of what happens during sex never really sunk in, aside from a roving thought bubble that popped into frame occasionally: "Watch out! You might get pregnant!" Pregnancy seemed, and was spoken about, as a negative consequence of sex, like getting an STD, rather than something sexual intercourse is intrinsically ordered to produce. I never fully apprehended—nor was it articulated to me—that in having sex I was joining my reproductive system with someone else's. All physiological systems are complete in a human individual, save one: the reproductive system. In order to procreate, two human beings with complementary reproductive systems have to join together and become one reproductive organism. As unsexy as that sounds, *that* is precisely what sex is. But in our cultural imagination, we've lost sight of the obvious.

In a Christian understanding of reality, sex does not have merely biological significance. During my interior conversion, I came to embrace the framework of a sacramental worldview, a recognition that our world was purposefully created and ordered and loved by God, and also designed in such a way that material realities become windows into the divine. Nowhere is this sacramentality more pronounced than in the human person, who, as an integrated whole of body and soul, is the very image of God. This Christian anthropology imbues the human body with sacred meaning, and the body itself speaks, through its design, a silent language that reveals its divine character.

In the act of sexual union, the body declares: *I give myself to you, the whole of my person, even my capacity to create new life.* A total self-gift is without reservation and implies permanence. The body, in sex, always speaks the language of gift, and when sex is removed from the context of a lifelong union, the language of the body becomes a lie. I've felt the pain of this lie many times in my life. I think of all the panicked pregnancy tests I've taken, waiting those agonizing two minutes to see if the plus sign will appear like an augur to proclaim that I've wedded myself permanently to someone I only meant to love in passing. My body had spoken its language of perpetuity—its wholehearted *yes*—at odds with my intentions, my *maybe*, my *just for now*.

I'd been tricked into thinking that sex is only about the momentary act itself, rather than its fruits: total self-gift and the possibility of new life. Reading the language of the body, this teleological meaning becomes clear. The pleasure behind sex is directed toward higher ends than a momentary surge of *jouissance*. Sex unites a man and a woman into a single whole, one that has the potential to generate a new human being. This is the full meaning behind the biblical language in Genesis of man and woman becoming one flesh: they become one flesh through a unique act of union, made possible by their sexual difference, and this union is not fleeting, temporary, but the sign of a permanent bond that has the possibility to become concretely "one flesh" in a child.

To use Catholic terminology, the twofold *telos* of sex is union and procreation. These two powers are not separate, but intertwined—and if we believe that God's design is not arbitrary, those powers are *meant* to be connected. The physical delights of sex are good and beautiful, but they do not exist for their own sake. Sex is meant to *lead us somewhere*, not more deeply into self-love, or even into an inward-facing, exclusionary romantic love, but into a love that is Christ-like and outward facing—a love that is synergistic and abundant, that spills over into the lives of others. Christianity, ultimately, is not about the elimination of sexual desire, but the orientation of it for the sake of love.

Sex, then, is not just about *pleasure*, it's about *persons*. Sex is how we participate in the transmission of human existence. *That* is why Christian tradition, for two millennia, has located marriage as the proper context for sex—and why, for two millennia, all of Christendom was united in its disavowal of contraception. This is not just an arbitrary rule, a scriptural mandate with no discernible purpose. To the contrary, the roots of this rule are grounded in the very heart of the Christian worldview, which asserts the divinely drawn goodness of the created order and an ethic of self-giving love.

* * *

When I discovered the Catholic view of sexuality, I was enamored with its sheer, beautiful sanity. But I was also chastened, because this vision of the world to which I wanted to belong was asking something from me. These weren't just lovely *ideas*, like so much of my feminist theorizing; this was an all-encompassing truth, which demanded not only my intellectual assent, but radical changes in my life.

You might assume that, as a married mother, I would already be living in harmony with Catholic sexual morality. But this wasn't true. I had to face the uncomfortable reality that I viewed my body, and even at times my husband, as instruments for my own fulfillment. Despite coming of age in an evangelical Christian context, I had been given no guidance on how to live out a holy sexual life within marriage. Evangelicalism, as it turns out, has little say on that topic, echoing the secular view of sex as primarily recreational. The only key difference is that evangelicalism situates that recreational activity within marriage. While there might be a general sense that children will come along eventually, the expectation, as I've encountered it, is that a couple will put off having children for a few years "to enjoy each other," and then have a few (but not too many!) children before being sterilized. Sex is only incidentally procreative. I never heard, as an evangelical, sex spoken of in teleological terms. Now that I had encountered that truth in its fullness, I had to clear out my bedside table, as it were, purging those thoughts and habits that took an instrumental, mechanistic view of sex for granted. Which is really difficult, by the way. Those toxic roots run deep.

This is where the prayer comes in. My conscience wasn't shaped by study alone, but through prayer—one prayer in particular, which I stumbled upon more or less by accident. While researching the Catholic view of conscience, I came across a homily on conscience by John Henry Newman, a famous cardinal and convert from Anglicanism. I don't remember anything about the homily, but within it was a prayer for the formation of conscience. I wrote it down by hand in my journal and began to pray it every night, for months, while I was wrestling with Catholic teaching on marriage and sexuality.

> I sacrifice to Thee this cherished wish, this lust, this weakness, this scheme, this opinion: make me what Thou wouldst have me; I bargain for nothing; I make no terms; I seek for no previous information whither Thou art taking me; I will be what Thou wilt make me, and all that Thou wilt make me. I say not, "I will follow Thee whithersoever Thou goest", for I am weak; but I give myself to Thee, to lead me anywhither. I will follow Thee in the dark, only begging Thee to give me strength according to my day. Try me, O Lord, and seek the ground of my heart; prove me, and examine my thoughts; look well if there be any way of wickedness within me; search each dark recess with thine own bright light, and lead me in the way everlasting.[20]

Of all the prayers I prayed that year, during my interior upheaval, this was the most dangerous. Night by night, it stripped away my cherished opinions, opinions that had been central to my identity as a progressive, a feminist, an academic. Soon after I began saying this prayer, I found myself in the throes of something that, months ago, I hadn't been able to conceive: a deep, internal conflict between my conscience and my emotions, specifically on the definition of marriage. On that particular issue, I was a bitterly reluctant convert.

Prior to my conversion, I had what you might call a revisionist-romantic view of marriage, marriage as an emotional, romantic, sexual bond between two people. This contrasts with the traditional-conjugal view of marriage, which begins with recognizing the realities of human procreation and sees marriage as an institutional response to that reality. In the romantic view, marriage is more exclusively about the couple; in the conjugal view, the bond of marriage creates a lifelong union for its own sake *and* for the sake of the children that may arise from that union. I had no conception of the conjugal view. I didn't even realize I was rejecting it. The romantic view was the only one I'd ever known: this was the view prevalent in secular culture, and also within evangelical culture, albeit with a biblical, heterosexual gloss.

Because I didn't see sex as intrinsically linked to procreation, I also didn't see procreative potential as a central feature of marriage. And if sex and marriage have no meaningful connection to procreation, why should sexual difference matter for either? This made same-sex marriage seem perfectly logical, and the traditionalist insistence on "one man, one woman" discriminatory. I never bothered to stop and consider why, if marriage has nothing to do with procreation, it should be limited to a "couple" at all, or why it should be an unbreakable, lifelong union—two features of marriage that indicate its reproductive logic. I reasoned that the only argument *against* gay marriage was an overly literalist reading of Scripture, which I'd long left behind.

When I began to follow the thread of Catholic teaching on contraception, it led me into the fabric of the Catholic cosmos itself, where my understanding of sex became both sacramental and teleological. The explanatory power of this new way of seeing was unexpected and thrilling, like digging through the attic for a lost sock and finding instead a priceless family heirloom. I felt freed to see myself as a whole person, and my fertility as a gift, rather than a shackle. I felt called into a higher love, a more radical kind of sexual intimacy.

At the same time, I began to feel uncomfortably aware that this discovery of the sacred significance of sexual complementary was extremely countercultural in my progressive milieu. How could I embrace this, and still maintain my affirming stance on gay marriage? Unlike, say, abortion and pornography, I had never felt any ambivalence about approving same-sex marriage, once I left biblical authority behind. My conscience was never piqued. In fact, I became quite zealous and self-righteous in my defense of it. This was a central part of my progressive identity.

I tried, at first, to find a loophole that would allow me to sneak gay marriage into this teleological worldview, where sex retains its twofold meaning. I pulled a trusty feminist trick: invoking the exception to upend the rule. What about infertility? There are plenty of married couples, after all, who simply aren't able to procreate. Yet, the Catholic understanding is that those marriages are just as valid. Is there any meaningful difference between a same-sex couple and an infertile heterosexual couple, when it comes to procreation? For a few weeks, I thought I'd found an inconsistency, and thus a solution to my dilemma, a way to stay faithful to both Catholic and progressive sexual creeds.

Then I started dabbling in Thomistic metaphysics—always a danger-ous pastime—and encountered the distinction between potentiality and actuality. If you've noticed, I've used words like *possibility of procreation* and *life-giving potential* throughout this chapter. This is because teleology is not the realization of a particular outcome or goal, but instead refers to an in-nate directedness or ordering toward that outcome. I, as a female human being, have certain potentialities that a man does not: namely the potential to gestate human life. My entire physiology is arranged according to that potential. I might have a condition that prevents that potential from ever becoming an actuality—but I retain the potential nonetheless. I am still a woman. (You can see how this helpful distinction between potentiality and actuality solves a perennial problem for feminist theory, which can never settle on a definition of "woman," its central subject of concern.)

In wanting to view a same-sex couple as indistinguishable from an infertile opposite-sex couple, I was focusing on *actuality*, but ignoring *po-tentiality*. Once, long before I was Catholic, I remember standing in line at the grocery checkout behind a young lesbian couple. They were buying a cartload of food, while I only had only item to purchase: a pregnancy test. As I stood there, idly watching the checker scan the groceries, it occurred to me, as a passing thought, that they would never be in my position, waiting in line to nervously buy a test for an unplanned pregnancy. There was a potential inherent to my sexual relationship that was completely absent in theirs.

That was the end of my reverie; I didn't follow the implications any-where, or begin to question my non-teleological view of sex. I simply made a quiet observation to myself and moved on. But looking back to that mo-ment, I can see that I was recognizing an important truth about sex: there is a potential for life in conjugal union that is not present in other sexual acts. This remains true *even if* that potential is not actualized, whether due to contraception or age or a condition like low sperm count. I was not actually pregnant back then, but the very act of buying that test was an indication that I had the potential to be.

A *telos* is an ultimate end or purpose toward which something is or-dered or directed, and conjugal union is inherently directed toward pro-creation, even if that potential is not actualized. I was forced to recognize, against my liberal sensibilities, that conjugal union between a man and a woman is different in kind than genital activity between people of the same sex. A man and a woman form a reproductive unit whether or not that par-ticular coupling results in a child. Even the phrase "infertile couple" signals an inherent potential that is being hindered by some obstacle; this is why infertility is often experienced as an intensely painful loss. It wouldn't make sense to speak of a gay couple as "infertile," because that potential was never there. Infertility, then, is not an argument *against* the teleology of sex as both unitive and procreative, but actually affirms it. What I had thought was a loophole brought me right back around to Catholic teaching.

At this point, I had to face what I'd been trying to resist: these two paradigms of sexuality are incommensurable. The Catholic paradigm sees the human person within the context of the natural order, an order brought and held into being by a loving Creator. The design of our bodies, our sexual complementarity and procreative potential, is not an error or an accident, but *purposeful*. This enables human beings to participate in the creative work of God by bringing new human beings into existence. Our bodies have a nuptial meaning. The capacity for conjugal love is written on them, spoken silently by them, and in a sacramental gesture, our bodies point beyond themselves, beyond the temporal order, toward the possibility of union with God. All this imbues sex with a profound, sacred significance.

To deny this, to say that sex has no purpose beyond the orgasm, is to step into a different world entirely. In this world, our bodies do not speak, because they have no intrinsic meaning to profess. They are not divine signs, but material objects, tools for us to wield. They are not part of a created order animated with divine intentionality. There is no givenness to our embodied humanity to which we are accountable.

This is the world I used to inhabit, and I came to see that it is not, at its root, a Christian world, but an atheistic one. The differences between these paradigms occur at the ground level. To inhabit one, I had to let go of the other. One cannot affirm a teleological view of sex and simultaneously deny it—which is what I would have to do, if I wanted to embrace the truth of Catholicism, while also arguing that it somehow doesn't apply to gay people. It would be oddly discriminatory, in fact, to extract gay people from the context of the created order and the sacred responsibilities it endows. If the twofold *telos* of sex is true, it is true for all human beings, regardless of our marital states or sexual histories, regardless of our complex and wayward desires.

Awakening to the truth of human sexuality was the most painful, wrenching, and disorienting part of my conversion. And it lasted for months. These scandalous ideas rattled around in my brain, and I both loved and loathed the sacred web they were revealing. The Newman prayer became a desperate incantation. *I sacrifice to Thee this cherished wish, this cherished opinion.* I wanted to belong fully to truth, to be overcome, swept away against my will, but on this one issue, I was Lot's wife, looking backward at the city I used to inhabit, the people I loved who remained there, even as I was being ushered along on the path of salvation. I was divided against myself, like Augustine describes in his account of conversion: *And so the two wills fought it out—the old and the new, the one carnal, the other spiritual—and in their struggle they tore my soul apart.* At last I understood, to my despair, what it means to have a conscience that is formed to external truth, rather than one that merely echoes my own sentiments and intuitions, because, to quote Augustine once more, *the day had dawned when I was stripped naked in my own eyes and my conscience challenged me within.*

This all came to a head in the summer of 2015. Something I had been anticipating for years was finally coming to fruition: the legalization of gay marriage. But by the time the Supreme Court decision was announced, I was unable to celebrate, because I had come to embrace what the Catholic Church teaches about sex. I recognized its ancient, eternal beauty and reoriented my life, my marriage around it, sacrificing my political commitments and a sense of moral satisfaction in the process. My mind was at rest, sated by truth, my conscience firm. But my emotions were a mess, my heart still unsettled.

I remember going to a park with some friends on the day the decision was announced. After a moment or two of small talk, while we watched our kids wrangle about on the playground, my friend burst out in exuberance, "Did you hear about the Supreme Court decision?" My other friend responded with enthusiasm, and I awkwardly slunk away, pretending my son needed help up the slide. These were good friends of mine, women that I respect and love. I wasn't so much fleeing from them as I was trying to avoid the specter of my former self, who they now mirrored back to me. I know what is thought and said about traditionalists like me, because I used to say and think those things.

In my more honest moments, I wonder if the real root of my intense angst during this time was vanity. I found it very comfortable to be on "the right side of history," a champion of the underdog, an advocate for love and equality, those cardinal virtues of progressive Christianity. Then, my worldview changed, and I was suddenly afraid of being found out by my liberal students and colleagues. When I thought about trying to articulate this new way of seeing, I was muted by the fear of being perceived as intolerant, bigoted. Those are the battle lines that have been drawn in this culture war, at least from the viewpoint I used to inhabit; one is either an ally or a homophobe. And it was much more comfortable and self-satisfying to be part of the groundswell of changing public opinion on this issue, rather than struggling to swim upstream.

Christianity, at its core, insists upon a radical commitment to the dignity of the human person. This is why the infinite value and God-bearing image of the gay person can never be questioned or undermined. Yet this is also why sexuality belongs within the context of a marriage that is open to life. Faced with either truth, we must not flinch.

Catholic teaching does not single out gay people in the way that often happens in conservative Protestantism, where married straights are allowed to turn sex into a recreational activity, but gay people aren't. In the Catholic understanding, everyone is called to redirect desire into self-sacrificial love. If we think marriage is easy and self-satisfying and the celibate life is difficult and self-denying, we've understood neither, at least not in the Christian sense. The cross is not imposed on gay and celibate people, but offered to all as a means to holiness. We are all asked to curb our sexual desires out of deference for human life and its genesis in human sexuality. For me, a straight married woman, this means I don't use contraception and try to respect the meaning of sex as self-gift. If I want to avoid pregnancy, I don't eradicate my fertility; instead, I abstain from sex. And I've come to discover that this kind of restraint, this kind of sacrifice, is itself a profound form of love. Rather than pulling me apart from my husband, it has made our union stronger.

Does recognizing the teleology of sex lead, necessarily, to the dehumanization of those whose desires are at odds with it? I have to believe that it doesn't, because I am one of them; I have plenty of desires that pull at the bit of Catholic sexual morality. But Christ, in his interactions with the various "others" throughout the gospels, enters into this tension and shows us a way through. So many of these encounters are with people who, like all of us to one extent or another, have unruly bodies and desires: the woman at the well, the bleeding woman, the harlot, the adulterer, the demoniac, the leper, the blind, the crippled, the corrupt tax collectors. In these encounters, Christ affirms their humanity and dignity, restores wholeness, and calls them into a harder, holier way of life. And lest I forget, when I cast myself into these stories, I must remember that I am the crippled man, I am the harlot. I am the one being healed.

* * *

As it turned out, my unexpected pregnancy was perfectly timed. While I was unthinkingly assuming that pregnancies should be either avoided or meticulously planned, God interrupted my life with an exquisite surprise. I had been buckling under the pressure of conflicting sexual norms, but once I became pregnant, I was able to suspend my struggles with NFP and take time, instead, to discover the *why* behind the Church's teaching. God didn't just want my compliance; he wanted to reshape my understanding of reality as a whole, which included my own sexuality. He didn't want to grant me the ability to fulfill those dueling and contradictory expectations that were tearing me apart; he wanted to free me from their thrall.

Margot's life, every moment of it, has been pure gift—not only for her precious, unrepeatable existence, but also for the conversion that accompanied it. Her conception was my spiritual quickening. Her gestation became my own: this was a time of discerning, listening, burgeoning, a time of hidden growth. I labored with her, as I labored with the faith that was struggling to birth within me. And when she was born, so was I. The overwhelming love and acute suffering of her arrival broke me open, down to the center of my being, so Love himself could enter and find the hardened seed that was hidden there, awaiting the only touch that could make it bloom into a *yes*.

Via Maria

Who was Mary to me as a child? I thought of her little, to be honest. I was not often asked to think of her at all. When I did, it was always within the tableau of a nativity scene. Mary, veiled and stooped over her divine child, Joseph by her side, a captive audience of shepherds, wise men, angels, and barn animals gathered around. That was where Mary always was, suspended in that single moment.

And it's an important moment, to be sure. This is the advent of the Incarnation—at least, when the Incarnation is made visible. The mystery of the Incarnation has already been made known to Mary, hidden and nurtured within her womb for nine months.

Let's just pause there, and let that sink in: consider the quiet intimacy Mary shared with Jesus for the better part of a year, before anyone else had glimpsed his face. She carried him under her heart. She felt his quickening, Life itself becoming life in the flesh. This is a special kind of knowing only a pregnant woman can experience: the paradox of loving a person that one has never seen or touched, but is also somehow always touching, in a mysterious and veiled way. This is not unlike the experience of faith; we see now darkly, through the veil, what we will one day see face to face. Yet even now we can love him, and before anyone else, she did. How can we contemplate this and simply pass by? How can we see her as only a transient figure, someone to be given a polite nod at Christmastime, and then disregarded completely?

The night Mary gives birth to the Incarnate Word is a culmination, yes, but it does not stand in isolation. Rather, this event is a bright star that casts light on other events, imbuing them with meaning: the angel's initial appearance and proclamation, Mary's encounter with Elizabeth, Simeon's harrowing prophecy, the flight into Egypt, the loss and recovery of the child Jesus in Jerusalem, Mary's intercession for the wedding guests at Cana, her vigil at the foot of the cross, her presence at the Spirit's outpouring in the

Upper Room—all of these are windows into the life of Mary and her role in the drama of salvation. Yet I was never invited to look through them. I never heard a sermon preached on Mary, even as an exemplar of faith. Abraham, Moses, David, Paul—these men were regularly lifted up as models for all to follow, but never was a woman similarly elevated. Not even the woman who gave birth to God.

Luke shines the widest spotlight on Mary, which grounds the other references to her in the Gospels. Her discreet, enduring presence can be traced throughout the arc of Christ's sojourn, his Incarnation, his childhood, his public ministry, his death, and the birth of his Church at Pentecost. This continuous nearness to Jesus is true of no other figure in the New Testament. To see Mary as insignificant disregards the testimony of Scripture and misunderstands both the profundity of the Incarnation and the meaning of motherhood.

Protestantism, to put it crassly, seems to regard Mary as a mere surrogate, not as a mother. In truth, giving birth is only the beginning of motherhood, not its end, and there is an intensely spiritual dimension to motherhood that goes beyond mere biology. Mary's maternal connection to her Son is not a relic of the past, but an eternal reality. Mary is bound to Christ in a unique, intimate, and indissoluble way. She is as close to God as it is possible for a creature to be.

The passages about her may be dispersed and compact, but they are deep pools of water into which one can plunge, and swim and swim, without ever brushing the bottom. The iridescence of these pools forms the constellation of a greater mystery. Bereft as I was from the tradition that has contemplated those passages for millennia, submerging into the depths, I was only ever able to skim along the surface.

Who was Mary to me later, as a feminist?

On the one hand, she moved from the margins to the foreground, as did any female figure or feminine metaphor. I viewed my work as a feminist critic like a kind of archaeology, digging down into the hardened, male-centered sediment of Christianity to uncover its buried feminine heart. During that period of my life, my feminism mushroomed to occupy the center of my cosmos; it was the sun around which all other bodies, religion included, revolved. I mistakenly assumed that my evangelical pedigree gave me the ability to speak from a place of knowledge and authority about Christian tradition as a whole, and so the relegation of Mary within evangelicalism signaled to me Christianity's fundamental patriarchal character. Christianity in general, and specifically Mary, had to be reinterpreted according to the mandates of my Western feminist orthodoxies.

In a sense, then, Mary became more prominent, but she was also compressed into a mere symbol. She was not a *person* I could come to know and love; she was a floating archetype, detached from anything real. The characters and mysteries of Christianity had become like cut flowers, rich and colorful blooms severed from their roots, from the stability of the soil, that could be endlessly rearranged. This revisionist work took on a sacred character for me. It became, in essence, my lone spiritual praxis, an act of worship to a theoretical divinity hidden behind the patriarchal mask.

Even during my decade of doubt, I was particularly intrigued by the story of the Annunciation, when Mary is visited by the angel and consents to bear the Incarnation. This episode from Luke's gospel is the center of my devotional life now, as a Catholic, and even then I was drawn to it. In my doctoral dissertation, I interpreted the Annunciation through the lens of feminist theory, concluding that Mary's assent to God was a denial of her own "spiritual becoming" as a woman. Her "yes" to God was a "no" to her own flourishing. I wanted to keep the dazzling idea of incarnation, but only as a conceptual tool, purged from any dogmatic truth claims—religious ones, anyway. I held fast to feminist creeds, to the veneration of autonomy and feminine self-actualization. Yet in trying to rescue Mary, I ironically demoted her. Instead of the mother of God Incarnate, the heroine in the drama of humankind's redemption, she became a trite emblem of the female ego turned in on itself, a woman gazing endlessly into a mirror.

Thus, in my first thirty years, my understanding of Mary careened between those two extremes: in the first extreme, Christ was cut off from his mother. In the second, Mary was cut off from Christ.

Pope Benedict XVI highlights those two polarities, and their relationship to one another, in his meditations on Mary's role in our salvation. On the one hand, he asserts that "we must avoid relegating Mary's maternity to the sphere of mere biology."[21] He describes how such a dismissal, characteristic of my upbringing, disregards the significance of the feminine dimension of salvation history and concludes that there is "nothing meaningful in the feminine line of the Bible stretching from Eve to Mary."[22] This gives rise to a feminist response, which Benedict regards as understandable in its motives, if ultimately misguided:

> Today's radical feminisms have to be understood as the long-repressed explosion of indignation against this sort of one-sided reading of Scripture—an explosion, however, that has indeed taken the step to truly pagan or neo-Gnostic positions: the rejection of the Father and the Son that occurs in these theologies strikes at the very heart of biblical witness.[23]

Benedict's analysis reveals that these extreme reactions to Mary, both of which I've embraced and experienced at various points in my life, seem to be locked in a reactionary dynamic: one is overly wary of the feminine and tries to suppress it; the other responds to this suppression by embellishing and exaggerating it. The Catholic understanding of Mary lives and thrives between these dialectic poles. The Church guides us between them. Her enduring witness enables us to:

> rediscover the feminine line in the Bible and its proper salvific content and to relearn that Christology does not exclude the feminine or repress and trivialize it and, conversely, that the recognition of the feminine does not diminish Christology, but that the truth about God and the truth about ourselves can appear only when the correlation of the two is correctly appreciated.[24]

In all that follows, keep that principle in mind: Mariology is born from an authentic Christology. Everything the Church teaches about Mary is ultimately about Christ.

* * *

When I contemplate my encounters with Mary, my own trek down that middle way, more deeply into mystery, five discrete episodes stand out in relief. I can picture them almost as three-dimensional scenes, like the Stations of the Cross that line the sides of every Catholic sanctuary—or like the *Via Matris*, with its seven stations that depict the sorrows of Mary. In a similar way, I have been walking, am walking, a Marian Road that leads into the heart of Christ. The stations along this road have not been sorrows, but marvels—steady lights on a nocturnal path.

I.

The first scene unfolds in a small, nondescript breakroom. Windows along one wall let in the purple twilight. There is a counter with a sink toward the front of the room, a sunken couch in the back, and between them a handful of young people have gathered. They are holding red prayer books and all facing the same direction, toward a small wooden cross resting on a table, a single white candle alight beside. With one voice, they offer up these words aloud:

> *My soul proclaims the greatness of the Lord*
> *My spirit rejoices in God my Savior*

For he has looked with favor on his lowly servant

From this day, all generations will call me blessed . . .

This is the Magnificat, the song of Mary from the Gospel of Luke. In the Anglican Book of Common Prayer, it is one of two canticles that can be selected as part of the Evening Prayer rite. For two years, during the heart of my college years, I gathered every weekday evening to pray this rite with a handful of other students and our philosopher-priest professor. We took turns leading, and whenever mine came along, I always selected the Magnificat, without fail. I had fallen in love with this prayer. Through it, Mary was emerging from the shadows.

This was where I began to know her, years before becoming Catholic, during my Anglican interlude, when I was stepping beyond the narrow borders of my childhood faith, toward the ancient, sacramental Church—before I shifted direction and began to move away again. Through the Song of Mary, I was catching hold of the "feminine line" Benedict XVI writes about, rediscovering a female genealogy of the faith that includes my beloved Old Testament women and runs through Mary into the Church, continuing through the Communion of the Saints. Hildegard, Catherine of Siena, Julian of Norwich—this was my initial exposure to the great cloud of witnesses, women and men, that extends beyond the pages of the New Testament.

God is not the God of the dead; he is the God of the living. The saints, Mary among them, are not dead. Now, in God's unfiltered presence, they are more alive than they've ever been. They are more alive than we are. To pray to a saint is not to worship that saint, but to beg for her intercession, to ask her to present a prayer, that golden bowl of incense, before the throne of the Lamb.

Why not pray directly to God? Why waste time asking for intercession? This logic would not only preclude the intercession of the saints, but all intercessory prayer. And this logic injects a competitive dynamic between God and his people, which cuts against the enduring witness of Scripture, in which the faithful continually intercede before God on one another's behalf. That is what the mystical reality of the Body of Christ is all about.

This Body, moreover, includes *all* the faithful. Death does not rend this Body, splitting it apart into the pilgrims on earth and the saints in heaven, a yawning chasm in between. That would make death more powerful than the Resurrection, more powerful than the divine life bestowed upon the Church that binds it into one whole. This binding together—this communion—is not temporary; it is not interrupted by the movement of souls from an earthly sojourn into eternal life. The scriptural mandate to intercede for one another, to pray for one another, is not suddenly abolished when a saint reaches heaven. Rather, it is intensified. We know from Scripture that the prayers of the righteous are particularly effective—they availeth much, as James testifies—and the most righteous men and women within the Body of Christ are those who have been purged from sin and are seated before the heavenly throne.

I was just beginning, during this Anglican interval, to discover the mysterious reality of the Communion of Saints. I was not yet praying to Mary, asking for her intercession, but through the Magnificat, I was praying with her. Her words became my own.

Still, she was not yet fully alive to me—my faith didn't quite extend that far. What I saw in Mary, and the other female saints, were models of a heroic feminine spirituality, female exemplars I could relate to and emulate. Mary's prayer was on my lips, but it would be years before I added my voice to the ongoing fulfillment of its prophecy: *For behold, henceforth all generations will call me blessed . . .*

2.

This scene takes place during a Mass, at the very beginning, after the priest has processed forward and is greeting the people. It is a Wednesday morning, but the sanctuary is almost full, unusual for a weekday Mass. The people are wearing light jackets and scarves, doused with spring rain. The sky visible through the windows is overcast and gray; there seems to be more light inside the church than out. Toward the back stands a woman, off to the side and apparently there by herself. She sits at a safe distance from other parishioners and, staring straight ahead, with an almost grim look, she cautiously pulls up one end of the gray scarf looped around her neck so it drapes over her head. When she hears the priest's greeting, she gasps aloud, only then glancing at the people around her, as if wanting someone else to witness and affirm whatever she's heard, whatever has elicited that cry of delight.

This was March 25, 2015, the month after the birth of my daughter. This was the onset of the intense, inward upheaval that began toward the end of my first year as a Catholic. I'd been praying those dangerous prayers, surreptitiously covering my head in the darkness of my room, and that morning I resolved to cover my head during Mass for the first time.

I chose a weekday, thinking there would only be a small, devout circle of attendees, less likely to cast a sideways glance at the veiled newcomer. As always, I was overly preoccupied with what others might think. When I pulled the scarf up over my head, I felt awkward and embarrassed, anticipating judgmental looks that might never come, already feeling them nonetheless. I pretended the veil was a sort of invisibility cloak and fixed my eyes toward the altar, trying to block out the anxious fantasies I was projecting onto the people around me.

Then I heard the priest's greeting, and in that moment I received a grace, one that came as a complete, unsolicited surprise. The priest unmasked what I assumed to be an ordinary day, revealing that it was a holy day, the Feast of the Annunciation. On this day, the Church celebrates and remembers the Yes of the Virgin Mary, the Yes that opened the way for our salvation. And this just happened to be the day that I'd taken upon myself a physical sign of my own desire to surrender to God. I wrote about this moment in an earlier chapter, without fully disclosing its Marian dimension. As soon as the significance of the day was unveiled, I immediately understood the gift. Christ was accepting my hesitant, half-hearted, wavering Yes, and directing me toward the perfect Yes of his mother.

In Luke's biblical scene, two of the deepest Christian mysteries are on display: the Incarnation and the Trinity. Mary assents to the will of the Father, who sends the Holy Spirit to come upon her, enabling her to give birth to the Son. This is the first unveiling of the Triune nature of God, and the descent of the *Logos* into flesh. And at the center of it all is Mary. Her Yes is the bridge between God and humankind that enables the Incarnation to take place.

This bridge is not built by Mary's willpower alone, but by the abundance of grace given to her from the beginning of her existence, to prepare her for this moment. This is the meaning of her Immaculate Conception. Her Yes is so absolute that it allows the Word to become flesh within her. A human will weakened by sin, curved in on itself, would have been unable to give such resolute consent—a Yes that expresses and offers the whole of her personhood, without reservation, to the will of God. This does not mean her Yes is coerced, compelled. The opposite is true. Mary, full of grace from her beginning, is uniquely free to give a consent that is wholehearted; she is free like a master musician is free, unencumbered by error, able to flawlessly harmonize her will with God's.

The Annunciation and the Incarnation—two mysteries that dazzled me even in my doubt. A two-fold cord that tethered me to Christianity during those restless years: with one hand I clasped onto it like a lifeline, with the other I cut it loose. In my feminist studies, I spent hours sitting with the Annunciation, mulling it over, analyzing it, interpreting it anew, playing my hermeneutical games. But I was only ever able to see it in the half-light, through a narrow, waning beam that followed only the face of Mary, leaving the Triune God in shadow.

That spring Mass was the beginning of Christ reintroducing Mary to me, so that I may know her as she really is, not as I'd imagined her to be. I came to realize that my feminist interpretation was a direct inversion of the truth: Mary's Yes is not some kind of denial of her selfhood, but rather its culmination. In actuality, I was the one denying my spiritual flourishing—by withholding my Yes from God and reserving it for myself.

That day, Christ gave me the gift of the Annunciation, newly illumined—not as a privilege, but as a charge: to live within that mystery, to let it invade my thoughts and affections, and, as much as I am able, to enter into Mary's Yes and make it my own.

3.

The third scene takes place in a church, but not inside the sanctuary—just outside it, in the parish hall. It is wintertime; the solstice is around the corner, so even though it is only eight o'clock, the sun has been down for hours. The glass windows and doors are black with night, revealing nothing of the outside world, only mirroring back the shapes and lights and movement of the hall's interior. And there is plenty to mirror: the ceiling is hung with strings of bright flags that spin out from a shared center, like the spokes of colorful wheel. The small flags, in bold shades of red, green, and white, carry silhouettes of biblical scenes, like images of the nativity. These are the decorations for the nine-day celebration of Las Posadas, which will culminate on December 12, the Feast of Our Lady of Guadalupe.

Mass ended a few minutes ago; the flood of exiting parishioners has ebbed to a few remaining stragglers, who have stayed behind to pray or light votive candles. One of these stragglers comes into the hall from the sanctuary, pausing briefly to splash holy water over herself in a hurried cruciform gesture, absentmindedly. She walks through the hall toward the front doors, then stops abruptly, looking up and around, as if she's heard something. But no one else is in the room. The flags stream above her and converge into a raised point, covering her like a tent. She stares at them for a moment, listening, then continues on her way.

This was December 8, 2015, the Feast of the Immaculate Conception. It is a holy day of obligation for Catholics, when attendance at Mass is required, so I made sure to go that evening. I lingered for a few moments afterward; one corner of the sanctuary was extravagantly decorated in a colorful scene depicting the miraculous appearance of the Virgin of Guadalupe to the Mexican Indian peasant, Juan Diego, in 1531—an encounter that precipitated a sweeping wave of conversions, almost ten million, in the Americas over the following decade. I looked at the display for a while, thinking about the Immaculate Conception, mulling it over, wanting to understand. I prayed a prayer I'd been praying for months, since last March: Jesus, show me your mother.

As I was walking out, I heard a voice say something to me. Not an audible voice—more like a thought proceeding into my mind from the outside, speaking to me in the interior of my heart. Yet, it was unmistakable, and it made me stop short and listen.

Consecrate yourself to me.

This wasn't the first time I heard that voice. It spoke to me once before, during Mass on another Marian feast day, the Assumption, on August 15. I had been praying that same prayer, asking Christ to introduce me to his mother, to help me know and understand the appropriate place she should inhabit in my spiritual life. And during that Mass, I heard: *I am the soul who magnifies the Lord.* This was a somewhat familiar phrase: the first line of the Magnificat—*magnificat anima mea dominum*—is literally "my soul magnifies the Lord." But the metaphor suddenly seemed new to me; I went home, wrote it down, and pondered its meaning.

Mary gives us a picture of a human soul so completely united to God that she becomes translucent; she shows us not herself, but God within her, the Word becoming flesh for our sake. In her person, she displays the essence of the Christian life—a creature who gives herself in complete trust to her Creator. Her humility and receptivity to God magnifies the scale of his redemptive work—the vast expanse he traverses to draw near to us, to pitch his tent among us. Mary, full of grace, exhibits a restoration of the *imago Dei*, the divine image etched upon the human creature.

But this new message—*consecrate yourself to me*—was strange and unsettling. I had not yet, in my Catholic sojourn, encountered the tradition of Marian consecration, so the language itself was alien. What could it mean? I wasn't sure I wanted to know, which exposed the deep-seated unease I still harbored toward Mary—the real Mary, not Mary *qua* feminist symbol.

For a while, I tried to dismiss the whole experience, write it off as some imaginative fancy. But I couldn't shake the way the thought had blindsided me out of nowhere, as if interrupting my stream of consciousness, rather than coming from it—and the fact that the voice asked me to adopt a devotional practice that was unknown to me at the time. So, with reluctance and ample doubts, I began to try and understand what was being asked of me.

Marian consecration, from what I could tell, was a practice of consecrating oneself—giving one's whole person—to Jesus through Mary. It involved taking Mary as a spiritual model and guide in order to grow in devotion to Christ. Some of this made intuitive sense to me. As a mother, I knew that Mary's love for Christ, and her commitment to him, is uniquely powerful and complete. She knows and loves him more perfectly than any other human could. Even before Christ was born, she shared an intimate, silent communion with him, and she followed him faithfully throughout his life, death, and resurrection. Perhaps, then, I could increase my own faith and love for Christ through her example and guidance.

The question of Mary having a mediating role was a little trickier. Isn't Christ the sole mediator between the Father and human beings? I was still plagued by the feeling that any explicit devotion or attention shown to Mary somehow detracted from or competed with my love for Christ. And that was my error: seeing those loves as competitive.

I considered my love for my husband and my love for my children. It is not as if, by loving my children, I am somehow loving my husband less, or vice versa. In fact, the opposite is true: these loves enhance each other. Similarly, if I love my mother-in-law, does that somehow decrease my love for her son, my husband? No—again, these loves have a synergistic rather than competitive relationship. Still, it *would* be a problem if I got those loves confused, because the ways in which I should love my children, my husband, and my mother-in-law are not interchangeable. So I began, slowly, to understand that my love for Mary does not detract from my love for Christ, but can enhance it—as long as I remember that my worship is reserved for Christ alone, as the Church has always emphasized.

Mary is not a mediator in the same way that Christ is a mediator. Mary is not divine; she cannot save us. And yet, she has been selected by God to play a unique role as the God-bearer. She is the human being chosen to bring Christ into the world—and this is a mediating role. Through Mary, the Incarnation is made known to us. Mary, then, is a mediator between Christ and humankind, in a way that is both analogous to and distinct from Christ's mediation to the Father. This notion of a human mediator to Christ is not actually that radical. No one encounters Christ in isolation; the gospel is always transmitted through other people. Even a common phrase in evangelical vernacular—"So-and-so led me to Christ"—demonstrates this. And who is better able to lead us to Christ than his mother?

Gradually, I began to feel more comfortable with the idea of dedicating myself to Mary as a means to deeper love for Christ, even as the wariness persisted. I had discovered, through my reading, that one completes the consecration on a Marian feast day, after a thirty-three day period of prayer and preparation. If I went through with this, I knew I would make the consecration on the Feast of the Annunciation, bringing this year of Marian encounters full-circle.

4.

The fourth scene unfolds in a sanctuary that has been stripped down to the bones. All the statues have been removed; the altar is bare; the corpus of Christ on the crucifix is covered with a shroud; the red candle beside the tabernacle that always burns as a signal of Christ's Eucharistic presence has been snuffed out. The tabernacle itself is empty, its door gaping open, giving a glimpse of the cavity within. The atmosphere of the room is solemn and silent—not a contemplative, restful silence, but the silence of absence.

The people have gathered; the liturgy has begun. A woman sneaks quietly in the back. She's late, and instinctively she dips her fingers into the font by the door, but she touches only air; the bowl of holy water has been removed. She slides into a back pew, joining the ongoing liturgy, but she's always a half-step behind, as if her body is too heavy, and her voice is slow to warm. She has a mantilla, but she hasn't pulled it over her head, instead letting it hang round her neck like a yoke.

This is March 25, 2016. Most years, this date is the Feast of the Annunciation of Our Lord, but this year that feast is displaced to make room for the Easter Triduum, which lasts from Holy Thursday through Easter Sunday. The Triduum is the summit of the liturgical year,

Easter Sunday is its highest point, when the Church celebrates the Resurrection. But first we must descend into the abyss of Good Friday, reliving the darkness before the Resurrection, when Jesus has died, and all seems lost.

This year, I was late to the service. Minutes before, I was sitting on my stairs, looking at the clock, which had just marked seven o'clock. I knew I had to go, but I felt immobilized, as if my body was made of dried clay that would crumble apart if I moved. I'd been feeling this way all week, Holy Week. This was the most sacred time of the year, when the darkness of Lent is shattered by the daybreak of Easter—a time of renewal and hope. Yet I was experiencing the inverse, a pervasive sense of spiritual desolation, a deep aversion to practicing my faith. When I tried to pray, the words felt like ashes in my mouth. When I thought about going inside a church, for any reason, I was overcome with spiritual lethargy so acute that it felt physical. I was almost nauseous when I thought about going to the Easter Vigil, the holiest, most beautiful Mass of the year—during which, this year, my mother was joining the Catholic Church.

To make matters worse, I was three weeks into my Marian consecration, which was set to end after the Easter octave, when the Annunciation would be celebrated on April 4. The consecration process was intense. I was following St. Louis de Montfort's guide, which had a selection of Scripture

readings and lengthy prayers for each day. Ideally, I suppose, one is supposed to meditate on the Scripture and pray with rapt, arduous attention,
but I was often rushing through it, or leaving parts out altogether. I felt like
an out-of-shape runner who had decided to start a marathon, and quickly I
was cramped and limping. The last two weeks of the consecration, around
the time of Holy Week and the Easter octave, were meant to focus on acquiring better knowledge of Mary and Jesus respectively, with the latter being
the culmination of the process, which is ultimately about growing in love for
Christ. It was during this time that my desolation hit in full force, reaching
its height on Good Friday, when it took all of my willpower to walk the few
blocks from my house to the church.

I came in late and sat in the back, feeling a sense of triumph that I
had somehow dragged myself there. A year earlier, I had been overwhelmed
with spiritual consolations during Holy Week, like an infant nourished with
the sweetest of milk. But now, I was cut off, weaned all at once, starved of
any consoling feeling or thought. The naked sanctuary, stripped of all its
beauty and sacred signs—even the Eucharist had been secreted away—this
was a mirror of the barrenness I carried within me. I felt, and this is the best
way to describe it, that there was a husk around my heart. A desiccated,
impenetrable shell. I sat in the pew and whispered the line from that Donne
poem—*Batter my heart, three person'd God*—hoping to summon God's violent return.

I thought of Mary's heart: open and willing, attuned to the divine hand
at work, brimming with love for her son. I thought of Simeon's prophecy
to her, when she presents the infant Jesus in the temple: *And a sword shall
pierce your heart also.* Christ's passion, his suffering unto death, was also
Mary's suffering. Her heart bears his scars. As a mother, I know this. Luke,
in his gospel, mentions Mary's heart repeatedly: hers is a heart that will be
pierced, and her heart is also a treasury that safeguards and continually
contemplates the divine mysteries of Christ. *Mary treasured all these words
and pondered them in her heart.* She is the first believer, the first Christian,
the first to be inhabited by Christ—not only in her body, but in the inward
center of her being.

Of all the dizzying, verbose prayers in Montfort's book, most of which
swirled around my head like cartoon birds, never quite landing anywhere—
there was one prayer, one line, that did land. I prayed it during that Good
Friday service, and I prayed it days later, when I completed the consecration,
because of all the things I still didn't understand about Mary, I understood
this: *Praebe mihi cor tuum, O Maria.*

O Mary, give me your heart.

5.

The fifth scene. A small chapel that feels like a cave. The walls and floor are made of stone. The air feels cool against the skin. The wooden ceiling hangs low, crossed by dark, heavy beams engraved with an intricate, colorful design that discloses key Marian symbols: Ark of the Covenant. Star of the Sea. At the front of the chapel, separated by a gate of wrought iron, is an alcove carved out of rock. Its center has been hollowed out to create a smaller niche, a cave within a cave, which holds a statue of Mary. She is made of rock, but nonetheless seems fluid, alive, her veil flowing down the length of her body, her folded hands draped with a rosary. This is the image of a famous Marian apparition—Our Lady of Lourdes—and there is something ethereal about it, as if it is made of light rather than stone. The center of the iron gate forms a cruciform shape, and looking straight on, the statue of Mary is hidden behind it, her gaze fixed upon it. In the darkness of the alcove, the statue seems luminous, reflecting a hidden beam from elsewhere.

At the foot of the gate, under the arched opening to the alcove, there's a small kneeler. A woman is hunched over it, weeping and mumbling the words to a prayer that is engraved across the top.

July 15, 2016, in the National Shrine of the Immaculate Conception in Washington, DC; I was back east for a conference, and I came a day early, to visit family and take a quick pilgrimage. I'd been to the Basilica several times before, but never as a Catholic.

My last visit, several years earlier, had been a strange mix of fascination and unease. I had been drawn to the rich, feminine imagery, abounding in the dozens of Marian chapels in the crypt level of the Cathedral, reflecting an array of depictions of Mary from around the world. The catholicity of Catholicism, its wide reach that stretches across the globe and back through time, was palpable there. But the corresponding masculine imagery unsettled me, especially the art in the interior dome of the Basilica itself, which depicted a Christ of fire and majesty—not the gentle shepherd Jesus, but the Jesus who comes to set the world ablaze, to bring not peace, but a sword. Even then, underneath my aversion, I felt a surge of nebulous longing. Entering the Basilica was like peeking inside the doorway to another world—a world that both repelled and attracted. Part of me yearned to enter, but I chose instead to pace beyond its reach.

To come to the Basilica as a pilgrim, then, as a Catholic native rather than a tourist, was an entirely different experience. G. K. Chesteron describes Catholicism as an immense cathedral that is larger on the inside than it is on the outside, and I experienced this optical illusion within the shrine's interior, whose halls and chapels were windows into infinity, into a divine reality that animates and encloses our small, earthly realm.

The upper level, with its fierce Christ, was under construction, and I was more than content to spend my time down below, in the crypt church, with its outskirt of seventy side chapels devoted to Our Lady. It had been three months since the Feast of the Annunciation, when I finished the consecration, and I was still unsure how to live it out. I felt as though I'd grown in my theological understanding of Mary, and I'd experienced the spiritual fruits of taking her as my model for living a life of faith. But I still wasn't sure I knew or trusted her *as a person*. It was hard to shake my feminist habit of thought that saw her, first and foremost, as a lovely symbol. The purpose of my pilgrimage, as much as I'd formulated it in my mind, was to meet Mary, to bring my whole person before her—not just my mind, but my heart.

First, I went to midday Mass in the crypt church. The beauty of the Basilica above is overwhelming, majestic, like the sounds of trumpets or a burst of gale-force wind. The crypt church, in contrast, is just as beautiful, but in an unobtrusive, hidden way, evoking the quiet intimacy of faith. Descending into the lower level of the Shrine was like entering into Mary herself, into the womb of the Immaculata, that space in which the Incarnation unfurled. Within this womb, I took the Eucharist, inviting Christ into the house of my body and asking him, once again, to show me his mother. After Mass, I asked my brother, who was with me, if I could have some time and space to wander around and pray.

I didn't get far, because just outside the crypt church, I saw the entrance to a side chapel off to my right. Unlike many of the other chapels, which boasted elaborate mosaics and dazzling colors, this entry was inconspicuous, its contents hidden. But I knew immediately that I needed to go in. I was being beckoned.

The door into the chapel opened up into the sacred; there's no other way to describe it. The bustle and energy beyond the door cut off abruptly. I could hear only the sound of my own breathing, the soft shuffle of my footfall. Miraculously, I was alone. This was the height of summer; the shrine was teeming with tourists, but this space had been cleared out, suspended, just for me. No one else came in until I was done praying—I wasn't sure how long that was, because time had receded altogether.

And yet I wasn't alone. That was also palpably clear.

For almost a year, I had been praying for Jesus to show me *his* mother. And that is where my contemplation of Mary centered—her relationship to Christ, and the implications of that eternal bond. But there was a leap, an extension of that motherhood that I had not yet embraced, one first revealed in the gospel of John, at the foot of the cross.

Just before his death, Jesus directs his mother to take the apostle John as her son, and for John to take Mary as his mother: *And from that hour, the disciple took her into his own home.* Christ's final gift before dying is to open Mary's motherhood to include his disciples, to those who love him. John's gospel is intensely theological, arguably more than the others; the details he includes in his portrait of Christ are meticulously chosen, numbering fewer than those included in the other accounts. To dismiss this moment, with its twofold gift, as having no enduring theological significance would be foolhardy. In fact, the beginning of the next verse—*After this, when Jesus knew that all was now finished*—reveals this to be the culminating act that completes his earthly ministry. Mary's role as a mother is rooted in her relationship to Christ, but extends beyond it; her maternal cloak has been cast over all the members of Christ's body. My prayer that Jesus would show me his mother was answered slowly, gradually, over the course of a year—and the final revelation was this: the mother I was seeking to know was not merely Christ's, but my own.

And meet her I did, as a veil was lifted and the Holy Spirit enabled me to feel her loving presence—not Mary the symbol, but Mary herself. I was overcome with emotion, like a child who rushes up for comfort, disclosing a fresh wound. I knelt and recited the prayer to Our Lady of Lourdes, each word a piece of flint that I struck against the sharp edge of my desire.

You see—I had come not just to meet Mary, but to give something to her, to entrust to her a secret grief. Within the written words, I enclosed another prayer: my heart's deepest longing, a prayer I carried around with me always, like a bullet caught between my ribs. I continually offered it to God, but could never actually let it go, as if God's generosity would be extended only in proportion to my pain. Part of the Marian consecration, I knew, was resting in her intercession, adopting a docile, childlike trust in the maternal role that has been divinely assigned to her.

Woman, behold your mother.

I reached into my heart, dug out that precious bullet, and handed it over.

The Edge of the Abyss

This is what haunts me now.

In the dream, I am looking at a landscape, a two-lane highway cutting through open land, rising steadily into mountains. My dream-self understands that this world, this land, is where I used to live. This is eastern Idaho, highway 20, running from the town of Ashton up to the scattered hamlet of Island Park.

The real highway 20 climbs out of a sprawling valley into the hills, flanked by forests and a mountainous horizon, toward Montana. Island Park is not a town *per se*; there is no center to it, only a series of small way-stations miles apart, places to stop for food, gas, and a fishing license. There are some homes, but they are hidden in the trees, far off from the highway. This is a place for passing through. This is a place of the in-between.

In the dream, I know that *this is where I used to live*, but it looks nothing like I remember it, nothing like that remote corner of eastern Idaho. Yes, there are mountains, trees, a highway rising—but once the highway flattens out, the land on one side of it drops away into a sheer, bottomless cliff. I am looking at this landscape from afar and above, a gods-eye kind of view, and I see a two-lane road running along the precipice, an occasional car zooming through, on the brink of death.

On the other side of the highway is another rock face, this one stretching upward. There is a row of cheery storefronts in bright Mediterranean colors along the road, doors and curtained windows carved into the rock itself. People live there, people drive by; they seem happy enough, and completely unaware that they are living on the edge of the abyss.

This scene fills me with complete terror. I feel the pull of vertigo, even from my omniscient perch; the sheerness of the cliff, its impossible depth, the fragility of those who move and live along its edge, unknowing.

This is where I used to live.

How can this be? This is not what I remember. This is not what it looked like back then. Yet, I lived here. I know this is true, a horrific epiphany, but I don't remember seeing the abyss.

I wake up terrified, a visceral kind of terror; my stomach feels hollow, the tips of my fingers bloodless and tingling. I can still feel the vertiginous pull, and that feeling hangs over me all day. I know the dream has named something, some deep terror within me, but I'm perplexed. It's clearly not a dream about Idaho, but what is it about?

This is where you used to live.

I don't understand until a couple of weeks later, one Friday afternoon. I'm meeting with some colleagues for a *fin-de-semaine* pint, and I start talking about this dream, the image of the cliffside village that continues to haunt me. That week, I'd had a series of conversations with students who are struggling with their faith, and in their faces I saw myself. I remembered the years I'd spent waiting in the darkness of the tomb like Mary Magdalene, mourning Christ and hovering between faith and unbelief. I tried to give my students advice, and felt like a fraud, as if I could understand how I've moved—have *been* moved—from that darkness into the dazzling light of the Resurrection, where the miraculous is not only possible but *real*, so real that it grounds all meaning. How can I explain this?

There I am, talking about these students, about the dream, and before I know it, I'm crying over the pain of this mystery. Why me and not my students? Why me and not my husband? Why have I been rescued from the abyss, while people I love continue to live there, on its yawning edge?

And I want to panic. I want to become a madwoman, running around and screaming and grabbing the cliff-dwellers and showing them the terror in my eyes *don't you see? Don't you understand? You cannot live here!* And I will run in circles because I feel the drag of black gravity and know that I can still free-fall if I let myself get too close but everyone else is walking calmly in straight lines, feeling sorry for me, because this is really such a nice town, the people are nice and the view is beautiful and I'm the one who doesn't see.

Him Whom I Love More Than All

The hidden longing that I entrusted to Mary, that day in the National Shrine, is the desire for my husband's conversion.

So much of my sudden and wrenching transformation was confined to the hollows of my inner life; it was something that happened to me and within me—deafening in its magnitude, yet quiet in its interiority. There's another story that unfolded simultaneously to this story of inward change, and that's the story of my marriage.

My conversion to Catholicism didn't just strike me in isolation; it happened also to my husband, and to a lesser extent, my friends and family. This sea change was disorienting enough to me, and I was experiencing it firsthand. I can only imagine how it must have seemed from the outside— perhaps like watching a loved one head off to war and come back a different person, only in this case the war was in my heart and will, concealed from those outside. Michael, as my counterpart, my confidant, was both an observer and a participant; he could not remain removed from the dramatic collapse of my worldview and its explosion into something new. The gravity pulled at him, too.

For the duration of our decade-long relationship, our religious differences had never been a source of strife. When we first married, we were in similar places spiritually—disaffected post-evangelicals, drifting away from our Christian origins, too in love with each other to bother much about God. From there, Michael settled into a worldview of scientific materialism, while I mucked around in the outer fringes of liberal Christianity. He had skepticism, I had feminism, and neither of us was much concerned with convincing the other, because in practice we were both effectively nonreligious. There was little, in our two worldviews, to be lived out; nothing really was asked of us. If I went to church on occasion, I went alone, because it was "my thing," and my faith was never robust enough to disturb the secular harmony of our domestic life.

We felt some initial tremors of discord when I was pregnant with our firstborn. The peaceable individualism at the core of our marriage was being threatened, because there would no longer be only two of us, but three—a brand new human was coming, one who would have to be ushered into the world of things and ideas and values. What would we teach him? Whose path would he follow? While I gave lip service to the pluralist platitude that our son should be free to choose his own religious identity, I had the growing sense that he should be raised within Christianity, rather than in some vague neutral zone, to enable him to understand religion from the inside. Michael wasn't opposed to this, but we were both hesitant, unsure how to proceed. The looming responsibilities of parenthood were forcing us both to face our existential uncertainties.

When I decided to begin RCIA, Michael was completely supportive. He'd witnessed my growing spiritual unease over the years, and he genuinely welcomed that I seemed, at last, to have found a home. By this time, our first son was about a year old, too young to be actively involved, and a whining, wiggling disaster during Mass, so we continued on in the individualistic grooves we'd plowed over the years, and I went to Mass by myself.

At first, I didn't mind this much at all. I was too enamored by the new sights and smells and consolations of Catholicism to feel alone. I actually felt much less alone than I had for the past decade, because I was part of a visible, approachable Church, a body extending over the world and through time that I could actually come to know and trust. In a way, to be Catholic is to never be alone—the saints are present, Mary foremost among them, and Christ is closer than ever, tangible through the sacraments. I was like an excitable infant in this unfamiliar world, transfixed by each color and sound, wanting to ferociously grasp the unfamiliar and bring it right up close, to taste it with zeal.

My initial desire for Michael's conversion, then, was born from this enthusiasm, akin to heartily recommending a great book. Oh, you just *have* to read this; it'll change your life! I had never before had the desire to share my faith with Michael, because my faith hadn't seemed worth sharing.

I remember once, in those first weeks of RCIA, when it dawned on Michael that a shift had occurred. We were sitting on our bathroom floor, giving Julian a bath. I was excitedly rambling about some aspect of Catholicism, which I did almost constantly during that period, and I said something that prompted Michael to pause, look at me, and ask, "Wait, does it upset you that I'm not becoming Catholic?" I hesitated for a moment, but then replied honestly. "Yes. Of course." Michael turned away from me, reaching into the bathwater to fish out the washcloth, and began to bathe Julian's already clean body. "That really bothers me," he said finally, "That you would want me to change. That what I believe is now somehow bad or wrong." I tried to reassure him, to explain that my desire was not a referendum on his beliefs, but more about wanting to share my newfound love with him. Yet even as I spoke I could sense that something between us had been disrupted. Our paths were no longer running side-by-side, like parallel lanes. We'd come to an intersection, and I had turned off onto another road.

At some point during this time, Michael read a self-help book, written by an atheist married to a Catholic, about how to have a successful marriage between a believer and a non-believer. The book featured case studies of several such marriages, some of which thrived, some of which failed altogether. The overall conclusion of the book, the author's secret to success, was essentially this: as long as the religious believer isn't very serious about faith, the marriage should work. But when religion becomes the fabric of that person's identity, the marriage will suffer. Neither of us found this answer encouraging. To Michael's credit, he did not wish for me to have a flimsy, sidelined faith—he realized, in fact, that this was precisely what I was escaping.

Admittedly, there were times when our diverging worldviews created conflict. One of our more memorable fights was over the issue of using condoms to combat AIDS in Africa—an issue that touched neither of us directly, but that evoked the growing philosophical chasm between us. This was a way, perhaps, for us to fight about religion at arm's length. Michael angrily interrogated the Church's stance, while I heatedly tried to defend it. This fight was punctuated not by raised voices and harsh gestures, but by long, frustrated silence. He sat on the couch, I sat on the floor, each of us staring in a different direction.

This issue of contraception was the first real test of our marriage after my decision to convert. The Catholic faith, when fully lived, can't be compartmentalized; NFP is not something that can be practiced in isolation, like popping a pill. For the duration of our marriage, I'd basically dealt with our mutual fertility by altering my physiology, enabling us to live within a paradigm of assumed sterility. Now, however, I was going to let my body return to its natural state, and I had these newfound religious tenets, which I was trying to follow, that also foreclosed the use of an alternative form of contraception, like condoms. I wanted to go *au natural*, all the way.

Michael respected my desire to quit hormonal birth control, and he was surprisingly amenable to the idea of practicing NFP. The reality that I'd been intentionally causing my body to malfunction was something we were both able to recognize as soon as the idea was presented to us, and he sympathized with my aversion. He seemed to understand the Catholic view of sex, and the logic of respecting its life-giving potential.

Our mutual agreement to embrace a principle of openness to life was a profound encouragement to me, a sign of the resilience of our love and the strength of our union. I was so grateful for his unswerving support, even though it meant reordering our sexual life—something that, surprisingly, created a more profound sense of closeness and vulnerability between us.

Yet this deepened intimacy, in turn, heightened my awareness of our spiritual distance. This was the paradox: the grace flooding through me was being channeled into our marriage; I was growing closer to Michael, increasing in love for him, but as that love intensified, so did the pain of our disunity. The more I loved him, the more I desired us to be truly, wholly one.

As my conversion escalated, this paradox became more pronounced. On the Feast of Corpus Christi, the summer after Margot's birth, Michael and I went to Mass at a Dominican parish in the heart of nearby Portland. I'd recently reconnected with a couple we knew in college who were also Catholic converts, and one of their daughters was receiving her first Holy Communion that day, so they invited us to attend.

This was my first foray into a more traditional parish, and entering that sanctuary was like entering another world, one shot through with the light of the Resurrection. The walls were a bright, luminous white; the ceiling was painted with a colorful mural depicting scenes from the life of Christ. As we waited for the Mass to begin, a rapturous polyphony burst forth above and behind us—clear, resonant notes that buoyed me upward. The entire Mass was sung in Latin, according to the Dominican rite, which was almost a thousand years old.

Even while my attention was transfixed at the altar during the Mass, I snuck glances at Michael, who listened to the polyphony with closed eyes. What was happening behind that veil, in the recesses of his being? Here he was, the one whom my soul loves and knows more than any other, and yet he's also a world unto himself, a living mystery. I had been hoping that the beauty of this ancient Mass would pierce Michael's heart, burning hotter within him than any doubt. My own conversion had seemed so sudden, so forceful and unlikely. What would it take for him to believe? I seized hold of this desire, harnessing my energy and attention into a sharp arrow of prayer, which I nocked and shot forth continuously throughout the Mass. *O Lord, make him see. O Lord, make him live.*

Michael was wearing Margot in a carrier against his chest, and when she started to stir, he went to the back, so he could pace around and soothe her to sleep. By this time the Mass was nearly over, but instead of reaching a normal conclusion, it transitioned seamlessly into a Eucharistic procession and adoration. The Dominican priest, in his hooded robe of gilded white, went to the tabernacle, where the consecrated hosts—the sacramental Body and Blood of Christ—are kept in repose. When he opened its doors, the people around me fell to their knees and I followed wordlessly, my eyes fixed on the tabernacle, which seemed lit up from within, light spilling out of it from an unknown, inward source, as if behind those golden doors was a window letting in the sun. And there was the sun itself! The monstrance, with its circular center enclosing the Host, and a surrounding ring of solid rays that signaled what it contained: the source of Light and Life himself, come to us now, hidden under the humble appearance of bread—Jesus Christ, the Word made flesh. Let us adore him.

After the procession ended, the Host was returned to the tabernacle, and the gathered crowd began to disperse. I got up slowly, as if emerging from a dream, still unclear where the dream ends and reality begins—but in this case, the dream of the Mass had been far more real than the ordinary world to which I was returning. The rich, enveloping texture of worship—I knew what it meant in a way that I hadn't before. I knew it not as a feeling, but as an encounter with an overpowering presence, to whom one cannot help but kneel.

I looked around for Michael, saw him still standing in the back, and after talking awhile with our friends, we got in our minivan to head back to my parents' house and pick up Julian. We drove in silence at first. I was desperate to know what he was thinking and feeling, too timid to ask. After a moment, Michael started to speak, and I felt my breath catch in my chest. Had he seen it? Had he felt it?

"That was a beautiful Mass," he said, "But *Jesus Christ*, it was long!" He grinned at me as he said this, in a familiar, fleeting way, as if we were sharing a private joke—completely unaware that his response was devastating.

The Mass had been long, this was true, almost two hours—and I had spent those hours in worship, adoring Jesus Christ and communing with him, offering myself to him, begging him to make himself known to my husband. To hear Christ's name as a casual expletive so soon after I had been kneeling before him gave me a physical jolt, like I'd brushed a live wire.

I was confronted, in that single phrase, with three distressing realizations. First: No, Michael had certainly not had a miraculous, mystical awareness of the Real Presence of Christ in the Eucharist. Second: I had long been a hypocritical Christian, one who rarely invoked the name of Jesus reverently, but used it freely as a curse word—so much that my husband had no reason to think I'd be bothered by it. And, lastly, the worst epiphany of all: there was a vast chasm between my husband and me, the expanse of an entire cosmos. And I had caused it. I was the one who had moved.

This disunity in my marriage became something of a quiet but constant grief, a stone I carried around in my pocket and kept accidentally touching. I was still going to Mass by myself, with the rare exception, and I began to feel a bitter bile well up inside me when I saw Catholic couples worshipping together.

One Sunday in particular, I was sitting right behind a young couple who were apparently—judging by the flashing rock on her finger—engaged to be married. It quickly became clear that he was Catholic and she was not. His voice and body moved with the flow of the Mass. He genuflected toward the tabernacle before finding his seat, moving his right arm in a seamless cruciform gesture. He knew when to sit and kneel, and spoke the words of the Creed from memory. She, on the other hand, seemed absolutely *terrified*. Her body was curved in on itself, her arms folded in a defensive posture. She glanced around like a startled bird whenever the congregation moved or spoke in unison, clutching onto her fiancé's arm with both hands. When I caught sight of her face once or twice, I saw a strained grimace, as if she was afraid of being contaminated by the people around her.

Instead of focusing on the Mass, I fixated on this couple, on the humble, devout piety of the man and the open disdain of the woman. And I began to hate her. I sent invisible beams of fury into the back of her blond head and fantasized about catching her arm after Mass, like a crazed, grizzled crone: *Do you have any idea how lucky you are, young lady, to have such a devout Catholic husband? Do you know how PRECIOUS that is? Do you?!* And then I would combust into a wailing, sizzling mess, my words drifting up from the sludge to latch onto her as a curse. *Do you have ANY IDEA . . .?*

Thankfully, I did nothing to her, aside from squeezing a bit hard when we exchanged the sign of peace.

After Mass ended, and my emotions settled down, I had the presence of mind to realize that this envy was getting out of hand. So I went to confession, and that became a turning point for me—not only because the marital envy dissipated thereafter, never to return, but also because I left the confessional armed with some sound advice, courtesy of Father Marcos: "If you want your husband to become Catholic, don't focus on his conversion. Focus on your own."

* * *

Around this time, I stumbled upon another person who would become a spiritual mentor and guide for me, a woman who knew firsthand what it was like to experience this unique paradox of love and sorrow, intimacy and separation. I first came across her early in my conversion, when I was googling around, trying to find saints who had been married to unbelievers. I was familiar with the story of St. Monica, who for decades prayed diligently for the conversion of her son, St. Augustine. Their story was inspiring to me, but I wanted to find something even closer to my situation, a story of a believing wife praying for her unbelieving husband.

After plumbing the depths of the internet, I read about Elisabeth Leseur, a French woman who died about a hundred years ago. She is a fairly obscure figure, not well known even in Catholic circles. She has not yet been declared a saint, although the process of her canonization was opened in 1990. I read her story, which I found fascinating, then promptly forgot about her—until months later, when I was in a moment of deep grief over the separation in my marriage. I was praying quietly, in the darkness of my room, more in groans than words, and her name flashed to my mind. That night, I downloaded a collection of her writings and began to read it by the glow of my phone, my infant daughter sleeping beside me.

Within the first few pages, I was in awe—her words gave voice to my longings, my struggles, my pain. Immediately, I felt less alone, a bridge formed between our two souls, a conduit of sympathy, something for which I'd been starved. I knew so few Catholics at the time; my social milieu was thoroughly Protestant and progressive. The isolation I often felt within my home was even more pronounced outside of it. And here was a woman whose earthly situation in many ways echoed mine; here was my own inner life, drawn out into language and handed back to me as a gift. We were separated by time, and the veil between this world and the next, but connected through a shared membership in Christ's body, that mystical communion. Here was a saint who could pray for me, who could understand the hidden desires of my heart.

In several key ways, our lives paralleled. We were both married at the young age of twenty-two, to men whom we loved deeply. Elisabeth's husband, Felix, was raised Catholic, but soon abandoned the faith when he began his medical studies, embracing a worldview of scientific materialism. Unlike Michael, Felix was an avid anti-Catholic, disdainful of religion in general, especially his native Catholicism. He actively tried to undermine his wife's faith, giving her books to read in liberal Protestant theology, which he figured would provide a nice gateway to agnosticism, and hopefully to a respectable atheism. (This strategy, based on my own history, is pretty sound.) For about a year, he seemed to have succeeded. Elisabeth fell away from her faith and was on the verge of abandoning religion, when, as her husband later describes, "she felt herself approach the abyss, and sprang backward." Ultimately, she was not convinced by the impoverished arguments supplied by her husband; in fact, they had the opposite effect of driving her into an immersive study of the Catholic tradition, through which she acquired a knowledgeable, substantive faith. Her reversion to Catholicism happened in her early thirties, the same era as my own conversion.

The journal Elisabeth began during this time opens with a description of an intense inner transformation, a period of "perpetual labor," which matured her mind, sharpened her convictions, and increased her love for souls. "I want to be Christian, Christian to the marrow," she writes, giving word to my newfound desire: "I want to live an entirely new life." I read, with great delight, her discovery of philosophy, which she asserts should be "the crown of all feminine education," as it "throws light on many things and puts the mind in order." Here was a kindred sister, to be sure.[25]

Elisabeth had very few confidants in her life; her social circle was decidedly secular, even hostile to religion at times, which gave her a profound sense of isolation. This did not, however, cause her to feel self-pity or resentment, or fuel aggressive attempts at evangelism. Instead, she felt love toward those who thought differently than she, and entrusted them to God:

> Spoke and discussed a great deal with some dear friends who do not believe. More than others I love these beings whom divine light does not illuminate, or rather whom it illuminates in a manner unknown to us with our restricted minds. There is a veil between such souls and God, a veil through which only a few rays of love and beauty may pass. Only God, with a divine gesture, may throw aside this veil; then the true life shall begin for these souls.
>
> And I, who am of so little worth, yet believe in the power of the prayers that I never cease to say for these dear souls. I believe in them because God exists, and because He is our Father. I believe in them because I believe in this divine and mysterious law that we call the Communion of Saints. I know that no cry, no desire, no appeal proceeding from the depths of our soul is lost, but all go to God and through Him to those who moved us to pray. I know that only God performs the intimate transformation of the human soul and that we can but point out to Him those we love, saying, "Lord, make them live."[26]

She expresses a "longing for deep sympathy," a longing she feels most intensely toward her husband, Felix. She writes continually of the pain she feels at their disunity; her journal is punctuated with sudden outcries to God on his behalf—"My God, wilt Thou give me one day the joy of this solitude for two, united in the same prayer, the same faith, and the same love?"[27]

What I immediately recognized within these cries was the paradox I described earlier, the intertwining of grief and love. Felix and Elisabeth, in one sense, do not have a strained marriage, but a singularly devoted one; the love, affection, and respect they share for each other is palpable in her writing. Elisabeth calls Felix's affection "the greatest happiness" of her life. Most often, when she writes about Felix in her journal, she doesn't use his name, instead referring to "him whom I love more than all." The depth of this love is precisely what creates the apex of her sorrow.[28]

Despite the compelling echoes between Elisabeth's life and my own, there are also stark differences. Elisabeth suffered from continual physical ailments, and she and Felix were unable to have children. Her health declined over the years, even as her spiritual vitality intensified. Eventually, she succumbed to breast cancer in middle age, dying in Felix's arms at the age of forty-seven. As her death drew near, she offered up her suffering and ultimately her life to God on behalf of her husband, for his conversion. Felix writes that she told him, "with absolute assurance," that after her death, he would become a Catholic priest.[29]

And this is what happened. Elisabeth died, and Felix discovered her secret diary, where she had disclosed her rich faith, her longing for his conversion, her continual prayers and offerings on his behalf. Not all at once, but slowly, Felix describes how he began to apprehend the splendor of his wife's faith: "The eyes of my soul were opening little by little."[30] Within a year, Felix did return to the Catholic Church. He joined a Dominican order, and was eventually ordained as a priest.

In the pages of her journal, I could see a lived example of the advice Father Marcos gave me. Elisabeth sought to bring about her husband's conversion not by preaching, cajoling, debating—but by retreating. She resolved "to be extremely reserved concerning matters of faith," to keep her spiritual life hidden:

> Let him see the fruit, but not the sap, my life but not the faith
> that transforms it, the light that is in me but not a word of Him
> who brings it to my soul; let him see God without hearing His
> name. Only on those lines, I think, must I hope for the conver-
> sion and sanctity of the dear companion of my life.[31]

This was something of a revelation to me. I had not—ahem—been particularly reserved about my revitalized faith. In the strongest throes of my conversion, when my worldview was being wrenched inside out, and my staunchest convictions upended, I had turned to Michael for support, afraid to share what was happening to me with anyone else. Night after night, sometimes for hours, I would lay on the couch, talking through my disorientation, while Michael listened patiently on the other end, tugging the ends of his beard and nodding. I joked that he was my liberal confessor, the one to whom I could expose my secret sins against progressive creeds.

Now, however, the earth had resettled; I found myself on steady ground again, and I decided to try and follow Elisabeth's lead, as best I could, to focus on my own inner transformation and express my desire for Michael's conversion through secret prayers and unseen penance.

But I couldn't completely hide. Michael and I had agreed, together, that our children would be raised Catholic. I couldn't totally sequester my Catholicism in some interior sanctum, because of my vocation as a mother, my duty to raise my children in the faith. This is where my state of life differed starkly from Elisabeth's, requiring me to live out my religion in a visible way, for their benefit. They were still quite little, far from the age of reason (to put it mildly), so we fumbled our way along, sometimes going to Mass as a family, but often I would still go alone. Nonetheless, I made a resolution, which I kept consistently but imperfectly, never to ask Michael to participate in any religious activity and only to speak of my faith if Michael raised the topic himself.

About a year after Margot's birth, I began praying the night prayer from the Liturgy of the Hours. I put together a simple altar in the bedroom—basically a wooden side table with a crucifix above, flanked by two icons, one of the Annunciation, the other of Christ. Most nights, I prayed there alone, by the wavering light of a single candle. But Margot, who still slept in my room, was entering a restless toddler phase, and even that small flame would interrupt her sleep. We have a small house, with no extra rooms and few spare corners, so I had to relocate the prayer altar to the living room.

I felt somewhat sheepish about this. The interior of our house was undergoing a gradual Catholic makeover. Icons, statues, crucifixes—these all provided windows into divine reality, a reality that is ever-present, imbuing and ordering all things, but all too easy to disregard. I needed those windows, prone to wandering as I am. They called me to prayer; they gathered my attention toward God. And Michael, for his part, didn't seem to mind, thanks to his medievalist sensibilities.

Still, I was a bit worried that a prayer altar in the living room was a little ostentatious—hardly fulfilling the Leseur principle of restraint. I waited to pray there until Michael was busy in the kitchen, doing the dishes after dinner. This meant praying a little earlier than I was used to, before the kids had gone to bed. I figured they'd be too busy playing to notice.

But as soon as I lit the candles they flitted over like moths, dazzled by the light and the way it flickered over the icons. I opened the prayer book and began singing the psalms for that day. I didn't know how to do actual plainchant, so I made up my own simple melody, while my toddlers danced around, running away, then zooming back over again; resting on my knee, then springing back up.

Just like that, a nightly tradition was formed. Over the weeks, I shortened and adapted the compline liturgy to accommodate the fact that I was no longer praying alone, but with two raucous attendants. At the end of night prayer, I sang the Salve Regina, a Marian hymn I'd been learning. This song, more than anything else, seemed to harness my children's attention. They settled into my lap and I reflexively began to sway back and forth, rocking them gently. The hymn is entirely in Latin, yet it transfixed them nonetheless. Before long—so quick it shocked me—Julian was able to sing along, and even Margot joined in on the syllables that she could discern, belting them out with gusto.

After awhile, Michael began to wander into the living room while we prayed. He'd sit on the couch and watch the antics of the children. I didn't know what was happening in his mind and heart; all I knew was that his presence brought a sense of comfort and completion to our prayer. Gradually, to my surprise, he began to participate here and there, singing the parts he knew. In early December, Michael brought home an advent calendar, one with tiny books for the days of advent, each containing a fragment of the nativity story, which we read together as a family. For Christmas, he gave me a small book of the Catholic night prayer liturgy. It included Latin translations of the prayers, and musical scores for singing plainchant. The English translations of the prayers were older, from the nineteenth century, and the beautiful, archaic language, the intimate Thee and Thou, breathed new life into the now familiar refrains. We began to use this book, praying together each night.

A few weeks later, I came home after a long workday to find the kids already scurrying to bed. Julian, on his way upstairs, announced perfunctorily that Daddy had already prayed with them, and they had prayed *the whole thing*. The next night, without a word or a discussion between us, as if we'd reached a secret understanding, Michael opened the compline book and began to sing: *O God, come to my assistance.* And I answered: *O Lord make haste to help me.* Then, together: *Glory be to the Father, the Son, and the Holy Spirit, as it was in the beginning, is now, and ever shall be, world without end, amen.* From that moment on, Michael led our nightly prayers as a family.

This wordless, organic transition from praying alone to praying with my children to praying as a family with Michael at the helm—this was a quiet miracle, a startling gift. When I was younger, still infatuated with feminism, I had chafed against the idea of male spiritual leadership in the home.

I'd found the idea sexist and offensive, a tradition to be purged. Words like *authority* and *submission* had seemed oppressive—but this reading misunderstands, entirely, the context of self-giving love that should be at the heart of married life.

When I experienced firsthand what it was like to try and shape the spirituality of my children on my own, I craved what I had once despised. Passages from the New Testament about marriage, like 1 Peter 3, now became my comfort, even though I had once wanted them excised from the Bible altogether: *Wives, in the same way, accept the authority of your husbands, so that, even if some of them do not obey the word, they may be won over without a word by their wives' conduct, when they see the purity and reverence of your lives.*

When Michael eased into leading our night prayer, it was like gears snapping into place and finally beginning to turn. There was nothing oppressive about that leadership, that initiating call to which I found myself delighted to respond. His presence brought a sense of harmony and order, a foretaste of the unity for which my soul longed. How removed and naïve my prior feminist angst seemed now. I had been preoccupied with the wrong question entirely, honing in on a speck and missing the fresco. The particular note I am singing doesn't matter; what matters is the song itself.

* * *

On our tenth anniversary, we are in Idaho, in that small lake town where I was born. My parents live here now, and we've left the wee ones in their care to get lost in the forest and be luxuriously alone. As we drive, I point at various sights that conjure dim childhood memories—so distant they barely exist, just hazy shades. This is the place where my memory begins. And I'm circling back now, all grown up, but still like a child in many ways, curious and prone to awe, only vaguely aware of how little I actually know.

We end up in a forest, but not at all lost, remaining in the civilized confines of a campground, in a rustic, one-room cabin. We crack open a bottle of wine and toast to each other, already drunk on the dizzying prospect of shared solitude, the promise of uninterrupted conversation.

There is a small hitch in the program. Fluent as I am in bodily lingo, I know that we're in that window of fertility, a time when any one-flesh union has a good chance of becoming incarnate in the body of a squirming, hungry new human. I don't know if I'm ready, if *we're* ready. We share the wine in comfortable silence, each of us mulling the same question, and decide to go for a walk.

Our forest is on a peninsula that juts into Payette Lake. We start off on a paved trail, the lake a visible backdrop behind the trees, and the water pulls us toward it, off the beaten path, until we find ourselves on the shore, in the hollow of a tiny beach sized for two that has been sculpted by the water, layer by layer, over time. We climb down and sit in the sand, facing out toward the far shore.

I begin first, launching into an unromantic practical analysis, ticking off the months on my fingers, weighing the pros and cons against the academic calendar and the possibility of an upcoming sabbatical. Underneath this relentless pragmatism, my resolve to remain rational and respectable, I conceal a longing that I fear to speak, a desire to open my arms to the unknown.

Then he responds. I don't want to be driven by a need for control, he says. I don't want our marriage to be motivated by fear of new life. Human life, he says, is fragile, unpredictable, but beautiful and innately valuable. I want to live in a way that welcomes life's chaos, with all its joy and suffering.

He takes my hand, and my heart surges *yes,* answering his, which I realize has become more open than my own. I'm aware now, of a mystery between and around us, the sacramental synergy of marriage that is changing, remaking us both. *I am my beloved's and my beloved is mine.*

Night is blooming; the light has almost drained from the sky, aside from a lingering rim of blue. The ridge of trees across the lake is now a jagged silhouette. We sit side by side, looking together toward that rugged horizon and the expanse that stretches in between. The water before us is dark but alive, dotted with circles rippling outward, as if a thousand tiny fish are swimming up to taste the strange and peaceful air.

Notes

Motherlove

1. Margaret Atwood, *Dancing Girls and Other Stories* (New York: Anchor, 1998), 242–43.

The Perfect Storm

2. Flannery O'Connor, *The Habit of Being: The Letters of Flannery O'Connor* (New York: Farrar, Straus and Giroux, 1979), 125.

Interlude: On Conversion

3. Saint Augustine, *The Confessions*, trans. Maria Boulding (New York: Vintage, 1997), 43.
4. Ibid., 157–58.

The Inner Altar

5. Joseph Cardinal Ratzinger, *Mary: The Church at the Source* (San Francisco: Ignatius, 2005), 15.
6. These quotes from St. Therese and St. John Damascene appear in the Catechism of the Catholic Church, in the section on prayer (2559).
7. St. Ambrose, a sermon on Cain and Abel, included in the Liturgy of the Hours, Office of Readings, October 11, 2017.

O Hidden God

8. Dom Anscar Vonier, *A Key to the Doctrine of the Eucharist* (Assumption Press, 2013), 3. Vonier draws heavily on the sacramental theology of St. Thomas Aquinas, and

his book has greatly shaped my understanding of the Eucharist.

9. Ibid., 36.

10. 1 Corinthians 11:28–29.

11. Justin Martyr, *First Apology*, Chapter 66. http://www.earlychristianwritings.com/text/justinmartyr-firstapology.html.

Mater Ecclesia

12. Pope Benedict XVI, in his *Introduction to Christianity*, uses a similar image to characterize the predicament of both the believer and the nonbeliever in modernity, though he takes the metaphor in a slightly different direction.

13. Robert Barron, "The Doritos Commercial and the Revival of Voluntarism." https://www.wordonfire.org/resources/article/the-doritos-commercial-and-the-revival-of-voluntarism/5081/.

14. G. K. Chesterton, *The Catholic Church and Conversion* (San Francisco: Ignatius, 2006), 113.

15. Jean Corbon, *The Wellspring of Worship* (San Francisco: Ignatius, 2005), 74.

16. Ibid., 112.

The Totality

17. Gertrud Von le Fort, *The Eternal Woman: The Timeless Meaning of the Feminine* (San Francisco: Ignatius, 2010), 3.

18. Ibid., p. 62.

The Language of the Body

19. Wendell Berry, "Feminism, the Body, and the Machine." http://www.crosscurrents.org/berryspring2003.htm.

20. John Henry Newman, "The Testimony of Conscience." http://www.newmanreader.org/works/parochial/volume5/sermon17.html.

Via Maria

21. Joseph Cardinal Ratzinger, *Mary: The Church at the Source*, 29.

22. Ibid., 43.

23. Ibid.

24. Ibid., 44.

Him Whom I Love More Than All

25. Elisabeth Leseur, *The Secret Diary of Elisabeth Leseur* (Manchester: Sophia Institute Press, 2002), 5, 24, 53, 5–6.

26. Ibid., 13–14, 69–70

27. Ibid., 33, 17.
28. Ibid., 38, 10, 15.
29. Ibid., xli.
30. Ibid.
31. Ibid., 69–70.

Made in United States
Troutdale, OR
09/17/2024

22900923R00127